"I enjoy reading Phil Moore's [illegible] *e*
Christian life with pe [illegible]
– Nicky Gumb [illegible]

"In taking us straight to th [illegible]
served us magnificently. We so need to get into the Scriptures and let the Scriptures get into us. The fact that Phil writes so relevantly and with such submission to biblical revelation means that we are genuinely helped to be shaped by the Bible's teaching."
– *Terry Virgo*, Founder of Newfrontiers

"Fresh. Solid. Simple. Really good stuff."
– *R.T. Kendall*, Author and speaker, former minister of Westminster Chapel, London

"Most commentaries are dull. These are alive.
Most commentaries are for scholars. These are for **you***!"*
– *Canon Michael Green*, Former evangelist, lecturer and apologist

"These notes are amazingly good. Phil's insights are striking, original, and fresh, going straight to the heart of the text and the reader! Substantial yet succinct, they bristle with amazing insights and life applications, compelling us to read more. Bible reading will become enriched and informed with such a scintillating guide. Teachers and preachers will find nuggets of pure gold here!"
– Greg Haslam, Westminster Chapel, London, UK

"A strong combination of faithful scholarship, clear explanation and deep insight make these an invaluable tool. I can't recommend them highly enough."
– **Gavin Calver**, Director of Mission, Evangelical Alliance

"The Bible is living and dangerous. The ones who teach it best are those who bear that in mind – and let the author do the talking. Phil has written these studies with a sharp mind and a combination of creative application and reverence."
– Joel Virgo, Leader of Newday Youth Festival

"Phil Moore's new commentaries are outstanding: biblical and passionate, clear and well illustrated, simple and profound. God's Word comes to life as you read them, and the wonder of God shines through every page."
– **Andrew Wilson**, Author of *Incomparable* and *If God, Then What?*

"Want to understand the Bible better? Don't have the time or energy to read complicated commentaries? The book you have in your hand could be the answer. Allow Phil Moore to explain and then apply God's message to your life. Think of this book as the Bible's message distilled for everyone."
– **Adrian Warnock**, Christian blogger

"Phil Moore presents Scripture in a dynamic, accessible and relevant way. The bite-size chunks – set in context and grounded in contemporary life – really make the Word become flesh and dwell among us."
– **Dr David Landrum**, Director of Advocacy & Public Affairs, Open Doors UK & Ireland

"Through a relevant, very readable, up-to-date storying approach, Phil Moore sets the big picture, relates God's Word to today and gives us fresh insights to increase our vision, deepen our worship, know our identity and fire our imagination. Highly recommended!"
– **Geoff Knott**, former CEO of Wycliffe Bible Translators UK

"What an exciting project Phil has embarked upon! These accessible and insightful books will ignite the hearts of believers, inspire the minds of preachers and help shape a new generation of men and women who are seeking to learn from God's Word."
– **David Stroud**, Leader of Christ Church London and author of *Planting Churches, Changing Communities*

For more information about the Straight to the Heart series, please go to **www.philmoorebooks.com**.
You can also receive daily messages from Phil Moore on Twitter by following **@PhilMooreLondon**.

CONTENTS

About the *Straight to the Heart* Series 9
Introduction: It is God Who Put You Here 11

PART ONE: GOD'S MAN IN BABYLON (Daniel 1–6)

The End of the World (Daniel 1:1–5) 16
How it All Begins (Daniel 1:3–8) 20
Tightrope (Daniel 1:8–16) 24
No Enemies? (Daniel 1:16) 29
Drilling and Blasting (Daniel 1:17–21) 33
On Their Backs (Daniel 2:1–13) 38
Live Ready (Daniel 2:14–23) 42
I Can't, But God Can (Daniel 2:24–30) 46
Everlasting Kingdom (Daniel 2:31–45) 50
Little Seeds (Daniel 2:46–49) 54
Chain Reaction (Daniel 3:1–12) 58
Two Forms of Faith (Daniel 3:13–18) 62
Cameo (Daniel 3:19–27) 66
The Wrong Words (Daniel 4:1–9) 70
Patience (Daniel 4:8–27) 74
The Garden (Daniel 4:28–37) 78
Unlikely Converts (Daniel 4:37) 82
The End of the Road (Daniel 5:1–12) 86
A Long Obedience (Daniel 5:13–29) 90
Nevertheless (Daniel 5:30–5:31) 95
Déjà Vu (Daniel 6:1–9) 99
Secret Weapon (Daniel 6:10–11) 103

Living God (Daniel 6:12–22) 107
Beyond (Daniel 6:23–28) 111

PART TWO: GOD'S PEOPLE IN THE WORLD (Daniel 7–12)
Fantastic Beasts and Where to Find Them (Daniel 7:1–28) 116
God Has a Son (Daniel 7:9–14) 120
Apocalypse Now (Daniel 7:15–28) 124
Manifest (Daniel 8:1–27) 128
Weapon #1: The Main Thing (Daniel 8:26–27) 132
Weapon #2: Scripture (Daniel 9:1–3) 136
Weapon #3: Fasting (Daniel 9:3) 140
Weapon #4: Prayer (Daniel 9:4–19) 144
Faster than Angels Can Fly (Daniel 9:20–27) 148
Weapon #5: Authority (Daniel 10:1 – 11:1) 152
What Must Soon Take Place (Daniel 11:2–20) 158
Twin Peaks (Daniel 11:21–45) 163
Weapon #6: Knowing God (Daniel 11:32–35) 167
Stars in the Night Sky (Daniel 12:1–13) 171

PART THREE: GOD'S WOMAN IN PERSIA (Esther 1–10)
Same Difference (Esther 1:1–8) 176
The Queen's Gambit (Esther 1:9–22) 180
Later (Esther 2:1–11) 184
Beauty Queen (Esther 2:12–18) 189
Providence (Esther 2:19–23) 194
Assassin's Creed (Esther 3:1–15) 198
The Answer is "No" (Esther 3:2–6) 202
Weapons of Persia (Esther 4:1–17) 206
Destiny (Esther 4:12–16) 210
More Drilling and Blasting (Esther 5:1–8) 214
Lasting Happiness (Esther 5:9–14) 218
Mordecai's Helper (Esther 6:1–14) 222
What Do You Want? (Esther 7:1–4) 226

The Greasy Pole (Esther 7:5 - 8:2) 230
Good News (Esther 8:1–17) 234
Good News Shoes (Esther 8:1–17) 238
Case Study (8:16 - 9:19) 242
Invisible God (Esther 8:17 - 9:3) 246
Purim (Esther 9:17–32) 250
Final Word (Esther 10:1–3) 254

Conclusion: It is God Who Put You Here 258

This book is dedicated to my amazing daughter, Esther. May God help you to look at every area of your life and to declare with faith: It is God who put me here.

Published by **Monarch Books**
www.lionhudson.com
Part of the SPCK Group
SPCK, 36 Causton Street, London, SW1P 4ST

ISBN 978 0 8572 1978 7
eISBN 978 0 8572 1979 4

First edition 2022

Acknowledgments
Scripture quotations taken from the Holy Bible, New International Version Anglicised. Copyright © 1979, 1984, 2011 Biblica, formerly International Bible Society. Used by permission of Hodder & Stoughton Ltd, an Hachette UK company. All rights reserved. "NIV" is a registered trademark of Biblica. UK trademark number 1448790. Both 1984 and 2011 versions (Anglicized) are quoted in this commentary.

Every effort has been made to trace copyright holders and to obtain permission for the use of copyright material. The publisher apologizes for any errors or omissions and would be grateful to be notified of any corrections that should be incorporated in future reprints of this book.

A catalogue record for this book is available from the British Library

Printed and bound in UK, January 2022, LH26

STRAIGHT TO THE HEART OF

Daniel & Esther

SIXTY BITE-SIZED INSIGHTS

Phil Moore

MONARCH BOOKS

About the *Straight to the Heart* Series

On his eightieth birthday, Sir Winston Churchill dismissed the compliment that he was the "lion" who had defeated Nazi Germany in World War Two. He told the Houses of Parliament that *"It was a nation and race dwelling all around the globe that had the lion's heart. I had the luck to be called upon to give the roar."*

I hope that God speaks to you very powerfully through the "roar" of the books in the *Straight to the Heart* series. I hope they help you to understand the books of the Bible and the message which the Holy Spirit inspired their authors to write. I hope that they help you to hear God's voice challenging you, and that they provide you with a springboard for further journeys into each book of Scripture for yourself.

But when you hear my "roar", I want you to know that it comes from the heart of a much bigger "lion" than me. I have been shaped by a whole host of great Christian thinkers and preachers from around the world, and I want to give due credit to at least some of them here: Terry Virgo, Dave Holden, Guy Miller, John Hosier, Adrian Holloway, Greg Haslam, Lex Loizides, Malcolm Kayes and all those who lead the Newfrontiers family of churches; friends and encouragers, such as Stef Liston, Joel Virgo, Stuart Gibbs, Scott Taylor, Nick Derbridge, Phil Whittall and Kevin and Sarah Aires; Joshua Wells and all the team at Monarch Books; my great friend Andrew Wilson – without all of your friendship, encouragement and example, this series would never have happened.

I would like to thank my parents, my brother Jonathan, and my in-laws, Clive and Sue Jackson. Dad – your example birthed in my heart the passion which brought this series into being. I didn't listen to all you said when I was a child, but I couldn't ignore the way you got up at five o'clock every morning to pray, read the Bible and worship, because of your radical love for God and for his Word. I'd like to thank my children – Isaac, Noah, Esther and Ethan – for keeping me sane when publishing deadlines were looming. But most of all, I'm grateful to my incredible wife, Ruth – my friend, encourager, corrector and helper.

You all have the lion's heart, and you have all developed the lion's heart in me. I count it an enormous privilege to be the one who was chosen to sound the lion's roar.

So welcome to the *Straight to the Heart* series. My prayer is that you will let this roar grip your own heart too – for the glory of the great Lion of the Tribe of Judah, the Lord Jesus Christ!

Introduction: It is God Who Put You Here

"Who knows but that you have come to your royal position for such a time as this?"

(Esther 4:14)

If you want to understand the message of the books of Daniel and Esther in the Old Testament, then it may help to think about a famous moment in the movie *The Imitation Game*. One of the Bletchley Park codebreakers cannot hide his frustration at being tucked away in a stately home, working on maths puzzles, while all his friends are away fighting on the battlefield. He seethes with frustration, and asks whether anyone realizes that there are actually soldiers who are *fighting* to win the war. His brother is risking his life in the navy. His cousins are RAF pilots. In his view, all his friends are contributing to the war whilst he is wasting his time, producing *nothing*.[1]

Benedict Cumberbatch and Keira Knightley hang their heads because they too suspect that this is true. There is little to show for their efforts to crack the German Enigma code. There are just as many bombs falling, just as many people are dying and there is just as little hope of a swift end to the war as when they began their lonely exile to Bletchley Park. The power of the scene, of course, lies in the fact that we know they went on to crack the code, shortening World War Two by over two years and saving over 20 million lives. Their frustration, while understandable, is utterly unfounded. They may constantly

[1] The codebreaker, Peter Hilton, in *The Imitation Game* (Black Bear Pictures, 2014).

doubt it, but they are in precisely the right place to change the course of history.

That's also how it was for Daniel, a young Jewish teenager torn from his hometown of Jerusalem and taken into exile in Babylon as a prisoner of war. Any dream of serving the Lord to save his nation from foreign invasion was cruelly dashed, and he was forced to serve as a civil servant in the evil empire that had just destroyed his hopes and his home. We know that Daniel wrote the book that bears his name, both from the book itself (Daniel 9:2 and 10:2) and from the words of Jesus (Matthew 24:15), yet – remarkably – we find in it no trace of self-pity or despair. Daniel saw things far too clearly for that. His book is listed among the *Major Prophets* because his insights into the future are amongst the clearest and most astonishing in the Bible.[2] Instead of looking back in anger, he looked forward in faith, believing that the Lord must have a better plan than his. Despite ample evidence to the contrary, Daniel reassured himself: *It is God who put you here.*

Daniel 1–6 tells the story of Daniel, revealing him to be **God's man in Babylon**. We discover that he was able to achieve far more by serving the Lord's plans for the Jewish nation in Babylon than he could ever have achieved had he remained in Jerusalem. First, his devout faithfulness rallies the Jewish exiles back to faith in the God of Israel. Then, his courageous witness persuades the evil King Nebuchadnezzar, the destroyer of Jerusalem, to surrender his own life to the God of Israel as well. When the Babylonian Empire is eclipsed by that of Persia, Daniel remains at his post and leads his new Persian master to faith in the God of Israel too. These are some of the most famous chapters in the Old Testament, and they were written to encourage us that we are also in the right place. Whenever

---

2 Ironically, this is why some modern scholars deny that Daniel wrote the book which bears his name. They insist that nobody could have prophesied so accurately about the next 400 years of history, which says more about their view of God than it does their view of the book of Daniel. *See Isaiah 41:21–24 and 46:8–11.*

we are tempted to doubt it, these chapters reassure us: *It is God who put you here.*[3]

Whenever we are tempted to imagine that we are living in the wrong city, attending the wrong church, working in the wrong job, married to the wrong person or investing in the wrong friends, the book of Daniel reminds us that the Lord's plans are always greater than our own. The Apostle Paul echoes the book of Daniel when he reassures us that *"God set the exact times and places where people should live."*[4]

Daniel 7–12 consists of a series of prophecies that apply this same message to **God's people in the world**. They predict in astonishing detail what will happen over the next few centuries of Jewish history until the coming of the Messiah, who will establish a far greater Kingdom than all the empires that will rise and fall in between. I am looking forward to studying those chapters with you because they are some of the most difficult chapters in the Bible to understand, and some of the most rewarding chapters when we do. Through them, the Lord includes us in Daniel's story. *It is God who put you here.*

The book of **Esther** forms a natural companion to the book of Daniel, since it records the story of **God's woman in Persia**. Esther had even more reason to despair than Daniel. Born a Jewish exile, she was orphaned young and brought up by a cousin. Her hope of marrying a nice Jewish boy was dashed when she was suddenly conscripted into the Persian emperor's harem. Horrified to find herself a plaything in a pagan palace, she was shaken still further to discover that her new husband had passed a law that would result in the massacre of the Jewish community across the Persian Empire. Her cousin echoes the book of Daniel when he asks her in Esther 4:14: *"Who knows but that you have come to your royal position for such a time as this?"* He reassured Esther: *It is God who put you here.*

---

[3] Daniel was written in the sixth century BC and Esther was written in the fifth century BC, yet the Apostle Paul insists in Romans 15:4 that these books were written to teach us *endurance*, *encouragement* and *hope*.

[4] This is my paraphrase of the Greek text of Acts 17:26.

The books of Daniel and Esther emphasize that the Lord is *omnipotent* – that he is the almighty and undisputed ruler of everything that happens everywhere. Daniel achieves this by telling us explicitly and repeatedly that the God of Israel is sovereign over every earthly kingdom. Esther takes a more subtle approach. By omitting to mention the name of God at all, while revealing his handiwork on every page, our eyes are opened to the invisible work of God in our own lives.[5] However godless and mundane the details of our life stories may appear to us, the sovereignty of God is written on every page.

The books of Daniel and Esther emphasize that the Lord is *omniscient* – that he is the all-wise and all-knowing architect of history. None of us could ever have guessed that the disasters which befell Daniel would give rise to a spiritual revival for the Jews and a surprise conversion for the king of Babylon. Nor could we ever have imagined that Esther's defilement by a Persian king would save the Jewish nation from genocide and lead to many more surprise conversions among the pagans. And yet the Lord planned it all.

So thank you for taking the time to journey through these two books of the Bible with me. You will not regret time spent discovering what they speak into our own lives today. As Christians, we inhabit the modern-day equivalents of Babylon and Persia, and we have many reasons to throw up our hands in despair. That's why, wherever you are and whatever your circumstances, the Lord wants to use these two books to invite you to acknowledge, with the same faith as Daniel and Esther, that *it is God who put you here.*

[5] This makes Esther the only book in the Bible not to mention God by name. Song of Songs can feel equally secular, but at least the Hebrew text of Song of Songs 8:6 refers to "*the flame of the Lord*".

Part One

God's Man in Babylon (Daniel 1–6)

The End of the World (Daniel 1:1–5)

"In the third year of the reign of Jehoiakim king of Judah, Nebuchadnezzar king of Babylon came to Jerusalem and besieged it."

(Daniel 1:1)

At the start of the twenty-first century, every CEO had a *2020 Vision* for their business. It was meant to be a play on words, a jokey claim that the CEO possessed a perfect vision of the future which ought to motivate employees to turn that vision into reality. But when 2020 arrived, the joke turned sour. Nobody had predicted that COVID-19 would devastate their business, eclipse their vision statements and silence their boasting. Their *2020 Visions* became sobering reminders of what the Bible says in James 4:13–14: *"Now listen, you who say, 'Today or tomorrow we will go to this or that city, spend a year there, carry on business and make money.' Why, you do not even know what will happen tomorrow."*

We don't know what Daniel would have written on his *605 BC Vision*, but what we do know is that 605 BC proved even more devastating to his world than 2020 proved to ours. For Daniel, the events of 605 BC must have felt like it was the end of the world.

The year 605 BC was the year that saw the rise of King Nebuchadnezzar of Babylon. First, the crown prince shifted the balance of power in the ancient world by crushing the Egyptian and Assyrian armies at the Battle of Carchemish. Then, just as the world became Babylon's for the taking, news arrived that King Nabopolassar had died. Nebuchadnezzar succeeded his father to become the greatest and longest-reigning king of Babylon. Like an unstoppable coronavirus, he spread his empire into every nation.

This was also the year that the nation of Judah definitively rejected the Word of God. We can read about what happened in Jeremiah 36, where King Jehoiakim is granted a private reading of a first edition of the book of Jeremiah.[1] Instead of repenting, he slices the book into pieces, throws the pieces on the fire and orders the arrest of the prophet. This violent rejection of God's Word marked a major turning point in Jewish history.

As a result, 605 BC became the year in which the city of Jerusalem fell to its enemies for the first time. A century earlier, the Lord had rescued the capital city of Judah from an Assyrian army due to the repentance of King Hezekiah and the prayers of the prophet Isaiah. King Jehoiakim's refusal to repent and to partner with the prophet Jeremiah meant that the city fell to the Babylonians after the Battle of Carchemish. Foreign soldiers plundered its royal palaces, its treasuries and its holy Temple. They also plundered its citizens by taking 7,000 young Jewish men into exile in Babylon – not just as trophies of war to sell at the slave markets, but as gifted students young enough to be brainwashed into serving as loyal officials for the growing Babylonian Empire.[2]

The opening verses of the book of Daniel inform us therefore that 605 BC was the year in which the gods of Babylon seemed to triumph over the God of Israel.[3] Since the name Nebuchadnezzar means *May-The-God-Nebo-Help-My-Crown-Prince,*

---

[1] Jewish historians counted part years as whole years, so 605 BC is the *fourth* year of Jehoiakim in Jeremiah 36:1. Like us, the Babylonians only counted whole years, so 605 BC is the *third* year of Jehoiakim in Daniel 1:1.

[2] The exile of 605 BC was the largest of the four Jewish deportations, involving 7,000 men, plus their families. The deportations of 597 BC, 586 BC and 581 BC involved 3,023 men, 832 men and 745 men, plus their families. See Jeremiah 52:28–30 and 2 Kings 24:14, where the figure of 10,000 combines 605 BC and 597 BC.

[3] By referring to Babylonia as Shinar, Daniel 1:2 takes us back to the Tower of Babel in Genesis 11:2. Daniel wants us to grasp that 605 BC looked like the triumph of the children of Babel over the children of Abraham.

it looked as though his father's prayer had been answered when he entered the Temple of the Lord and took back some of its sacred objects as plunder to the temple of his own idol in Babylon.[4]

Daniel was among the 7,000 Jewish young men who were carted back to Babylon with the treasures from God's Temple, so 605 BC must have felt like the end of the world for him personally. It dashed any dream that the teenager might have had of working with the prophet Jeremiah to bring spiritual revival to the Jewish nation.[5] It ruined any hope that he might have had of his aristocratic family securing him a post at the royal palace, from which he might become a godly influence on the kings of Judah. Instead, he was forced to serve the monstrous empire that had just torn him away from his parents and from the Promised Land. It took several months to travel from Jerusalem to Babylon, so it must have felt like the end of the world to Daniel in every way.[6]

Have you got that? Then you are ready for the message of the book of Daniel, because the Lord does more than dash the hopes and dreams of CEOs for their businesses. He also dashes the hopes and dreams of his followers for how they can serve him. The book of Daniel demonstrates that God is not looking for generals who can assist him with clever strategies for the advance of his Kingdom. He is looking for foot soldiers who trust that he alone knows the best strategy and who say a simple "yes" to his commands. The year 605 BC felt like the end of the world for Daniel and his contemporaries, but these opening verses hint at two ways in which it would spell revival for the Jewish nation.

---

[4] *Nebo* (also known as *Nabu*) was worshipped as the son of *Bel* (also known as *Marduk*), who was the patron god of Babylon. Daniel 4:8 suggests that the Babylonian idol referred to in 1:2 is Bel, rather than Nebo.

[5] The age of the 7,000 exiles is not given, but the Hebrew text describes them literally as *"lads"*. Daniel 6 tells us that he was still working in government in 538 BC, so he must have been a teenager in 605 BC.

[6] It took four months for the news of the fall of Jerusalem to reach Babylonia in Ezekiel 33:21. It also took four months for some of the exiles to return from Babylon to Jerusalem in Ezra 7:8–9.

First, these opening verses tell us that the events of 605 BC granted Jewish believers access to the throne room of Babylon. The breaching of the walls of Jerusalem did not mark the end of Jewish history. It marked the moment when its faith went global. The arrival of 7,000 Jews in Babylon marked one of the greatest missionary moments in the Old Testament. It was the beginning of the Jewish conquest of Babylon.

Second, these opening verses tell us that the events of 605 BC sowed the seeds for the return of the Jewish exiles to the Promised Land. The sacred articles that are plundered from the Lord's Temple by King Nebuchadnezzar become very important later. We are informed in Daniel 5 that the Lord regarded the mistreatment of these vessels as mistreatment of himself, so when the king of Babylon used them to raise a toast to his own idols, it directly caused the fall of Babylon to the Persian army in 539 BC.[7]

From that perspective, 605 BC was not the end of the world for the Jewish nation. Like the famous Trojan Horse in Greek mythology, it marked the moment when God's people breached the walls of Babylon. We must never forget that God marches to victory on the death-and-resurrection highway. Even when he looks defeated, he knows precisely what he is doing.

So if your own world feels like it is in tatters right now, be encouraged. If your own plans for serving God have ended in failure, then do not despair. Whenever you find yourself in a hopeless place, remember the message of Daniel: *It is God who put you here.*

---

[7] Ezra 1:7–11 tells us that all of these sacred articles were returned to Jerusalem in 538 BC. The Lord is able to recover all of his lost property! Acts 9:4–5 echoes Daniel 5 by informing us that Jesus also views the mistreatment of his followers, who are his New Covenant Temple, as mistreatment of himself.

How it All Begins (Daniel 1:3–8)

"But Daniel resolved not to defile himself with the royal food and wine…."

(Daniel 1:8)

King Nebuchadnezzar had a plan for how it would all begin. When news of his father's death arrived at his army camp, he performed a quick calculation in his head. There were not enough gifted men in the city Babylon to administer an empire as large as the one that he imagined, so he conscripted some of the finest captives from his Carchemish campaign and created a civil service finishing school for them in Babylon.

Nebuchadnezzar commanded the headteacher to exact a strict admissions policy. The students were to be the children of foreign royalty or nobility. They were to be fit, healthy and handsome. They were to have razor-sharp minds. There were to be no commoners or struggling students in the class of 605 BC. Most of all, the students were to be young enough to be brainwashed easily. A three-year immersion in the language, literature and culture of Babylon had to be enough to turn them into loyalists who remembered nothing of their former homes, their former culture or their former values. They were to become automatons of the Babylonian Empire. Nebuchadnezzar dreamed of world domination and this finishing school was how it would all begin.

First, the students were given a crash course in the everyday language of Babylon. Chaldean Aramaic used the same alphabet as Hebrew and shared much of its vocabulary, which made things a little easier for Daniel and the other Jewish students.[1] Then came lessons in literature, which meant reading texts in Sumerian and Akkadian too, the ancient languages of Babylon. For three years, Daniel and the other Jewish students were forced to dedicate their minds to pagan myths and culture, so that they would forget the story of the people of the God of Israel.[2]

The Devil tempts people from the outside in. He targets our eyes to incite fleshly desire, which will result in sinful action that damages our souls. King Nebuchadnezzar therefore supplied the school canteen with the best food and wine from his royal table. The meat had not been butchered in accordance with the strict regulations in the Law of Moses. It had been dedicated to the gods of Babylon, along with the wine, but what was that to hungry students? It looked tasty, and three years of allowing their eyes to rule over their bodies ought to be enough to make the students loyal citizens of Babylon.[3]

Last of all, King Nebuchadnezzar commanded his officials to rename all of the students at his finishing school. People tend to live up to what the most important people in their lives speak over them, so the Jewish students were to be given names which supplanted any memory of the God of Israel with a pledge to serve the gods of Babylon.

Daniel means *The-Lord-Is-My-Judge* or *The-Lord-Will-Vindicate-Me,* so the headteacher renamed him Belteshazzar, which means *Bel-Will-Protect-The-King*. Something similar happened to his three close school friends. Hananiah means *The-Lord-Has-Shown-Me-Grace,* so he was renamed Shadrach which means *Commanded-By-The-Moon-God-Aku*. Mishael means *Who-Is-Like-God?,* so he became Meshach which means *Who-Is-Like-Aku?* Azariah means *The-Lord-Is-My-Helper,* so he

[1] *Chaldeans* is the true ancient name for the Babylonians – for example, in the Hebrew text of Daniel 1:4.

[2] Daniel focuses on the Jewish students at the school, but Nebuchadnezzar must also have conscripted students from amongst his other prisoners of war: from Egypt, Assyria, Phoenicia and elsewhere.

[3] Leviticus 17:10–14; Deuteronomy 12:15–16; 1 Corinthians 8:1–13 and 10:18–33. Note the order when Revelation 18:13 teaches us literally that the goal of Babylon is to enslave *"the bodies and souls of people"*.

became Abednego which means *Servant-of-Nebo*. Every trace of Jewishness was erased from their names.

This was a vital moment in Jewish history. Although they didn't know it at the time, this initial group of exiles in Babylon was deciding what cultural values would shape the Jewish community during its exile and after its return to the Promised Land. Within two decades, the nation of Judah would be wiped off the map, leaving its future in the hands of the Jewish exiles in Babylon.[4] If they succumbed to Nebuchadnezzar's attempt to brainwash them and to paganize their culture, then the history of Israel was over. But it was here in the schoolrooms of Babylon that a great Jewish spiritual revival began.

Daniel dared to be different. He shifted his eyes away from the odds that were stacked against him. Looking up to heaven, he concluded that one believer plus the God of Israel was a winning team.[5] He decided to resist the king of Babylon and, amazingly, he won. For Christians, who are called to live at the heart of modern-day Babylon, this raises an important question. What was the secret of Daniel's revival? How did it all begin?

We have already noted that the Devil tempts people from the outside in. He targets their eyes to entice their bodies, so that their flesh attempts to dominate their inner being, instead of being governed by it.[6] This is the spiritual battle highlighted in Proverbs 4:23 – *"Above all else, guard your heart, for everything you do flows from it"* – and which the Exodus generation of Israelites lost, forfeiting the Promised Land because *"their hearts were devoted to their idols."*[7] Whenever we feast our eyes

---

[4] Jeremiah 24 and Ezekiel 11 warn the Jews left behind in Jerusalem not to consider themselves the "lucky ones". God would rebuild their nation, not through them, but through the Jewish exiles in Babylon.

[5] The fact that Daniel's dreams had just been shattered through his exile to Babylon makes his refusal to doubt the Lord's goodness all the more remarkable here.

[6] For example, in Genesis 3:6 and 6:2; Joshua 7:21; 2 Samuel 11:2–4; Psalm 119:37; Matthew 5:28 and 6:22–23; James 1:14–15 and 1 John 2:16.

[7] Ezekiel 20:16. Character is formed by little heart decisions. If we are ever going to stand our ground over big issues in the future, then we need to stand our ground over small issues now. Daniel and his friends were laying a foundation for their lives, and in doing so they laid a new foundation for their nation.

on things that entice our flesh to dominate our spirit, we end up losing our battle against temptation.

Daniel therefore decided not to fix his eyes on the meat and wine in the school canteen. He refused to let his study of Babylonian culture make him forget what it meant for him to have been born into the Jewish nation. He resolved not to let the new name that his pagan schoolteachers had given him dilute what he believed about his identity in God. We are told literally in verse 8 that *"Daniel* ***set his heart*** *not to defile himself with the royal food and wine".* That's how it all begins when it comes to spiritual revival. Holiness flows from the inside out.[8] One of the greatest Jewish revivals in history began when Daniel resolved deep within his heart that he would live as God's man in Babylon.[9]

These words were written down for us. They explain how the Jewish nation was granted a second Exodus from Babylon. They also teach us how we can work for a great revival of the Church in our own generation. It all begins with a resolution in our hearts that we will serve the Lord and the Lord alone. The great nineteenth-century preacher and revivalist Charles Spurgeon explains it this way:

> *The Christian is no more a common man... If you and I are tempted to sin, we must reply, "No, let another man do that, but I cannot. I am God's man; I am set apart for him; how shall I do this great wickedness and sin against God?" Let dedication enforce sanctification.*[10]

---

[8] The New Testament explains this further. When God's Spirit unites himself with our spirit (1 Corinthians 6:17), his holiness flows out from deep within us – from *spirit* to *soul* and to *body* (1 Thessalonians 5:23).

[9] Similar resolutions of the heart are commended to us in Job 31:1; Psalm 17:3; Luke 21:14 and Acts 11:23.

[10] From a sermon entitled "Threefold Sanctification", preached at the Metropolitan Tabernacle in London on 9 February 1862. The reference is to a similar heart resolution made by Joseph in Genesis 39:9.

Tightrope (Daniel 1:8–16)

"Daniel resolved not to defile himself with the royal food and wine, and he asked the chief official for permission not to defile himself in this way."

(Daniel 1:8)

On a recent trip to the park with my youngest son, we stumbled upon a would-be tightrope walker who was attempting to learn his trade. He had fastened a low rope between two tree trunks and was wobbling, first to one side then to the other, as he perfected the difficult art of balancing. Judging by the number of times that he fell off his tightrope, he evidently had a fair amount of practising left to do.

For Daniel and his school friends, living as devout Jews in Babylon must have felt a lot like learning to become a tightrope walker. To accept the thinking of their pagan teachers would spell disaster for the Jewish nation, but to reject everything that came from Babylon would mean expulsion from the school – or worse. Daniel's headteacher is not exaggerating in verse 10 when he warns him to be careful of the royal executioner.

The New Testament encourages us to learn from Daniel's example in these verses. It depicts the non-believing world we live in as our own Babylon.[1] If we allow its culture and its values to shape our thinking, then we will never reap the spiritual harvest that Jesus has promised to all those who follow him.

---

[1] Explicitly in 1 Peter 5:13 and Revelation 17–18; implicitly by quoting from Isaiah 52:11 in 2 Corinthians 6:17.

At the same time, if we fear the world and retreat into the Christian subculture, we will miss out on the harvest too. To be a fruitful Christian means becoming a successful tightrope walker. Don Carson explains:

> *Every culture has good and bad elements in it... In every culture it is important for the evangelist, church planter, and witnessing Christian to flex as far as possible so that the gospel will not be made to appear unnecessarily alien at the merely cultural level. But it is also important to recognise evil elements in culture when they appear and to understand how biblical norms assess them. There will be times when it is necessary to confront culture.*[2]

Daniel walks that tightrope expertly in these verses. He is surprisingly flexible towards the culture of Babylon, sacrificing any aspects of his Jewish culture that are man-made and that might get in the way of serving as God's man in Babylon. Learning Aramaic is fine; it will help him to proclaim the Lord to his new pagan masters.[3] Studying pagan literature is also fine; it will help him to dress God's Word up in the right clothing to reach as many Babylonians as possible.[4] If his headteacher wants to take away his Hebrew name, which points to the God of Israel, and replace it with a name that points to the gods of Babylon, then even this can be endured.[5] Just as a boxer gladly

---

[2] D.A. Carson in *The Cross and Christian Ministry: Leadership Lessons from 1 Corinthians* (2004).

[3] It would also enable him to write Daniel 2:4b – 7:28 in Aramaic. These verses refute the idea that Christians ought to avoid a secular education. As in Daniel's case, a secular education can often prepare a Christian to accomplish the specific work that the Lord has created them to fulfil (Ephesians 2:10).

[4] This is known as "contextualization". It presents the timeless Gospel in a timely way to a specific group of people, like the British missionary Hudson Taylor when he dressed in Chinese clothing to reach the Chinese.

[5] Daniel happily calls them Shadrach, Meshach and Abednego in chapter 3, but here in 1:11 he emphasizes that their new names have not altered their identity. They are still Hananiah, Mishael and Azariah to God.

accepts a few punches to get close enough to land a knockout blow, so the missionary gladly sacrifices many of their personal preferences in order to gain a hearing for the Gospel.

But to eat meat that has not been butchered in the way the Lord commanded in the Law of Moses? To dine on food and drink that has been dedicated to the demon gods of Babylon? That wouldn't be to flex on the tightrope, but to fall off it! Daniel declares that he would rather lose his life than disobey the Lord's command for his people to separate themselves from paganism out of reverence for the God of Israel. He knows that such a decision may cost him his life, but he believes that any missionary who is willing to defile himself to win the praise of non-believers is as good as dead already.

Tim Keller observes that:

> *Every human culture is an extremely complex mixture of brilliant truth, marred half-truths, and overt resistance to the truth. Every culture will have some idolatrous discourse within it. And yet every culture will have some witness to God's truth in it. . . If you forget the first truth – that there is no culture-less presentation of the gospel – you will think there is only one true way to communicate it, and you are on your way to a rigid, culturally bound conservatism. If you forget the second truth – that there is only one true gospel – you may fall into relativism, which will lead to a rudderless liberalism. Either way, you will be less faithful and less fruitful in ministry.*[6]

Daniel walks this tightrope well when he seeks permission from the headteacher to replace the non-kosher food of Babylon with simple vegetables and water instead. When the headteacher says "no", because he fears King Nebuchadnezzar, Daniel proposes a

[6] Timothy Keller in *Center Church* (2012).

compromise to his class teacher instead.[7] If he can be permitted to abstain from pagan portions in the school canteen for just ten days, then he will happily ask the teacher to inspect his students at assembly on the eleventh day and to decide if obedience to the God of Israel creates weaker students than those who serve the deities of Babylon.

This chapter is not about vegetarianism. It isn't really about food at all. It describes what happens when a believer embraces suffering for the Lord, instead of chasing after fleeting worldly comforts and the momentary pleasure of popularity.[8] When the teacher assembles his students on the eleventh day, he is shocked to discover that Daniel and his three friends are the healthiest looking of them all. It isn't clear in verse 16 whether *"their"* refers to Daniel and his three friends or to the other students in the school, but I personally take it to mean that the teacher is so impressed that he decides to overhaul the menu at the school canteen. There will be no more meat and wine for anyone.

The Lord wants to use verses such as these to build our own confidence to live as believers in Babylon. Whenever you feel overwhelmed by the worldliness of your workplace, of your studies, of certain groups of friends, of social media, or of the political arena, then these verses are meant to reassure you: *It is God who put you here.*

They are also meant to teach us how to walk the tightrope of Christian mission to the world. They cheer us on whenever we flex one way by sacrificing some of the man-made comforts of our Christian subculture in order to get close enough to non-believers to gain a hearing for the Gospel. They cheer us on again when we flex back the other way by insisting that the Word of God isn't ours to change. It can wear different clothes

---

[7] Daniel is not confrontational and holier-than-thou towards his teacher. He is reasonable and willing to compromise. *How* we make a stand for the Lord often matters just as much as *what* we make a stand about.

[8] Hebrews 11:24–26 points out that Moses made this same decision at Pharaoh's palace in Egypt.

for different cultures, but it must not be diluted or defiled. It is the eternal Word of God.

Studying these verses trains us to walk the same tightrope as the Apostle Paul, who explains his missionary methods in 1 Corinthians 9:20–23.

> *To the Jews I became like a Jew, to win the Jews. To those under the law I became like one under the law . . . so as to win those under the law. To those not having the law I became like one not having the law . . . so as to win those not having the law. To the weak I became weak, to win the weak. I have become all things to all people so that by all possible means I might save some. I do all this for the sake of the gospel.*

No Enemies? (Daniel 1:16)

"So the guard took away their choice food and the wine they were to drink and gave them vegetables instead."

(Daniel 1:16)

Before we move on from Daniel's first year at finishing school in Babylon, let's take a moment to reflect on how his fellow students must have felt about him. Young men from the conquered cities of the ancient world were not so different from the young men of today. They must have dearly loved feasting on meat and wine fit for a king. When their teacher suddenly informed them that from now on, thanks to Daniel, the school canteen would serve only vegetables and water, it can't have gone down very well.

Jerusalem was not the only conquered city to send students to the school. There were many pagan students who saw no problem with consuming non-kosher food and drink that had been dedicated to the gods of Babylon. They must have bitterly resented the way that their dinner menu had become collateral damage in Daniel's quest to remain faithful to the God of Israel.[1] We can often assume that the best way to win non-believers to Christ is to become liked by them, but Daniel pursues a very different strategy here.

Even the Jewish students at the school cannot have been impressed with Daniel. Over time, his example would convict them of their sin and spark a spiritual revival among the Jews in

---

[1] I'm not speculating here. Daniel's colleagues hate him so much that they try to murder him in 6:1–9.

Babylon. But in the short term, his courageous action exposed their own lack of devotion to the Lord. When Daniel and his three friends emerged from their ten-day trial looking healthier than the other Jews, it must have provoked some jealousy.

Walking the tightrope of Christian mission may win us friends. We are told in verse 9 that *"God had caused the official to show favour and compassion to Daniel".*[2] But it may also win us enemies, and we must not be surprised at this. We follow in the footsteps of a Messiah who was crucified. If our Master was hated for his obedience to his Father, then how can we expect to follow him without people hating us too?

The Scottish radical Charles Mackay asks in one of his most famous poems:

You have no enemies, you say?
Alas, my friend, the boast is poor.
He who has mingled in the fray of duty
That the brave endure, must have made foes.
If you have none, small is the work that you have done.
You've hit no traitor on the hip.
You're dashed no cup from perjured lip.
You've never turned the wrong to right.
You've been a coward in the fight.[3]

As Christians living in modern-day Babylon, we need to recognize that this is true. Otherwise our attempts to win a hearing for the Gospel will morph into something more sinister. We will find ourselves altering the Gospel in order to win acceptance for ourselves. It is crucial that we grasp that walking the tightrope of contextualizing the Christian message is never about giving people what they want to hear. It is about

---

[2] The Hebrew words *hēsēd* and *rahamīm*, which mean *loving kindness* and *compassion*, are normally used in the Old Testament to describe the Lord. Daniel 1:9 is therefore telling us that God imparted something of his own love for Daniel to the guard.

[3] Charles Mackay was a Chartist who lived from 1814 to 1889. He entitled this poem simply No Enemies.

communicating the Bible's answers to the questions that they are asking in a language that they can understand, and in the most compelling manner – but they may dislike those answers intensely. Tightrope walking means that, even when they reject those answers out of hand, what they reject is the Gospel itself, rather than the fact that it has come to them dressed in the wrong clothes.

I have never met a Christian who did not long to see the same rapid expansion of the Church that we read about in the book of Acts. But our yearning for New Testament Christianity tends to overlook Acts 28:22, *"people everywhere are talking against this sect."*

I have never met a Christian who did not long for the same spiritual fervour to grip the Church today as enabled it to conquer the Roman Empire for Christ. But how many of us are willing to share the conviction of the leaders of the Early Church that *"The blood of the martyrs is the seed of the Church"*?[4] How many of us would truly wish the Lord to grant us the same courage as Polycarp? When a Roman governor threatened to execute him unless he offered incense to the emperor as a god, he retorted, *"You threaten me with fire which burns for a moment and is quickly extinguished. But you are ignorant of the fire of the judgment that is coming and of the eternal punishment that is reserved for the ungodly. What are you waiting for? Do what you want to me!"*[5]

These ancient examples are not unusual. Spiritual revival in the Church has invariably been accompanied by bitter hatred and persecution. Sometimes this has come from non-believers who hate the Christian message. Harder to bear, it has often come from within the Church, as nominal believers react with anger to the exposure of their shallow faith or as leaders fear that the revival will threaten their position. The sixteenth-

---

[4] Tertullian said this in about 197 AD in his *Apology* (chapter 50).

[5] Quoted by the early Christian historian Eusebius of Caesarea in his *Church History* (4.15).

century reformer Martin Luther knew this pain personally and concluded that:

> *Jesus Christ lived in the midst of his enemies. At the end all his disciples deserted him. On the cross he was utterly alone, surrounded by evildoers and mockers. For this cause he had come, to bring peace to the enemies of God. So the Christian, too, belongs not in the seclusion of a cloistered life but in the thick of foes. There is his commission, his work. The Kingdom is to be in the midst of your enemies. And he who will not suffer this does not want to be of the Kingdom of Christ; he wants to be among friends, to sit among roses and lilies, not with the bad people but the devout people. O you blasphemers and betrayers of Christ! If Christ had done what you are doing who would ever have been spared?*[6]

So before we move on from Daniel's ten-day school test in Babylon, let's take a moment to consider how much it cost him. Walking the tightrope of presenting the timeless Gospel to people in a timely manner will win us friends, but it will also win us bitter enemies. Not just in ancient Babylon, but in modern-day Babylon too.

In 2 Timothy 3:12, the Apostle Paul encourages us to resolve ahead of time that this is true:

> *Everyone who wants to live a godly life in Christ Jesus will be persecuted.*

---

[6] Quoted by Dietrich Bonhoeffer in *Life Together* (1939). Bonhoeffer would go on to be executed by the Nazis.

Drilling and Blasting (Daniel 1:17–21)

"The king. . . found none equal to Daniel, Hananiah, Mishael and Azariah. . . In every matter of wisdom and understanding. . . he found them ten times better."

(Daniel 1:19–20)

The walls of Babylon were said to be unbreachable. If we can believe the Greek historian Herodotus, then they were thicker than a tennis court is long, enough to make any would-be besieger retreat in despair.[1] Daniel and his friends must have felt the same way about breaching Babylonian culture with the Word of God, but the Lord had not called them to become his strategists. He had merely asked them to obey him as his happy foot soldiers and to trust that he would find a way to breach the walls of Babylon.

Sure enough, the Lord had spotted an entry point for the Gospel long before Daniel and his friends arrived at Nebuchadnezzar's finishing school.[2] A clue can be found in the name of the king of Babylon, which means *May-Nebo-Help-My-Crown-Prince*. Another clue can be found in the new name that was given to Azariah, since Abednego means *Servant-of-Nebo*. Nebo was worshipped by the Babylonians as the god of wisdom,

[1] Herodotus says that the walls were 25 metres thick in his *Histories* (1.178).

[2] I am not being anachronistic by referring to "the Gospel" before the arrival of Jesus. Hebrews 4:2 and 4:6 tell us that *"we also have had the good news preached to us, just as they did."* See also Galatians 3:8.

literature, learning and prophecy.[3] The Lord had chosen this to be his way of breaching the walls of Babylon, just as Babylon had breached the walls of Jerusalem.

In the most reliable Greek manuscripts of 1 Timothy 1:17, the Apostle Paul describes the Lord as *"the only wise God."* Nebo was therefore an imposter, a demon who was duping people into offering him worship that rightfully belonged to the Lord.[4] For Daniel to say that outright would be to fall off the tightrope without gaining a hearing for the God of Israel, so he spoke that truth more positively.[5] He decided to affirm what was good in Babylonian culture. He presented the Lord to his new masters as the true God of wisdom that they were looking for.

Tim Keller describes this process as "drilling and blasting". If you are building a road and you need to remove a massive boulder in your way, then you have to drill a shaft into the centre of the rock which you fill with explosives to detonate the boulder from within.

> *If you drill the shaft but never ignite the blast, you obviously will never move the boulder. But the same is true if you only blast and fail to drill. . . All drilling with no blasting, or all blasting with no drilling, leads to failure. But if you do both of these, you will remove the rock. To contextualise with balance and successfully reach people in a culture, we must both enter the culture sympathetically and respectfully (similar to drilling) and confront the culture where it contradicts biblical truth (similar to blasting). If we simply 'blast' away – railing*

---

[3] *Nebo* was also known as *Nabu*. See Isaiah 46:1 and Jeremiah 48:1. His massive influence on ancient culture can be detected from the fact that, even in Old Testament Hebrew, the word for *prophet* is *nābī'*.

[4] In Babylonian art, Nebo's father, Marduk, was pictured walking with a dragon. Paul explains in 1 Corinthians 10:20–21 that this was a none-too-subtle clue that demons were at work behind ancient deities.

[5] This is why Paul seems so surprisingly positive about Athenian idolatry in Acts 17:22–23. It is also why he shocks us in Acts 17:28–29 by treating certain Greek beliefs about Zeus as genuine insights into the Lord.

> *against the evils of culture – we are unlikely to gain a hearing among those we seek to reach. Nothing we say to them will gain traction; we will be written off and dismissed. We may feel virtuous for being bold, but we will have failed to honour the gospel by putting it in its most compelling form.*[6]

Daniel and his friends therefore resolve to regard reverence for Nebo as a positive aspect of Babylonian culture.[7] They devote themselves to pagan literature and learning. They complement this with the Jewish Scriptures that reveal the God of Israel to be the author of all wisdom. When Daniel senses that the Lord has granted him prophetic gifting through the Holy Spirit, he does all he can to fan that gifting into flame. When King Nebuchadnezzar pays the school a visit to inspect its students, it immediately becomes obvious to him that Daniel and his three friends are the wisest of them all. The dating of chapter 2 reveals that he allowed the four friends to graduate early.[8] Not because they badmouthed the false god Nebo, but because they affirmed the Babylonian thirst for wisdom and proved that the Lord was the true God of wisdom they were looking for.

Without a similar positive approach towards our own culture, we will fail to gain a hearing for the Gospel. But merely affirming our culture is unlikely to convert anyone. Our "drilling" needs to lead to "blasting", which is what Daniel and his friends do next. We are not just told that Nebuchadnezzar found these four Jewish students to be wise. Verse 20 makes a deliberate comparison. *"In every matter of wisdom and understanding about which the king questioned them, he found them ten times better than all the magicians and enchanters in*

---

[6] Timothy Keller in *Center Church* (2012).

[7] This wasn't as easy as it sounds. The Hebrew words in 1:20 that are translated *magicians* and *enchanters* can also mean *occultists*, *diviners*, *conjurers* and *necromancers*.

[8] Daniel and his friends arrived in Babylon in 605 BC, but chapter 2 shows that they had graduated into the royal palace by 603 BC. Nebuchadnezzar evidently concluded that his school had nothing left to teach them.

his whole kingdom." Daniel and his friends began exposing the weakness of the Babylonians when it came to wisdom. They started sowing doubts about Nebo.

"Drilling" and "blasting" is all about recognising that every non-believer thirsts for something that only the real God can give them. It means resisting our innate desire to tell people that they are wrong. It means choosing to affirm wherever they are right, while challenging them to recognise that they are looking for good things in the wrong places. This is how Daniel and his three friends were allowed to graduate early into King Nebuchadnezzar's elite circle of royal soothsayers.[9] He could tell that they honoured his goals but had found a better manner of achieving them than any of the wise men of Babylon. By "drilling" and "blasting", Daniel became God's man in Babylon, moving into position for the events of chapter 2, where his prophetic gifting would start to convince the king that Nebo was nothing and that the God of Israel was everything.

If your own culture appears unbreachable by the Gospel, then these verses should encourage you to think again. If the Lord was able to find an entry point for the Gospel in ancient Babylon, then he is able to find similar entry points for you and me today.

Take sex, for example. Many of the non-believers in modern-day Babylon are lonely and longing for love. That's why apps such as Tinder are so popular. People have been sold the lie that sex can cure their loneliness, but it doesn't take much "drilling" to be able to begin "blasting". People know that sex without commitment makes them feel even more lonely – used and discarded, like a cheap item of clothing that is quickly thrown away.

This is just one of the many ways that the Lord has found to breach the walls of modern-day Babylon through us. Whether

---

[9] Daniel 1:19 only tells us that they were accepted into the civil service. Daniel 2:12–13 adds that Nebuchadnezzar allocated them posts among the Magi, the prestigious order of wise men of Babylon.

we choose to target our culture's god of sex, or its god of popularity or its god of consumerism – we find that its walls are surprisingly shaky. Let's learn from Daniel and his friends how to "drill" and "blast" our way through each of these potential breaches because, if the Lord could reveal himself to the ancient Babylonians as the true God of wisdom, then he knows how to reveal himself to our friends as the true God that they are looking for today.

On Their Backs (Daniel 2:1–13)

"In the second year of his reign, Nebuchadnezzar had dreams; his mind was troubled and he could not sleep."

(Daniel 2:1)

In the Netflix series *House of Cards*, Frank Underwood complains that he's always detested the need to sleep, regarding it like death – that "*puts even the most powerful of men on their backs.*"[1]

King Nebuchadnezzar was the most powerful man in the world. He had dispatched every foreign rival to his empire at the Battle of Carchemish. Back at home, people trembled at his words and he casually executed anybody who dared to disagree with him.[2] But one night in 603 BC, the Lord put Nebuchadnezzar on his back. He gave him such a vivid dream that he woke up in a sweat, unable to go back to sleep until he knew its meaning. He immediately summoned the wise men of Babylon to interpret it for him.

The Lord used this summons to put the wise men of Babylon on their backs too. Many of them were powerful priests and prophets of Nebo. The first three Hebrew words that are used to describe them in verse 2 can be variously translated as *magicians, occultists, enchanters, diviners, astrologers, necromancers, spiritualists, mediums, wizards* and *conjurers*. Such words are meant to emphasize that many of these men were demonized, possessing supernatural power from the evil

---

[1] *House of Cards*, Season 2, Episode 10 (2014).

[2] For example, in Daniel 1:10, 2:5–13, 3:1–6, 3:29 and 5:19.

one. The fourth Hebrew word that is used to describe them in verse 2 simply means *Chaldeans* or *Babylonians*, so some of these men were just deep thinkers, rather than demon worshippers, but they all shared a belief that their order was all-powerful – until the king demanded that they interpret his dream.

Nebuchadnezzar is so troubled in his spirit that he makes an entirely unreasonable demand.[3] He will not tell the wise men of Babylon his dream in case they concoct plausible interpretations of their own. If they are truly wise, and if they truly have access to the God of wisdom, then it ought to be no problem for them to receive a revelation of the dream and its interpretation as one job lot together. This is how Nebuchadnezzar will know for certain that what his wise men say is true. If they rise to the challenge, he will reward them handsomely. If they cannot, then he is better off without them. He will execute them all, before destroying their houses and their families too.[4]

The wise men of Babylon faint with fear when they hear this. They confess to the king that nobody in Babylon enjoys this kind of access to the god of wisdom. *"There is no one on earth who can do what the king asks!"* they complain. *"What the king asks is too difficult."*

This is the cue for Daniel, but note how much these verses emphasize that he and his friends are on their backs too. They are asleep when the king has his dream. The spiritual breakthrough that takes place in this chapter does not come from a shrewd plan of their own. It is divine initiative all the way. Rather than persuading a reluctant God to bless their own plans, they discover that *it is God who put us here.*

Daniel and his friends are not present when the king briefs the wise men of Babylon. We know that they are counted among them, because the royal executioner includes their four names

---

[3] We saw in Daniel 1 that the Devil tries to tempt us to sin from the outside in. The Hebrew text of Daniel 2:1 and 2:3 states the flipside of this. God stirs the king's *rūach*, or *spirit*, in order to save him from the inside out.

[4] Daniel 6:24 explains that the destruction of their houses would include the slaughter of their families too. See also Daniel 3:29; Ezra 6:11; and Esther 7:10 and 9:7–10.

on his kill list, but it is significant that the first time they hear about the king's dream is the moment when the executioner comes knocking on their door.[5] The events of this chapter will transform the fortunes of the Jewish community in Babylon and begin the process by which King Nebuchadnezzar, the evil destroyer of Jerusalem, repents of his sins and finds salvation in the God of Israel. Yet none of this is initiated by Daniel and his friends. Remember, God is not on the lookout for human generals who can assist him in finding the right strategies for winning non-believers to salvation. He is on the lookout for obedient foot soldiers who are listening for his orders. We don't have to make anything happen for the Lord. We just need to believe that he put us here.

Our English Bibles tend to overlook a dramatic moment in the story. The Old Testament is written almost entirely in Hebrew yet, when the wise men of Babylon begin to speak halfway through verse 4, the text suddenly switches from Hebrew into Aramaic. The text then continues in the language of Babylon until it switches back to Hebrew in Daniel 8:1.[6] This is meant to emphasize that the God of Israel has decided to reveal himself as the God of Babylon. Only a few years later, the prophet Ezekiel would witness God's glorious presence abandoning his Temple in Jerusalem in response to the Jewish nation's sin.[7] Meanwhile, God is revealing his glorious presence to a pagan nation within the palace of Babylon.

The first thing that the wise men of Babylon say in Aramaic is *"May the king live forever!"*[8] That's ironic, because the message of the king's dream is precisely that he will *not* live forever.

[5] 2:12–13. The executions were already starting by the time they heard the news. Daniel 2:13 tells us literally that *"The sentence went forth and the wise men were being slain, so men sought Daniel and his friends to put them to death."*

[6] The only other sections of the Bible written in Aramaic are Jeremiah 10:11, and Ezra 4:8–6:18 and 7:12–26.

[7] This took place on 17 September 592 BC and is recorded in Ezekiel 9:3, 10:3–5, 10:18–19 and 11:22–25.

[8] 2:4. This was the normal court etiquette for addressing the kings of Babylon and Persia. See Daniel 3:9; 5:10; 6:6; 6:21, and Nehemiah 2:3.

These verses are recorded in Aramaic because the dream is a solemn warning that the Babylonian Empire will soon give way several others. Only the Kingdom of God, which is revealed at the end of Nebuchadnezzar's dream, will truly last forever.

The wise men of Babylon then declare in Aramaic that *"What the king asks is too difficult. No one can reveal it to the king except the gods, and they do not live among humans"* (verse 11). This becomes the confession upon which the Lord can breach the mighty walls of Babylon. When the priests and prophets of Nebo confess that the king's dream has put their false god on his back, it paves the way for the Lord to reveal himself as the true God of wisdom. The Babylonians know as little about finding Nebo as they do about the movie *Finding Nemo*, but they are about to discover that the God of Israel is powerfully present among them through his Holy Spirit, deep at work within Daniel and his Jewish friends.[9]

Nebuchadnezzar is on his back. The wise men of Babylon are on their backs. The false god Nebo is on his back too. This humiliation of the powerful brings Daniel centre stage in Babylon. His three friends whisper to him nervously: *It is God who put you here.*

[9] In the Aramaic text of verse 11, the wise men complain literally that *"The dwelling of the gods is not with flesh."* Don't miss the glorious reversal of this when God promises in Joel 2:28, *"I will pour out my Spirit on all flesh."*

Live Ready (Daniel 2:14–23)

"Daniel spoke to him with wisdom and tact. He asked the king's officer, 'Why did the king issue such a harsh decree?'"

(Daniel 2:14–15)

In William Shakespeare's *Julius Caesar*, Brutus pleads with his friends to seize the opportunity that is offered them, or else suffer the regret of losing it forever.

There is a tide in the affairs of men,
Which, taken at the flood, leads on to fortune;
Omitted, all the voyage of their life
Is bound in shallows and in miseries.
On such a full sea are we now afloat,
And we must take the current when it serves,
Or lose our ventures.[1]

Daniel seems to have had no inkling that a high tide moment in Jewish history was about to come in like a flood upon him. He had no time to get ready for action when the executioner knocked on his door, but it didn't matter. Daniel had learned to live ready.

Brutus is right. Had Daniel succumbed to self-pity, he would have missed this high tide moment and regretted it

---

[1] *Julius Caesar* (Act 4, Scene 3).

forever. It is easy for us to spot now that the disasters of 605 BC were all part of God's perfect plan, yet history is full of people who allowed life's disappointments to rob them of many years of active service to God. Daniel had no idea that almost all of those he left behind in Jerusalem would be slaughtered when the city fell to the Babylonians again, in 597 and 586 BC. For now, he could only feel the unfairness of his exile. Nevertheless, instead of feeding his self-pity, Daniel chose to feed his faith on the thought that the ruin of his own plans must mean that the Lord had far greater plans for him. When opportunity knocked on Daniel's door, against all odds, it found him ready.

Daniel had been furnished with another reason for self-pity just before this high tide moment in Jewish history. At the end of chapter 1, he and his three friends had won the favour of King Nebuchadnezzar. They had been permitted to graduate early and initiated into the elite circle of royal soothsayers.[2] But the start of chapter 2 suggests that the wise men of Babylon were unwelcoming towards the four new arrivals. The fact that Daniel and his three friends only learn about the king's dream when the royal executioner knocks at their door suggests that their new colleagues had excluded them for being far too young, far too Jewish and far too threatening.

Added to this came the dangers of luxury. History is strewn with devout believers who climbed the greasy pole of politics, only to compromise their beliefs once they found themselves in positions of power. How many leaders of church denominations, promoted as a result of their radical faith in Jesus, have lurched immediately towards comfort, compromise and conservatism? The promotion of Daniel and his three friends to the royal palace of Babylon was therefore a dangerous moment for them, but they remained true to their calling. When opportunity knocked on his door, Daniel was ready.

---

[2] Some readers assume that the friends are not with the other wise men of Babylon in 2:2 because they remained part-time students. But this fails to acknowledge that they are awarded full-time jobs in 2:49.

Daniel was ready when this crisis reared up without warning. His reaction was not fear or flight, but faith. He knew precisely what to do. First, he checked the facts. Then he negotiated for time so that he could bring the problem to the Lord in prayer. Next, he gathered other devout believers around him so that they could wrestle in prayer together. As a result, he was able to return to the king of Babylon knowing precisely what to say. Daniel models godly crisis management for us here. Daniel was ready to stand up to a bully. We are told that he spoke to his executioner *"with wisdom and tact"*, voicing what the man was thinking but dared not speak out loud: *"Why did the king issue such a harsh decree?"* When Daniel took the time to listen to his executioner's answer, he was granted an audience with the king, during which he offered a compromise to Nebuchadnezzar. If the king would grant a temporary reprieve to the wise men of Babylon, then Daniel would accept his challenge. He would consult the God of wisdom and return with the details of the dream and its interpretation.

Daniel was ready to make good on this promise. He took personal ownership of the crisis, rushing back to the house that he shared with his three Jewish friends.[3] We were told in 1:17 that Daniel possessed prophetic gifting from the Holy Spirit, so he was in no doubt that the Lord would grant him revelation where the servants of Nebo had failed. It is too late to get ourselves ready when opportunity comes knocking at our door. We need to live ready, like Daniel, who had already stirred his gift of prophecy into flame. That very night, in response to his fervent prayer with his three friends, Daniel received a vision from God that revealed to him everything he needed to know.[4]

---

[3] Note that Daniel 2:17 uses their Jewish names and not their new Babylonian names. The fact that Daniel goes to his own house to find them suggests that they all lived together.

[4] The Aramaic text of 2:19 describes this revelation as a *vision of the night*. It is possible that Daniel was awake and fretting, but a more obvious translation is that he received this revelation as a dream while he slept. Like Peter in Acts 12:5–6, Daniel prayed then went to bed. Those who pray can let God do the worrying!

Daniel was ready to put his complete trust in God. He did not wait to check that his vision was correct before he started worshipping the Lord.[5] He praised him straightaway as the true God of wisdom and as the only deity who *"gives wisdom to the wise and knowledge to the discerning."*[6] He proclaimed ahead of time that the idol Nebo had been exposed as an imposter because the Lord alone *"reveals deep and hidden things"*.[7] Daniel did not wait to verify his vision with Nebuchadnezzar before declaring in faith that *"You have made known to me what we asked of you, you have made known to us the dream of the king"*.[8]

So let's learn from Daniel. Let's not wait for the moment when opportunity knocks on our door to get ready to serve the Lord. If we do, then it will be too late. We will miss our high tide moment and find ourselves languishing in the shallow waters of regret. We cannot afford to allow the regrets and disappointments of the past to rob us of our readiness to serve the Lord today. Like Daniel, let us live ready.

---

[5] Daniel mirrors the faith of the Israelite leaders in Exodus 4:29–31, when they worship the Lord for his promise to deliver them from Egypt, even though their Exodus has not yet begun.

[6] 2:21. Daniel's description in this verse of the Lord deposing and raising up kings is more than just an abstract reference to the sovereignty of God. It echoes Nebuchadnezzar's dream, which Daniel has just seen.

[7] When Daniel read the scroll of Jeremiah many years later (9:1–2), he discovered that the Lord had been teaching his fellow prophet something similar back in Jerusalem. Jeremiah 33:3 echoes Daniel 2:20–23.

[8] 2:23. Note Daniel's humility here, remembering to give credit to his three friends in his prayer. Daniel was the one chosen to receive this vision, but it was *"made known to **us**"* in response to *"what **we** asked of you"*.

I Can't, But God Can (Daniel 2:24–30)

"Daniel replied, 'No wise man, enchanter, magician or diviner can explain to the king the mystery he has asked about, but there is a God in heaven'..."

(Daniel 2:27–28)

If you want to access the files on my computer, then you need to know the password. Get it right, and you can access everything. Get it wrong, and the computer is useless.

These verses teach us that this is where the problem lies for many Christians today. They have all of the hardware that they need to witness spiritual breakthrough, in the form of the plans and promises of God. They have all of the software that they need, in the form of the blood of Jesus, by far the most powerful operating system in the world. Nevertheless, they struggle to activate any of what the Lord has placed at their fingertips, because they have no idea of the correct password. As Daniel steps into the throne room of Babylon, he reveals this password to us. We need to watch him carefully, because the Lord is still as able and as willing to grant us similar breakthroughs in our own Babylon.

Arioch, the royal executioner, can tell from the look in Daniel's eyes that he knows the secrets of Nebuchadnezzar's dream. He tries to steal some of the credit by informing the king that it was his idea to ask for help from the Jewish exile. If one of the most senior figures in the Babylonian Empire feels the need to fawn like this over his king, then Daniel surely needs to cower even further.[1] But he doesn't. It is a rhetorical question when the king asks, in verse 26, *"Are you able to tell me what I saw in my dream and interpret it?"* Nobody dares to say "no" to a dictator. But Daniel's goals are far greater than merely walking back out of the palace alive. He sees this as his high tide moment to prove once and for all that the God of Israel is the true God of wisdom. If he is to expose Nebo as an imposter, then Daniel cannot afford to let his ego get in the way. Daniel shocks Nebuchadnezzar by declaring that *"No wise man, enchanter, magician or diviner can explain to the king the mystery he has asked about, but there is a God in heaven who reveals mysteries"* (verse 27–28).

This is the password that unlocks the power of God's Kingdom for his people. It is the statement: *I can't, but God can.* Our hopes of spiritual breakthrough are never thwarted by the fact that the Lord is too weak. They are only ever thwarted by the fact that we believe ourselves too strong.[2] The Lord longs to reveal his glory to the world, but he will not allow his people to steal any of it, as Arioch attempted to do with Daniel. Our inflated egos are our own worst enemies. They get in the way of what God wants to do.[3]

Most of us instinctively deny that this is true. That's because ego is the carbon monoxide of sin. It kills our dreams silently and slowly, without our ever being aware of it. The great Christian writer A. W. Tozer explains that *"The meek man is not a human mouse afflicted with a sense of his own inferiority. Rather. . . he has stopped being fooled about himself. He has accepted God's estimate of his own life. He knows he is as weak and helpless*

---

[1] The post of *captain of the guard* was a very senior position in the Babylonian Empire. Arioch's successor to the post, Nebuzaradan, would preside over the destruction of Jerusalem in Jeremiah 39:9–14 and 52:12–16.

[2] The Lord points this out to Gideon when he tells him in Judges 7:2, *"You have too many men. I cannot deliver Midian into their hands, or Israel would boast against me, 'My own strength has saved me.'"*

[3] The Lord warns us that this is true in Isaiah 42:8 and 48:11; James 4:6 and 10; and 1 Peter 5:5–6.

as God has declared him to be, but paradoxically, he knows at the same time that he is in the sight of God more important than angels. In himself, nothing; in God, everything. That is his motto."[4]

If you need more help to grasp this, then note the deliberate similarities between Daniel's audience with the king of Babylon here and Joseph's audience with the king of Egypt in Genesis 41. Both men are Hebrews who have been carried away from the Promised Land and forced to serve pagan masters in a foreign land. Both have received prophetic gifting from the Lord which has opened doors for them into the corridors of power. Both are asked to interpret a horrifying dream and both use the same password to activate spiritual breakthrough. When Pharaoh asks Joseph the same question that Nebuchadnezzar asks of Daniel, he replies in Genesis 41:16, *"I cannot do it. . . but God will give Pharaoh the answer he desires."* It's the same password: *I can't, but God can.*

Nebuchadnezzar isn't listening to Daniel. He treats his answer as part of the hyperbole of the royal palace, rather like the way in which his courtiers keep on wishing that their king will live forever. Daniel therefore repeats himself until his words are taken literally.

First, he describes the Lord as *"the God of heaven"*. This is a phrase that occurs twenty-two times in the Old Testament, nearly always when recording events that take place in Assyria, Babylon or Persia. The phrase appears to have been one of the primary ways in which the Jews communicated that their God was far greater than any of the pagan deities. Daniel refuses to reveal what the dream means until the king recognizes that he is more than just another messenger of Nebo. Daniel is a prophet of the God of Israel.

Second, he describes the Lord as *"the revealer of mysteries"*. Since he is speaking in Aramaic, he uses the word *rāz*, which is often featured in the boasts of Nebo. It is the equivalent of the Greek word *mustērion* which is used throughout the New

---

[4] A. W. Tozer says this in his book *The Pursuit of God* (1948).

Testament to describe a secret that God has hidden and revealed only to his friends. Daniel uses this name because Nebo was like the Greek god Hermes, the Roman god Mercury and the Egyptian god Thoth – all of them worshipped as messenger gods to the world. Daniel wants to emphasize to Nebuchadnezzar that Nebo's mailbag is empty. The only messenger in his throne room who has anything to say is a servant of the God of Israel.

Third, as if suspecting that the stubborn king is still not listening, Daniel repeats that *"This mystery has been revealed to me, not because I have greater wisdom than anyone else alive".* Nebuchadnezzar needs to take his eyes off Daniel to see the glory of the God of Israel, who is everything that Nebo claims to be but isn't – and so much more besides.

I can't, but God can. It is such a simple password. And yet its five simple monosyllables can seem so difficult for us to say. We find it far too easy to act like Arioch, trying to share a little of the credit with the Lord. But ego stands for **E**dging **G**od **O**ut. Instead of stealing credit, we rob ourselves of experiencing the true power of the Lord.

Rivers flow to the sea because the sea is lower than they are. In the same way, God's grace flows towards anyone who sides with him against their ego. This was Daniel's secret. It was Joseph's secret. It has been the secret of every person who has stewarded any of the breakthroughs in Church history. It is only when we are willing to parade our own weakness that the Lord is able to entrust us with his glory and his power. The password that activates God's plans and promises is very simple: *I can't, but God can.*

Everlasting Kingdom (Daniel 2:31–45)

"The great God has shown the king what will take place in the future."

(Daniel 2:45)

It says a lot about Nebuchadnezzar that a bad dream could render him sleepless. Although he was feared as a bloodthirsty tyrant, he suffered from secret insecurities. Something he saw while in his pyjamas touched a raw nerve and terrified him.

Nebuchadnezzar feared what every dictator fears – that his rule would be toppled and his kingdom be destroyed. He had witnessed the Assyrian Empire come to a violent end, and he lost sleep over the idea that his own empire would eventually go the same way. The Lord gave him a dream which exposed this secret fear because he wanted to satisfy the king's deep longing for an everlasting kingdom.

Daniel is full of respect for Nebuchadnezzar. In these fifteen verses, he addresses him four times as *"your Majesty"* or as *"the king"*, and a fifth time as *"the king of kings"*. This was a Babylonian way of describing an emperor – a ruler whose conquests were so extensive that they needed to rule the world through a network of lesser, vassal kings.[1] Daniel's speech is sensitive to Nebuchadnezzar's insecurities, but he doesn't pull any punches when it comes to describing the dream itself. If it made him tremble, then good. It was precisely the kind of dream that ought to make a king of Babylon afraid!

---

[1] Ezra 7:12 Ezekiel 26:7 and Daniel 2:37. The New Testament takes this name and applies it to God himself in 1 Timothy 6:15, and in Revelation 17:14 and 19:16.

Daniel reveals that the nightmare which terrified the king was a dream about an enormous statue. He describes it for him without stopping to fact-check all the details. He has already weighed his prophetic interpretation with his three Jewish friends, so he is supremely confident that what he speaks is a supernatural revelation from the Lord.[2]

The statue had a head of pure gold. Daniel explains that this represents the splendour of King Nebuchadnezzar and his Babylonian Empire. The statue's chest and arms are made of silver because Daniel explains, to the king's great horror, that the rule of Babylon will be eclipsed by another. The Persian Empire will be weaker than the one it conquers, and it will in turn be destroyed by another. The statue's belly and thighs are made of bronze to represent Alexander the Great and his conquests, the largest empire that the world had ever seen. The statue's legs are made of iron to predict that it too will be eclipsed by the mighty Roman Empire. The statue's feet are made of iron and clay (materials that cannot mix) as a prediction of the inherent weakness of Roman rule. The corruption of its emperors will be its fatal flaw. The Roman Empire too will fall.

King Nebuchadnezzar dreamed of being part of an everlasting kingdom, so this statue represented his worst nightmare. Not only did it mean that his empire would end, but it predicted the same fate for those that followed it. The Lord sent him this horrifying dream because it is only when we despair of our own plans that our eyes are opened to the far better plans of the Lord. Nebuchadnezzar needed to grasp that the rule of Babylon would pass away so that he would start looking for God's everlasting kingdom.

Now for the great crescendo of the king's dream. Daniel reveals that a rock struck the statue, smashing it into tiny pieces, before growing into a mountain which filled the entire

---

[2] Shadrach, Meshach and Abednego are not in the throne room with Daniel, yet he sees himself as spokesman for a larger team. He declares in 2:36, *"This was the dream, and now **we** will interpret it to the king."*

earth.[3] It represents a very different kind of empire, one not founded *"by human hands"* but by the God of heaven. As a result, it will become the world's only ever truly global empire and the world's only ever truly everlasting kingdom. It will be what Nebuchadnezzar is secretly longing for. *"The God of heaven will set up a kingdom that will never be destroyed, nor will it be left to another people. It will crush all those kingdoms and bring them to an end, but it will itself endure forever."*

Daniel has just proclaimed the God of heaven to King Nebuchadnezzar in a language that he can understand and in a manner that addresses his deepest longings. Now comes the moment of truth. Was he actually correct in his description of the dream? If he was, will the king treat his prediction of the fall of Babylon as an act of treason or as good news about an even better kingdom? Will Nebuchadnezzar respond with fury or with faith? Anyone who has ever shared the Gospel with a non-believing friend knows a little of how Daniel feels at the end of interpreting the king's dream.

Astonishingly, the non-believing king of Babylon believes. He treats the fact that Daniel knows the detail of his dream as proof that Daniel is indeed a prophet. Since none of the worshippers of Nebo have been able to do this, he accepts that the God of Israel must therefore be the true God of wisdom. Nebuchadnezzar does not try to contest Daniel's claim in verses 36–37 that it was Israel's God who gave him victory at the Battle of Carchemish, paving the way for the extension of his empire across the world.[4] Instead of getting angry that a Jewish courtier should dare to predict the demise of his own rule, he responds with excitement to this news about another, everlasting kingdom. He believes Daniel when he informs him that *"The great God has shown the king what will take place in the future. The dream is true and its interpretation is trustworthy."*

---

[3] Daniel predicts in 2:44 that the Messiah will come to establish this Kingdom of God *"in the time of those kings"* – that is, during the days of the Roman emperors. See Luke 2:1–7.

[4] The Lord refers to *"my servant Nebuchadnezzar king of Babylon"* in Jeremiah 25:9, 27:6 and 43:10.

King Nebuchadnezzar's reaction to Daniel's courageous witness is truly remarkable, so let's not take Daniel's words less seriously than the non-believing king of Babylon. If we are ever tempted to doubt that the Kingdom of God has already broken out on the earth, let's remember the rock in this dream.[5] If we are ever tempted to despair of the Church and to imagine that its best days lie behind it, let's note that the growth of the rock is unstoppable.[6] Daniel assures us that the Kingdom of God will keep on advancing and growing throughout the entire earth until Jesus returns.[7]

The Lord gave Nebuchadnezzar this nightmare in order to deliver him from empty dreams about his Babylonian Empire. He intended it to lift the king's eyes up from his own rule so that he could see a better hope than Babylon. So let's reflect on what his dream tells us about the Kingdom of God and let's worship, like Nebuchadnezzar. The Lord is the only wise God and, right now under our noses, he is establishing the only truly global and truly everlasting Kingdom.

---

[5] Matthew 12:28 and Luke 11:20 tell us that the Kingdom of God came to earth with the first coming of Jesus.

[6] Daniel tells Nebuchadnezzar literally in 2:28 that his dream describes *"what will happen in the last days"*. That phrase is used to describe the whole of AD history in Acts 2:17; 2 Timothy 3:1; Hebrews 1:2; James 5:3 and 2 Peter 3:3.

[7] Matthew 6:10; Luke 19:11–12 and Revelation 11:15 tell us that the Kingdom of God will only come in all its fullness with the second coming of Jesus. We live in a moment between the two comings of Jesus, and we should expect it to be a time of great advance and expansion for God's Kingdom throughout the world.

Little Seeds (Daniel 2:46–49)

"The king said to Daniel, 'Surely your God is the God of gods and the Lord of kings and a revealer of mysteries, for you were able to reveal this mystery.'"

(Daniel 2:47)

Last summer I created a vegetable garden with my two youngest children. When we planted the little seeds in the ground, it was difficult to imagine that they would ever grow into something that we could eat for our dinner. But little seeds are mighty things. We are still eating those prize-winning vegetables now.

King Nebuchadnezzar's dream has planted a little seed of faith in his heart. He is not yet converted, but don't miss how much distance he has travelled in just a few verses. At the start of the previous chapter, he was plundering God's Temple in Jerusalem and taking its sacred treasures back as booty to the temple of his own false god in Babylon. Now he is bowing down to Daniel as the prophet of the God of Israel and declaring, *"Surely your God is the God of gods and the Lord of kings and a revealer of mysteries, for you were able to reveal this mystery."* It is a stunning turnaround!

Nebuchadnezzar still has a long way to go before we can consider him to have been genuinely converted to the Lord. For a start, he brings a grain offering to Daniel as a god and burns incense before him as an act of worship – not exactly what Daniel was hoping for in response to his Gospel presentation! Nebuchadnezzar still regards the God of Israel as *"your God"*, rather than his own God, and he will still command his subjects to bow down to his idol in chapter 3. Nevertheless, we must not despise these small beginnings. Little seeds can grow into something massive. Nebuchadnezzar has never needed to bow down to anybody in his life other than his father, so the fact that he bows down before Daniel is a massive milestone in his journey towards repentance. His confession that the God of Israel is greater than the deities of Babylon is a major milestone too. Every great planting of the Lord starts out as a little seed.

The events of this chapter have also planted a little seed of faith in the hearts of Daniel and his three Jewish friends. Only two years earlier, they arrived in Babylon as down-and-out prisoners of war, so these verses mark a massive turnaround for them. Their permission to graduate early from school at the end of chapter 1 seems like nothing compared to their fast-track promotion at the end of chapter 2. Daniel becomes the governor of Babylon, the wealthiest and most powerful province in the empire. His three friends are made chief ministers to assist him in his new role. Daniel is also put in charge of King Nebuchadnezzar's elite circle of royal soothsayers. Four poor Jewish immigrants now find themselves in the top ten most powerful people in the world!

Every time we make a successful stand in obedience to the Lord, it plants another little seed of faith in our hearts. It might be nice to imagine that we can learn to trust God more deeply by reading paperbacks about him while sitting in a comfy chair, but it simply isn't true. The Pentecostal revivalist Smith Wigglesworth taught that *"Great faith is a product of great fights. Great testimonies are the outcome of great tests. Great triumphs can only come after great trials."*[1] These verses ought to convince us that this is true. The fact that they have trusted in God together and been delivered for a second time gives Daniel

[1] Quoted by Jack Hywel-Davies in *Baptised by Fire: The Story of Smith Wigglesworth* (1987).

and his friends a growing courage to keep on standing up for God in Babylon.[2]

The events of this chapter have also planted a little seed of faith in the hearts of the Jewish community in Babylon. They were taken into exile two years earlier because their nation rejected the Word of God. It worshipped pagan idols, intermarried with its pagan neighbours and thought nothing of defiling itself with the sinful ways of the world. The fall of Jerusalem to the Babylonians compounded this national sense of disaffection towards the God of Israel. Other than Daniel and his three friends, none of the Jewish exiles protested at being served non-kosher food in the school canteen. They would have lost their sense of national identity and been absorbed into Babylon had not the promotion of Daniel and his friends transformed their view of the Jewish Law and its call to pursue spiritual purity. How had four Jewish exiles in their late teens or early twenties managed to become some of the most powerful men in the world? It could only be because the God of Israel still honoured those who honoured him.[3]

Like King Nebuchadnezzar, the Jewish exiles still have a long way left to travel on their journey to revival. In the next chapter, most of them will worship a pagan idol, rather than be persecuted for their faith in the Lord. But we must not despise the little seeds of faith that were planted in their hearts through the events of this chapter. Those little seeds will prove decisive in determining whether their exile in Babylon will turn out to be a period of further backsliding and compromise, or a period of repentance and renewed devotion to the God of Israel. The Hebrews had worshipped the idols of their slave masters in Egypt. They had worshipped the idols of the Canaanites after entering the Promised Land. Even after the final destruction

---

[2] This must surely have been what gave Daniel's three friends the courage to stand up for the Lord in chapter 3, in the face of death threats, even without Daniel.

[3] 1 Samuel 2:30. Only twelve years after this, the prophet Ezekiel would honour Daniel by naming him as one of the greatest Old Testament believers of all time (Ezekiel 14:14, 14:20 and 28:3).

of Jerusalem in 586 BC, the handful of Jewish survivors still persisted in their idolatry.[4] It was only because of the contagious devotion of Daniel and his three friends that the beleaguered community of Jewish exiles in Babylon chose to take a very different road.

As a result of this, the events of this chapter planted little seeds of faith in the hearts of the pagans throughout the Babylonian Empire. When they witnessed how willing the Jewish exiles were to live set apart from the rest of the world for the sake of their God, they either hated them or loved them for it. For every pagan that persecuted them, there was another pagan who came knocking on their door with questions about how they might come to know the Lord too.[5] Rather than destroy their faith, the Jewish exile in Babylon became the most successful missionary endeavour in their nation's history.

This should not surprise us. This chapter is about the massive power of little seeds. Nebuchadnezzar dreamed of a rock that quickly grew into a mountain until it filled the entire earth. When Jesus came to earth to launch the rule of his Kingdom through the first church in Jerusalem, he taught his followers that this is how his Kingdom always grows. He told them a famous parable about the power of little seeds. *"The kingdom of heaven is like a mustard seed, which a man took and planted in his field. Though it is the smallest of all seeds, yet when it grows, it is the largest of garden plants and becomes a tree, so that the birds come and perch in its branches."*[6]

---

[4] Ezekiel 20:6–8 and Jeremiah 44:15–18. This may be why Daniel praises the Lord in 2:23 as the *"God of my ancestors"*. His nation was too backslidden for him to feel he could call the Lord the current God of Israel.

[5] For examples of these two opposite reactions, see Esther 3:8–9 and 8:17.

[6] Matthew 13:31–32. This parable also echoes Nebuchadnezzar's second dream. See Daniel 4:12.

Chain Reaction (Daniel 3:1–12)

"There are some Jews whom you have set over the affairs of the province of Babylon – Shadrach, Meshach and Abednego – who pay no attention to. . . your gods..."

(Daniel 3:12)

When Daniel delivered his Gospel presentation to the king of Babylon, it triggered an important chain reaction. The Devil was appalled to witness God's Word flourishing in Babylon, so it provoked him to launch a counter-offensive of his own.

Satan derives perverse pleasure from taking any object that we use to worship the Lord and transforming it into an idolatrous substitute instead. He did this with the bronze snake which the Lord used as a prophetic picture of the cross of Jesus for the Hebrews in the desert.[1] He did it with the Law of Moses, when the Jewish scribes rejected Jesus for questioning their interpretation of it. He still does it today whenever people pray to the apostles as saints instead of studying their words and obeying them. He does it through a superstitious view of communion bread and wine, or of the water at a christening service. He even did it with Daniel's Gospel presentation to the king of Babylon.

Nebuchadnezzar orders the construction of an enormous statue on one of the open spaces just outside the city.[2] We are

---

[1] Numbers 21:4–9; 2 Kings 18:4 and John 3:14–16.

[2] We are told that it was 2.7 metres wide and 27 metres high, which would make it a very skinny statue. Most likely, this height included a large base, meaning that the statue itself was of natural proportions.

not told what this image was explicitly, but there are several clues which suggest that it was a reconstruction of the statue in his dream. We are told that it was made of gold, just like the top section of the statue in chapter 2, which represented Nebuchadnezzar and his Babylonian Empire. We are told that the statue is something distinct from the gods of Babylon, but which must nevertheless be worshipped.[3] Satan must have laughed with delight as he turned a statue that was meant to convert the king of Babylon into something that would compromise the Jews.

The chain reaction spreads to the wise men of Babylon. They see this as their chance to rid themselves of Jewish students who have risen out of nowhere to rule their nation.[4] It is possible that they suggested to Nebuchadnezzar that he construct the statue for this reason, like the royal courtiers in chapter 6, but a more natural reading of these verses is that the chain reaction spread the other way. Seizing upon the king's idea, they waste no time in denouncing their Jewish colleagues to the king.[5] The Devil tries to use their hatred as a way of uprooting the little seeds of faith that God has planted in the hearts of the Jewish exiles.

Soon the chain reaction spreads to the entire city. You don't need to know the difference between a *satrap*, a prefect, a governor, an advisor, a treasurer, a judge, a magistrate and an official. These eight words in Aramaic are simply meant to convey a sense that the entire government of Babylon sided with the king and with his statue. You don't need to know the difference between a horn, a flute, a zither, a lyre, a harp and a pipe either. Those six words are merely meant to show us that every people group in the city complied by offering their

---

[3] Nebuchadnezzar is told that the three friends *"**neither** serve your gods **nor** worship the image of gold"* (3:12).

[4] The word *Astrologers*, or *Babylonians*, in 3:8 was used as shorthand for the wise men of Babylon in 2:10.

[5] The Aramaic metaphor that is used in 3:8 and 6:24 for *denouncing* people means literally to *chew pieces off* them. This is what happens when we slander people. We leave their reputation mauled and bleeding.

diverse types of worship to the golden statue.[6] *"All the nations and peoples of every language fell down and worshipped the image of gold"* (3:7).

Things look pretty dire for the Jewish faith in Babylon, but we discover that the Lord has launched his own chain reaction too. Daniel is nowhere to be seen in these verses. His government duties have evidently taken him out of town. But if this emboldened the king to think that he could get away with his statue, then he has a big surprise in store. Daniel had never been a lone ranger for the Lord. He took a lead in chapter 1 but asked his teacher to include his three friends in his school test. He took a lead in chapter 2 but gathered his four friends to pray for revelation and to weigh his vision together. Daniel insisted in verse 36 that he was the spokesman for a wider team. *"This was the dream, and now* ***we*** *will interpret it to the king."* After being promoted at the end of chapter 2, Daniel's first action was to request similar promotions for his friends.

As a result, once Daniel leaves town and the king constructs his statue, we see the vital importance of teamwork to effective ministry. In the novel by H. G. Wells, the invisible man laments, *"I made a mistake . . . a huge mistake, in carrying this thing through alone. I have wasted strength, time, opportunities. Alone – it is wonderful how little a man can do alone!"*[7] Daniel has worked with others from day one. It doesn't matter that the Aramaic text refers to his three friends by their new Babylonian names – Shadrach, Meshach and Abednego – because Daniel has already shown them how to act as Jews behind enemy lines, perfectly devoted to the God of Israel.

This is how spiritual revival spreads. Note the four generations of Christians that are mentioned in 2 Timothy 2:2, when the Apostle Paul commands: *"The things you have heard me say in the presence of many witnesses entrust to reliable*

---

[6] These two detailed descriptions of the civil servants and the musical instruments of ancient Babylon should also build our confidence in the eyewitness historicity of the book of Daniel.

[7] H. G. Wells in his novel, *The Invisible Man* (1897).

people who will also be qualified to teach others." Paul imparted his faith to Timothy and encouraged him to impart his own faith to reliable people, who could in turn impart their faith to others. This is about more than mere multiplication. If Daniel had been the one who rejected the king's command then it would have had an impact on the Jewish exiles, but the fact that three different voices spoke now with the same courage must have impacted them more. Better than the symphony of horns and flutes and zithers and lyres and harps and pipes, the sound of many diverse believers singing the same song of courageous commitment to the Lord with different voices is enough to bring down the spiritual walls of any city.

Suddenly it becomes clear that the Devil's chain reaction has backfired. Nebuchadnezzar constructed his enormous statue as a triumphant declaration that he was the ruler of the world and that he knew the secret to an everlasting kingdom. Instead of looking powerful in these verses, however, he looks very small. He is manipulated by his courtiers, like a puppet, into attacking some of his best officials. He loses his temper like a spoiled child when Shadrach, Meshach and Abednego expose his secret insecurities by declaring that their primary allegiance isn't to him, but to God's everlasting Kingdom.

The Devil's strategy has failed. This episode isn't going to spell disaster for the Jews in Babylon. It will simply serve to spark a chain reaction by which Daniel's devotion to the God of Israel will spread to his friends, to the other Jewish exiles and to the world.

Two Forms of Faith (Daniel 3:13–18)

"The God we serve is able to deliver us... But even if he does not, we want you to know, Your Majesty, that we will not serve your gods or worship the image of gold..."

(Daniel 3:17–18)

Shadrach, Meshach and Abednego were men of faith - they needed to be, in order to defy the king's command to worship his statue. Everybody knew that Nebuchadnezzar was a tyrant who thought nothing of beheading a teacher for meddling with the menus in the school canteen or of slaughtering courtiers who failed to measure up to his unreasonable demands.[1] When the three Jewish friends refused to worship the king's statue, they knew that they were issuing their own death warrants. Even so, they were determined to express their faith in the God of Israel in either of its two forms.

We are meant to spot a demonic parody of the Gospel in the angry response of King Nebuchadnezzar to Shadrach, Meshach and Abednego. When Jesus describes hell in Matthew 13:42 and 13:50, he uses words that are taken directly from the Greek Septuagint translation of these verses that describe the king's *blazing furnace*. Nebuchadnezzar essentially boasts to these three Jews that he holds the power to throw them into hell unless they worship his golden statue. He forgets his own confession of faith in 3:15 when he carries on by boasting: *"Then what god will be able to rescue you from my hand?"*

---

[1] There is nothing hyperbolic about Daniel 1:10, 2:5, 3:29 and 5:19.

Nebuchadnezzar has thrown down the gauntlet to the God of Israel. Shadrach, Meshach and Abednego therefore refuse to stall for time. They do not soften their position to pacify the king's anger. They do not ask for time to go away and pray before coming back with a more considered answer.[2] Instead, they declare that they are ready to display their commitment to the God of Israel in either of faith's two forms.

The first form of faith in God is when we trust him to deliver us from the need to pass through a particular evil. Shadrach, Meshach and Abednego express this first form of faith when they tell the king that *"If we are thrown into the blazing furnace, the God we serve is able to deliver us from it, and he will deliver us from Your Majesty's hand."*

The second form of faith in God is when we trust him to deliver us from evil, even if his perfect plan should necessitate that we pass through it. The three friends express this second form of faith when they continue: *"But even if he does not, we want you to know, Your Majesty, that we will not serve your gods or worship the image of gold you have set up."*[3]

It is vital that we recognize both of these two forms of faith if we are to take the same courageous stand in modern-day Babylon. If we equate successful Christian witness with miraculous deliverance, then we will never tread the path that has led so many of the great men and women of Church history to sacrifice everything for the Lord.

We will celebrate the faith of Martin Luther who, when threatened with execution unless he backtracked on his Gospel preaching, famously retorted, *"My conscience is captive to the Word of God. I cannot and I will not recant anything, for to go against conscience is neither right nor safe. Here I stand. I can do*

---

[2] The Aramaic text of 3:16 can just as easily be translated, *"We do not need to come back to you on this matter."*

[3] Note how little time they require to arrive at this bold decision together. Like Daniel in 1:8, they have already resolved to obey the Lord at any price. They lived ready to embrace their high tide moment.

no other. So help me God."[4] But unless we recognize that faith has two forms, we will tell the story of Martin Luther's deliverance and of his sixteenth-century revival as if it were how every showdown of faith ought to end.

Yet what about Jan Hus, the fifteenth-century church leader from Prague, who was also threatened with execution for his Gospel preaching? Unlike Martin Luther, he wasn't friends with powerful politicians who rescued him from the flames. Instead, his communion cup was snatched from his hands and he was tied to a stake to be burned. Unless we grasp that there are two forms of faith, we will view what happened to Jan Hus as a tragic tale which lacks the proper happy ending. We will see no glory in his defiant declaration, *"I trust in the Lord Almighty God. . . that He will not take the cup of His salvation from me. I have the firm hope that I shall today drink of it in His kingdom. . . Most joyfully will I confirm with my blood that truth which I have written and preach."*[5]

The truth is that triumphant Christian faith has two forms. For every story of God delivering his people ***from*** evil, there is another story of his delivering them ***out of*** evil. The execution of Jan Hus provoked such a backlash that his writings spread more after his death than they ever had while he was alive. Just before he made his own stand of faith, Martin Luther confessed to a friend how much Jan Hus had inspired his own spiritual revolution. *"We are all Hussites without knowing it."*[6]

Unless we grasp that there are two forms of faith, and that both of them represent successful Christian witness, we will struggle to understand Hebrews 5:7, which tell us that *"During the days of Jesus' life on earth, he offered up prayers and petitions with fervent cries and tears to the one who could save him from death, and he was heard because of his reverent submission."* We

[4] Quoted by Roland Bainton in *Here I Stand: A Life of Martin Luther* (1950).

[5] Quoted by Paul Roubiczek and Joseph Kalmer in *Warrior of God: the Life and Death of Jan Hus* (1947).

[6] Martin Luther wrote this in a letter to George Spalatin in February 1520.

will fail to fathom how Jesus' prayers "were heard" when he was tortured, crucified and killed. We won't grasp that this verse is telling us that Jesus exhibited two forms of faith, and not just one. He prayed to be saved ***from*** death, but once he saw that his death would do more to further God's plan of salvation than his deliverance, he embraced being saved ***out of*** death instead.[7]

I have never met a Christian who did not long to see a spiritual revival of the Church in their nation like the one that has brought millions to Christ over the past few years in China. There are now more Chinese Christians than there are Chinese communist party members, and there are many miraculous tales of God delivering Chinese preachers from their would-be persecutors. But if we want to see spiritual revival like the one in China, then we also have to be prepared to embrace the second form of faith too.

Watchman Nee laid much of the foundation the Chinese revival. He was arrested by the communists in 1952. Although he prayed to be released, he died two decades later in a filthy bunk bed in a labour camp, never having been set free. When a family member went to the labour camp to collect his remains, one of the prison guards handed her a scrap of paper which he found hidden under Watchman Nee's pillow. Just before he died, the old man had written: *"Christ is the Son of God who died for the redemption of sinners and was raised after three days. This is the greatest truth in the universe. I die because of my belief in Christ."* [8] He had learned the truth that Shadrach, Meshach and Abednego attempt to teach us in this chapter. Faith in God has two forms, and we each need to have them both.

---

[7] The Greek phrase *ek thanatou* in Hebrews 5:7 can be translated as either *"from death"* or *"out of death"*.

[8] Witness Lee in *Watchman Nee: A Seer of the Divine Revelation in the Present Age* (1991).

Cameo (Daniel 3:19–27)

"Look! I see four men walking around in the fire, unbound and unharmed, and the fourth looks like a son of the gods."

(Daniel 3:25)

There have been some pretty stunning cameo appearances by directors in their own films. There's Martin Scorsese as a passenger in *Taxi Driver*. There's James Cameron as a bystander in *Titanic*. There's Peter Jackson as a peasant in *The Lord of the Rings*. There's Alfred Hitchcock in just about any movie he directed. But all of these are nothing compared to what happens in these verses. Jesus suddenly shows up in ancient Babylon.

Nebuchadnezzar isn't expecting to come face to face with the ruler of the everlasting Kingdom which formed the grand finale to his terrifying dream. He is too busy terrifying Shadrach, Meshach and Abednego with what will happen to them if they refuse to bow down and worship his golden statue. The kings of Babylon were a bit like James Bond baddies. It was never enough for them merely to murder their enemies. They always had to do it in strange and needlessly elaborate ways – a giant-sized oven or a pit full of lions – and this time the king of Babylon is taking no chances. He demands that his blazing furnace be made seven times hotter than usual. So hot, in fact, that the executioners die simply from standing too close to it.[1] When Shadrach, Meshach

---

[1] These soldiers were not weaklings. The Aramaic phrase that is used to describe them in 3:20 can be translated *"mighty men of valour"*. Their deaths proved there was no way for the three friends to survive.

and Abednego are tied up and thrown into the furnace, it looks like it is game over for Daniel's three friends.

But Nebuchadnezzar has not counted on the ruler of God's everlasting Kingdom making a sudden appearance in the story. As he gazes into the furnace, he asks his advisors in amazement, *"Weren't there three men that we tied up and threw into the fire?"*[2] He knows that this is true, but his eyes tell a different story. *"Look! I see four men walking around in the fire, unbound and unharmed, and the fourth looks like a son of the gods."*

The Hebrew word *elōhīm* and its Aramaic counterpart *elāhīn* are both plural nouns, translated as gods when describing pagan deities and as God when describing the Lord. This was an Old Testament clue that the Lord was one God in three Persons, but it also serves an important purpose here, because the king is speaking far more truly than he knows. This is not a cameo appearance by a pagan deity, such as Nebo, who boasted that he was the son of Marduk. This is the Son of the Lord God of Israel. It is the ruler of God's everlasting kingdom, whose arrival was represented by a rock demolishing the statue in Nebuchadnezzar's dream. Centuries before he ever walked out onto the stage in Galilee, the baby of Bethlehem put in a surprise cameo in Babylon.

King Nebuchadnezzar leaps to his feet in amazement. He is suddenly reminded of how he felt when he heard Daniel's miraculous interpretation of his dream. He commands Shadrach, Meshach and Abednego to step out of the blazing furnace, addressing them as *"servants of the Most High God"*.[3] Instead of making people tremble at his orders by executing Daniel's three friends, it is now the king himself who trembles before the Lord.

---

[2] The Aramaic text of 3:23 says that the three men *"fell"* into the blazing furnace – presumably from a hole in the roof. There was evidently another hole at ground level too, through which the king of Babylon could see.

[3] It required a fresh step of faith for the three friends to come out of the blazing furnace, since it had become for them the safest place in the whole world. They had to trust God that the king's change of heart was real.

These verses are meant to encourage us whenever we experience persecution for our faith in modern-day Babylon. Theologians still debate whether Jesus descended into hell for three days between his crucifixion and his resurrection, but we should be in no doubt that he descends into our own hell with us whenever we suffer for his name. In Philippians 3:10, the Apostle Paul describes finding fellowship with Jesus in his sufferings. Most of us assume he means that we draw closer to the cross of Jesus when we are persecuted for him. While this may be true, the message of Daniel 3 is that Jesus draws closer to where we are in the midst of our sufferings too.

"I will never leave you or forsake you," the Lord promises us. *"When you pass through raging rivers, I will be with you. When you walk through the fire, you will not be burned. The flames will not set you ablaze, for I am with you."* The promises God makes in Deuteronomy 31:6 and Isaiah 43:2 are vividly illustrated here. They reassure us that the Lord is with us in all of our afflictions. Whether he comes bodily or spiritually, and whether he comes to save us from death or out of death, we never suffer for him alone.

When King Nebuchadnezzar inspects his three Jewish officials, he is amazed still further. The flames have burned away the ropes with which his soldiers bound their hands and feet. That's how they were able to walk around freely in the furnace. But their *robes* and *trousers* and *turbans* and *other clothing* have not been singed at all.[4] Nor has a single hair on their Jewish heads been burned, despite the way in which the furnace charred the Babylonian flesh of the soldiers who stood too near. Shadrach, Meshach and Abednego's clothes don't even smell as yours or mine do after we have been sitting by a bonfire.

The king therefore changes his tune. He concludes that the cameo appearance he has just witnessed must have been that of

---

[4] This list of four types of Babylonian clothing (3:21) goes together with the lists of eight types of Babylonian official (3:2) and six types of Babylonian musical instrument (3:5) to affirm the historicity of the book of Daniel. This chapter can only have been written by a contemporary eyewitness.

an angel of the Most High God of Israel.[5] He worships the Lord for this, *"for no other god can save in this way."* Then he praises Shadrach, Meshach and Abednego. He actually commends them for having had the courage to resist his rash command to commit idolatry! He promotes the three friends to the top positions within the province of Babylon, which is the richest and most powerful province of the world's richest and most powerful empire.

King Nebuchadnezzar is not yet converted to the Lord. The cruelty of his royal decree in verse 29 demonstrates that his sinful heart remains largely unchanged. But this is now the third time that he has witnessed the power of God at work in Babylon. The fire in his furnace is gradually subsiding, but the fire of the Gospel is spreading. Nebuchadnezzar declares to his subjects, from every people group and language of his empire, that the God of Israel is greater than any of the deities of Babylon.

We can only imagine what effect this announcement had on the Jewish exiles and on their pagan neighbours. We are left to guess how much it contributed to the spiritual revival that they experienced in Babylon. We are left to ponder what the Lord might do in our own day if his people truly preferred to die than compromise his name.

The message of this chapter is very simple. Whenever we allow the Gospel to consume us, its fire spreads.[6]

---

[5] We are not told that it *was* an angel – simply that Nebuchadnezzar assumed it must be an angel.

[6] Daniel 3:27 says literally that *"over their bodies the fire had no power"*. That's great news when it refers to the fire of Babylon, but it is tragic whenever sleepy Christians become flame-retardant to the Gospel.

The Wrong Words (Daniel 4:1–9)

"He is called Belteshazzar, after the name of my god . . . I said, 'Belteshazzar, chief of the magicians, I know that the spirit of the holy gods is in you. . .'"

(Daniel 4:8–9)

The Bible has over forty authors. Many of them are quite surprising. But far and away the most surprising of them all is the person who wrote the fourth chapter of Daniel. He was the destroyer of ancient cities. He was the erecter of a golden idol. He was the tyrant of Babylon. Yes, incredibly, King Nebuchadnezzar actually wrote part of the Bible.[1]

In the original Aramaic text, the first three verses of chapter 4 are the final verses of chapter 3. These are the words that King Nebuchadnezzar sent out across his empire after seeing the Lord deliver Shadrach, Meshach and Abednego. Since he had sent out a herald to command the *"nations and peoples of every language"* to bow down to his statue, Nebuchadnezzar uses similar wording in these three verses to explain why he is now rescinding that order. A series of astonishing miracles have led to his discovery that the God of Israel is *"the Most High God"*, far above any of the deities of Babylon. He is no longer calling people to bow down to his dream that the Babylonian Empire might become an everlasting kingdom. He now recognizes that

---

[1] Daniel remains the editor of chapter 4, but its format is unusual, collating both his own words and those of the king. First, the king writes in the first person to describe his second dream (4:4–18). Daniel then interjects in the third person to give his interpretation (4:19–27) and an account of the king's final encounter with the Lord (4:28–33). The king then returns to share a first-person testimony of his surrender to the Lord (4:34–37).

this will only ever be the case for God. The Lord deserves all worship, because *"His kingdom is an eternal kingdom"*.

In 4:4–27, the timing changes but the subject matter doesn't. Many years have passed since he threw three of his Jewish courtiers into the blazing furnace, yet the king reveals that the fire of the Gospel is still burning brightly in his heart.[2] He has received a second dream that terrifies him as much as the first one. He has shared it with the wise men of Babylon and they have once more come up short, so he turns again to Daniel and to the God of Israel. Before we hear the contents of his dream, let's pause for a moment to marvel at the faithfulness of Daniel. Many years have rolled by, but he is still present at the palace, living ready for the next high tide moment in God's salvation story.

In verse 8, we catch a sense of how difficult this must have been for Daniel. The king refers to him as *"Belteshazzar, after the name of my god"*. How disappointing. By now, we might have expected him to have renounced all ties with Bel, the patron deity of Babylon, or at the very least to have stopped all that nonsense about renaming Daniel with a moniker that means *Bel-Will-Protect-The-King.* The events of the past three chapters ought to have convinced him that the name Daniel is significant, since it means *The-Lord-Is-My-Judge* or *The-Lord-Will-Vindicate-Me.* But no. Nebuchadnezzar is sharing his personal testimony as it really happened, and the truth is that old habits die hard. Frustrating though it was for Daniel, the king kept on using all of the wrong words.

In verse 9, he does so again. He refers to Daniel as his *"chief of the magicians"*, using an Aramaic word which can mean occultist, enchanter, wizard or conjurer. It is one of the four words that he also uses in verse 7 to describe Daniel's pagan colleagues as magicians, astrologers, diviners, necromancers, spiritualists, mediums and sorcerers. After all that he has been through, how

[2] Daniel 4:22 suggests that he received this second dream after he had completed much of his conquering.

can Nebuchadnezzar still regard the Lord's prophet as a common conjurer? For Daniel, it must have been terribly disappointing.

It gets even worse. In both of these two verses, the king asserts that Daniel is wise because *"the spirit of the holy gods is in him."*[3] The Aramaic word here is *elāhīn*, a plural noun, which is translated gods when describing pagan deities and God when describing the Lord. English Bible translators opt for the former here because it's fairly obvious that Nebuchadnezzar is expressing his old pagan worldview.[4] He still sees Bel as his real god. He still regards the God of Israel as a sideshow. If you have ever winced to hear your non-believing friend express how "lucky" you are to have a faith in God or how "magical" it felt when you prayed for them, then you know a little of how Daniel must have felt here. Nebuchadnezzar uses all of the wrong words.

So why does Daniel put up with it? Why does he make no attempt to correct the king's grating language and to teach him the right words to use when describing the God of Israel? It must be because of what we learned about "drilling" and "blasting". Daniel is less concerned about correcting the king's language than he is about learning the right language by which he can connect with the king. Whenever he felt discouraged, he reminded himself that he was a missionary in Babylon: *It is God who put you here.*

Let me try to explain with a modern-day example. One of the missionaries that I most admire has planted many churches across Japan, which is generally regarded as a tough mission field. Initially, he found this to be true, since he was preaching from the traditional Japanese translation of the Bible, which translates the word *sin* with a Japanese word that means "lawbreaking". Whenever he preached the Gospel to Japanese people and asked them to raise their hand if they needed

---

[3] Nebuchadnezzar goes on to make this same mistake for a third time in 4:18.

[4] When the king confesses that Bel, who was also known as Marduk, is still his god, it could hardly be more serious. Bel was usually depicted in Babylonian art accompanied by a dragon. In case this isn't enough to convince you that he was demonic, note that the Canaanites referred to him as *Baal*. See 1 Kings 18.

forgiveness, nobody did so. In an honour culture like Japan, he discovered, nobody admits to being a lawbreaker.

The missionary went back to the drawing board. He decided to preach less and to listen more. When he did so, he discovered that Japanese people used different words to express their spirituality (rather like a king of Babylon saying *gods* when he really meant God, or *magician* when he really meant prophet). Some of their words were actually more biblical than his own. They used a far better word to describe sin. They didn't call it lawbreaking. They called it falling short, which is far closer to the actual meaning of the Hebrew word *hāṭā'*. The missionary raised his own hand to repent of the cultural blindness that had made him use the wrong words to describe the right things.

To his immense surprise, when he began to preach the Gospel as a call to confess to God that we have *fallen short*, a forest of Japanese hands went up in the air. The teenagers felt that they were a disappointment to their parents. The parents felt that they were a disappointment to their bosses at work. When they heard that God was not disappointed with them, but had sent his Son to earth to save them, it truly sounded like Good News to them. The missionary now has a network of churches across Japan.

So don't miss the way that Daniel handles his disappointment when the king uses the wrong words in these verses. It is a vital aspect of the message of the book of Daniel. If we imagine that the book is a non-stop call for Christians not to compromise with Babylon, then we are only reading half the story. Daniel also calls us to listen to non-believers, without judging them for using the wrong words, so that they might teach us to use the right ones. Then, and only then, will we be able to breach the walls of Babylon and to lead many of its citizens to salvation.

Patience (Daniel 4:8–27)

"Daniel came into my presence and I told him the dream. . . 'Here is my dream; interpret it for me.'"

(Daniel 4:8–9)

Eventually, Daniel's patience with King Nebuchadnezzar pays off. We are not told when the king has his second dream, but we can tell from verse 22 that it is quite some time after the Battle of Carchemish. By now he has conquered much of the known world.[1] Daniel has been serving the king for many years, but he is still standing faithfully at his post in the palace. He is still living ready for a fresh high tide moment in history.

Nebuchadnezzar's testimony pivots on a few simple words in verse 8 – *"Daniel came into my presence and I told him the dream."* It turns out that the biggest contribution we can make to God's plans is simply remaining where he has placed us. Daniel has had many moments over the years when he might have given up on serving the king of Babylon, but here he is still standing at his post when opportunity comes knocking. How many times must he have needed to remind himself? *It is God who put you here.*

Daniel's example brings to mind the Rule of St Benedict, which teaches that the secret to spiritual fruitfulness lies in a commitment to what Benedict calls stability.[2] A rolling stone

---

[1] This probably means that Nebuchadnezzar dreamed it after sacking and destroying Jerusalem in 586 BC. We are not told how Daniel persevered through this. He just kept on witnessing patiently for the Lord.

[2] Benedictine monks take three vows: *obedience*, *stability* and *openness to being challenged*.

gathers no moss, and nor does a Christian who is too busy flitting from one place to another to make any discernible impact on anywhere. The most important thing that Daniel does in this chapter is simply staying where God put him. His high view of God's purposes has helped him persevere through many setbacks and disappointments. His stability flows out of his faith in the sovereignty of God: *It is God who put you here.*

As a result, this fresh Gospel opportunity finds Daniel at his post and ready for action. He listens to the king's second dream and, by the time Nebuchadnezzar has finished, he feels every bit as terrified as the king. He hesitates, wondering how to explain that this dream about a tree is a continuation of his previous dream about a statue.[3] The tree's wide and lofty branches represent King Nebuchadnezzar's glory.[4] He is even greater now than he was when he received his first dream. His mighty empire is unlike anything that the world has ever seen. It is now *"visible to the ends of the earth" and* encompasses *"every creature"*.[5] But sadly, world domination has gone to the king's head.

Over the years, Daniel has patiently perfected the art of "drilling" and "blasting". Note how he communicates timeless truth to Nebuchadnezzar using timely words that the king can understand. In verse 23, rather than use the Aramaic word that corresponds to the Hebrew word for *angel* throughout the Old Testament, he repeats the two Aramaic words that the king just used in verses 13 and 17.[6] If Nebuchadnezzar prefers to refer to angels as watchmen or holy ones, then that is fine by Daniel. He

---

[3] Daniel's hesitation springs from genuine affection for Nebuchadnezzar. But it also springs from knowing that the king is not a man to take bad news lightly and that his dream is very bad news indeed.

[4] Archaeologists have unearthed an ancient inscription that refers to Babylon as a *"spreading tree"*. God is therefore modelling for us here how to use the right words to communicate truth to specific non-believers.

[5] Jesus echoes this dream when he deliberately uses language from 4:12 and 4:21 to describe his own everlasting Kingdom in Matthew 13:32; Mark 4:32 and Luke 13:19.

[6] The Aramaic word *mal'ak*, in 3:28 and 6:22, corresponds to the Hebrew word *mal'āk* throughout the Bible.

has learned the importance of learning the right words to use to connect with non-believers.

Daniel does it again when he refers to the Lord in verses 24 and 25 as *"the Most High"*, which is the phrase that Nebuchadnezzar used to describe him in verses 2 and 17. Daniel is determined to dress up God's Word in the language of the king's own heart. It would be one thing for Nebuchadnezzar to reject the Gospel for its own sake, but it would be quite another for him to reject the Gospel because Daniel dressed it up in Jewish clothes.

Remember the words of Tim Keller that we read together earlier. *"All drilling with no blasting, or all blasting with no drilling, leads to failure . . . To contextualise with balance and successfully reach people in a culture, we must* ***both*** *enter the culture sympathetically and respectfully (similar to drilling)* ***and*** *confront the culture where it contradicts biblical truth (similar to blasting)."* After "drilling", Daniel therefore takes a big gulp and starts "blasting".

He informs Nebuchadnezzar that the Lord has decided to deal with his stubborn pride. If ego stands for **E**dging **G**od **O**ut, then the Lord has determined to edge himself back in. Nebuchadnezzar is about to be driven from his throne by a lengthy bout of madness. We can tell from a later chapter that *"seven times"* refers here to "seven years".[7] The king will believe that he is an animal, eating grass and sleeping out in the open, until he finally acknowledges the message of his first dream – that his mighty empire is a gift from the Lord.[8] Only then will his madness be lifted so that he can reassume his throne.

Tightrope walking isn't easy. Those who are the best at communicating sensitively with non-believers ("drilling") can

---

[7] The significance of the phrase that is used in 4:16, 23 and 25 will be explained later, in Daniel 7:25.

[8] Daniel 4:17 and 4:25 deliberately echo 2:37–38. To the Lord, he is merely *"my servant Nebuchadnezzar king of Babylon"* (Jeremiah 25:9, 27:6 and 43:10).

often be the worst when it comes to delivering the punchy Gospel challenge that they need to hear ("blasting"). Daniel therefore models for us how to walk the tightrope when he gives the king both barrels of God's judgment in verse 27. Nebuchadnezzar was at the height of his powers when he dreamed this second dream. Jeremiah 4:7 describes him as *"a destroyer of nations"*, so he would think very little of destroying an outspoken courtier. Yet Daniel is less worried about emerging from the king's palace alive than he is about seizing the opportunity for which he has been waiting patiently. Throwing caution to the wind, he accuses Nebuchadnezzar of being a wicked sinner, a persistent wrongdoer and a cruel oppressor. Daniel tries to be winsome about it, but he still displays enormous courage. *"Therefore, Your Majesty, be pleased to accept my advice: Renounce your sins by doing what is right, and your wickedness by being kind to the oppressed. It may be that then your prosperity will continue."*[9]

Silence falls on the palace. The royal courtiers can hardly believe their ears. They now understand why Daniel was so perplexed and terrified about the dream. They hold their breath to see how Nebuchadnezzar will respond to Daniel's interpretation.

Sadly, the king does not repent, even after this second Gospel presentation from Daniel. We are told that, twelve months later, his ego was still edging God out, and that he had to come to faith in the Lord the hard way. Nevertheless, it only happened then because Daniel was found at his post in the palace to interpret Nebuchadnezzar's second dream. Once again, opportunity had found him ready when it knocked on his door. It found Daniel to be a man of *stability* and *patience.*

---

[9] Verse 27. Daniel's example suggests that Christians today have not proclaimed the Gospel to people and found them unreceptive. Compared with Daniel, we have pulled our punches and not proclaimed the Gospel at all.

The Garden (Daniel 4:28–37)

"Twelve months later, as the king was walking on the roof of the royal palace of Babylon. . ."

(Daniel 4:29)

Nebuchadnezzar was not just a bloodthirsty destroyer. He was also a sensitive gardener. His Hanging Gardens of Babylon were so amazing that they were listed among the Seven Wonders of the Ancient World.

Nebuchadnezzar had married a foreign princess named Amytis of Media. She loved her new life in Babylon but she dearly missed the forested mountains of her home, so her husband demonstrated his love for her by building her a man-made mountain in downtown Babylon. He constructed an enormous palace which had several storeys. He planted trees and vines on each of its tiered rooftops and allowed their branches to hang down the sides of the palace, making it look and feel like an enormous green mountain to remind the queen of her home.[1] A better translation for Nebuchadnezzar's creation is the Overhanging Gardens of Babylon.

The Lord was very patient towards the great gardener of Babylon. He gave him twelve months to repent after receiving his second dream.[2] Only then did the Lord enact what he had

---

[1] The first-century Jewish historian Josephus tells us this story in *Against Apion* (1.19).

[2] The Lord gave Nebuchadnezzar twelve months to repent, but then his judgment fell suddenly. This is how it will be with the second coming of Jesus. God is very patient now, but then his judgment will be immediate.

threatened. The narrative of verses 28–33 is in the third person, as Daniel explains to us what happened next to the king. He was walking in the garden on his palace rooftop, when his heart was filled with arrogance towards the Lord. What other ruler could have created a man-made mountain like the Hanging Gardens of Babylon? What other king could have built a city like the one that he looked out onto below? Forgetting everything that the Lord had tried to teach him through his two dreams, Nebuchadnezzar boasted out loud, *"Is not this the great Babylon I have built as the royal residence, by my mighty power and for the glory of my majesty?"* [3]

No sooner had he spoken these words than a voice from heaven boomed out a reply. Nebuchadnezzar would be gripped by madness for seven years until his stubborn heart grew humble enough to confess that the message of his two dreams was true: *"The Most High is sovereign over all kingdoms on earth and gives them to anyone he wishes."* [4] Nebuchadnezzar had filled his rooftop garden with a menagerie of animals. For seven years, he would now join them, eating the grass in his garden like common cattle and sleeping rough under the stars until his hair became matted and his nails became as hardened as the feathers and the talons of one of the eagles in his garden.[5]

Perhaps this scene is meant to remind us of a different garden. Like Adam and Eve, Nebuchadnezzar refused to listen to a warning from the Lord. They were led astray by a snake; he is led astray by a deity who is depicted as walking with a

---

[3] Nebuchadnezzar's boast in verse 30 is a direct denial of 2:37–38, 4:17 and 4:25. The issue is not his pride with regard to other men. He really had achieved more than any other ruler. The issue is his pride with regard to God.

[4] Note that the Lord uses Nebuchadnezzar's own words when he describes himself as *"the Most High"*. He is even more committed to contextualizing the Gospel than Daniel. He knows exactly the right words to use.

[5] Modern medicine has recorded rare examples of something similar today. *Boanthropy* is a personality disorder which causes the sufferer to believe that they are a cow or ox, and to act accordingly.

dragon. Their eyes tempted them to eat forbidden fruit in order to become like God; his eyes tempt him to speak blasphemously that he has already become like God. Adam and Eve were ejected from their garden; Nebuchadnezzar becomes a wretched prisoner in his.

One of the most famous pictures by the British artist William Blake depicts the madness of Nebuchadnezzar. He appears naked and bestial, but there is a look of despair in his eyes – as if he is suddenly coming to his senses and recalling the great heights from which he has fallen. By God's grace, the king's descent into madness is not the end of the story. In verses 34–37, he resumes his role as our narrator. He shares his testimony about the glorious moment when he finally came to his senses and was set free.[6]

> *At the end of that time, I, Nebuchadnezzar, raised my eyes towards heaven, and my sanity was restored. Then I praised the Most High; I honoured and glorified him who lives forever. His dominion is an eternal dominion; his kingdom endures from generation to generation . . . Now I, Nebuchadnezzar, praise and exalt and glorify the King of heaven, because everything he does is right and all his ways are just. And those who walk in pride he is able to humble.*

This confession of faith is a high point in the book of Daniel. In many ways, it summarizes the book's message. Nebuchadnezzar admits that the message of his two dreams is true.[7] The Lord is the only true Ruler of the earth, who presides over the only truly everlasting Kingdom that the world will ever see. The Lord is utterly sovereign over the powers of heaven and the peoples of the earth. He is uninhibited by any pagan deity or by any earthly king. *"He does as he pleases . . .*

---

[6] *"My sanity was restored"* reminds us of a similar moment in the Parable of the Lost Son, in Luke 15:17.

[7] Daniel 4:34–35 is meant to be a direct echo of 2:37–38, 2:44–45, 4:3, 4:17 and 4:25–26.

No one can hold back his hand or say to him: 'What have you done?'"[8] King Nebuchadnezzar finally surrenders his heart to the message of the book of Daniel: *It is God who put you here.*

The moment that Nebuchadnezzar makes this confession of faith, it paves the way for his restoration. When his courtiers come to feed him in his Hanging Gardens, they discover that his madness is no more. They bring him back downstairs into the palace. They trim his nails and hair. They declare to the Babylonian Empire that Nebuchadnezzar is back on the throne. The seven years of regency are over. The Lord restores to him all of his former fame and splendour. The king tells us in verse 36 that the Lord made him even greater than before, which is probably a nod to his conquest of the Egyptian Empire in 567 BC. It's amazing how much the Lord can elevate us once we confess freely that we are nothing. He wants to lift us up, not pull us down.

I wonder how much of our frustration in modern-day Babylon can be traced back to this same principle. If I am honest, my greatest failures in life have usually been preceded by an overinflated view of my own talents. I may not have boasted out loud like Nebuchadnezzar, but I have entertained similar thoughts in my head. I have forgotten the message of the book of Daniel. *It is God who put you here.*

When I look back on my greatest triumphs, they have usually been preceded by a right view of my own weakness and a right sense of the greatness of the Lord. Perhaps this is the main thing that God is looking for in his servants. Perhaps the secret to achieving many of our dreams is to learn from the two dreams of Nebuchadnezzar. Perhaps the Lord is simply waiting for us to confess that what Colossians 1:16 says about him is true: *"In him all things were created: things in heaven and on earth, visible and invisible, whether thrones or powers or rulers or authorities; all things have been created through him and for him."*

[8] Nebuchadnezzar's question in verse 35 echoes Job 9:12 and Romans 9:20. His literal reference in 4:35 to *"the army of heaven"* is perhaps a reflection of the fact that he saw an angel in 4:13. He is in awe that God should command such beautiful beings.

Unlikely Converts (Daniel 4:37)

"Now I, Nebuchadnezzar, praise and exalt and glorify the King of heaven . . ."

(Daniel 4:37)

Readers of the book of Daniel cannot agree on whether or not King Nebuchadnezzar was actually converted. Did he come to genuine faith and surrender to the Lord, or is this just another of his knee-jerk declarations which later prove shallow? Let's look at some of the evidence that he wasn't converted, then at some of the evidence that he was. Then we can reflect on four reasons why our view on this issue really matters.

The greatest reason to doubt that Nebuchadnezzar was converted is that there is little historical evidence to suggest he was. No record has survived of any royal edict ordering the closure of pagan temples or declaring that there is a new God of Babylon.[1] Even if there were, the king's testimony here seems quite deficient. He has a good grasp of God's greatness and of his own sinfulness, but there is little understanding here of how God has atoned for our sin.

One of my favourite places to take my children for a day out is the British Museum. I can't defend the rightness of so many objects from the ancient world being on display in my home city, but studying them gives us a better perspective on history. Take, for example, the failure of King Sennacherib of Assyria to capture Jerusalem in 701 BC. The siege is recorded

---

[1] That is, unless we include this one. We actually have very few surviving records at all from the second half of Nebuchadnezzar's reign. The book of Daniel is the most reliable history book for that entire period.

three times in great detail in the Bible yet it is not mentioned in the royal records of Assyria.[2] It seems like an open-and-shut case of the Bible's account being a fairy story – until you step into the room in the British Museum that displays the massive wall carvings that Sennacherib created to record his siege and capture of the town of Lachish, just down the road, earlier that same year.

Lachish was a very minor fortress in comparison to Jerusalem. Its capture hardly warranted the enormous wall carvings in the British Museum – unless, of course, King Sennacherib was desperate to deflect attention from his failure elsewhere. As any good historian will tell you, the absence of evidence is not evidence of absence! It should not surprise us that the scribes of Nebuchadnezzar dared write nothing in the royal annals about his seven years of madness and his subsequent surrender to the God of Israel.

It is easier to make a strong case that Nebuchadnezzar had a genuine change of heart. For a start, Daniel seems to include the king's personal tract in chapter 4 precisely to communicate that this is what happened! Nothing less than a genuine change of heart could have motivated him to send such a humble and God-glorifying letter to all his subjects right across his vast empire. As for the complaint that Nebuchadnezzar speaks too little about God forgiving sins through atoning blood – well, that is to expect the wrong words from somebody who has grown up speaking the language of Babylon.

Although Daniel challenged the king over his sin in verse 27, this was never his primary approach to proclaiming the Good News of the Gospel to Nebuchadnezzar. The king's greatest nightmare was that his own empire would come to the same violent end as the empire of the Assyrians. His deepest longing was to be part of an everlasting kingdom, so this is how the Lord chose to reach out to him. When he praises God that *"His dominion is an eternal dominion; his kingdom endures from*

[2] 2 Kings 18:13–19:37; 2 Chronicles 32:1–23 and Isaiah 36–37.

generation to generation", it is as clear a conversion testimony as one can get in the language of an ancient king of Babylon.

This really matters for four reasons. First, because these verses are meant to challenge the very scepticism which makes us doubt that the king truly changed. These verses head our scepticism off at the pass by allowing the king to become one of the authors of the Bible. Let Nebuchadnezzar tell his turnaround story in his own words! Daniel wants to build his readers' faith that God is able to save absolutely anyone, even the most hardened sinners. This is the man who destroyed God's Temple along with Jerusalem. This is the man who slaughtered the people of Judah along with many other ancient people groups too. If the Lord proved himself merciful and powerful enough to save a man like Nebuchadnezzar, then Daniel reasons that there should be no doubt that he is merciful and powerful enough to save anybody in any generation.

Second, it matters because our doubts over the king's profession of faith reveal how much we can be like him. God has given us a great proof that he is able to save anyone – it is called looking in the mirror! It is therefore ironic how quickly we can start believing that our conversions were only to be expected – it is everybody else's that are surprising. We seldom voice it like that. As good Christians, we know better. But in our hearts we can entertain thoughts that sound quite similar to Nebuchadnezzar's boast in verse 30.

Imagine how Peter and the other disciples from the fishing town of Capernaum must have felt when Jesus called their local tax collector, Matthew (the very man who had swindled them for years!), to become one of his disciples with them. They must have been tempted to protest that Jesus was making a huge mistake. It's for such moments that Daniel allowed Nebuchadnezzar to write these verses. We mustn't ever resist the fact that God's grace can reach absolutely anyone.

Third, it matters because Nebuchadnezzar's testimony is meant to teach us that conversion is a process which takes time. These verses are the grand finale of four long chapters that have trained us in how to "drill" and "blast" with non-believers in modern-day Babylon. Nebuchadnezzar reigned from 605 to 562 BC, so Daniel and his three friends shared their faith with him for over forty years. This ought to stop us from giving up when our friends and family are not converted right away. These four chapters contain crisis moments, confrontations and crazy miracles but, for the most part, they just involve Daniel and his friends waiting around. Stay at your post, Daniel encourages us. Pursue patience and stability. Live ready for the moment when opportunity comes knocking on your door.

Fourth, it matters because this is how the Gospel begins to spread rapidly throughout the world. Non-believers must become more than converts. They need to become missionaries themselves. Whether it is the Apostle Paul or Saint Augustine or Francis of Assisi, many of the great advances in Church history have been spearheaded by great sinners who have encountered an even greater Saviour. When people laughed at William Booth, the founder of The Salvation Army, and asked him where he would find enough workers to expand across the world, he quickly retorted: *"We shall get them from the public houses. Men who have felt the fire will be the best men to rescue others, and we shall never fail in getting the right men."* [3]

So let's pause to reflect on the fact that the king of Babylon became a child of Zion, and that the builder of the Hanging Gardens of Babylon found a place in the paradise of God.

[3] Charles T. Bateman in Life of General Booth (Press, 1912). Booth became famous for his speed at sending drunkards and prize fighters back out into the mission field.

The End of the Road (Daniel 5:1–12)

"They brought in the gold goblets that had been taken from the temple of God in Jerusalem, and the king and his nobles, his wives and his concubines drank from them."

(Daniel 5:3)

A lot of miles are travelled between the end of Daniel 4 and the start of Daniel 5. If you don't know the history of the six kings of the Babylonian Empire, then this little list may help you. The story has fast-forwarded over twenty years, and it is 6 October 539 BC.

Nabopolassar	(626–605 BC)
Nebuchadnezzar	(605–562 BC)
Awel-Marduk	(562–560 BC)
Neriglissar	(560–556 BC)
Labashi-Marduk	(556 BC)
Nabonidus	(556–539 BC)

Nebuchadnezzar's son ruled for only two years before he was murdered and supplanted by his brother-in-law.[1] That new king died after four years and his son reigned for only two months before Nabonidus murdered him and seized the throne. Nabonidus saw himself as a "king of kings" and left the day-

[1] One of the events of his brief rule is mentioned in 2 Kings 25:27–30 and Jeremiah 52:31–34.

to-day running of Babylon in the hands of his favourite vassal king and eldest son Belshazzar. Although he ruled for seventeen years, Nabonidus spent most of them away from his capital on military campaigns. Constantly moving, he had no idea that his empire was reaching the end of the road.

Nebuchadnezzar's nightmare was about to come true. A new power had risen in the region and its army had set up camp outside the walls of Babylon. Instead of preparing to repulse them, the ancient historians tell us that Belshazzar threw a massive dinner party to drown his sorrows with a thousand courtiers.[2] Daniel adds that, midway through the feast, Belshazzar suddenly remembered that Nebuchadnezzar plundered some exquisite goblets from the Temple of the Lord in Jerusalem.[3] With total disregard for what Nebuchadnezzar subsequently learned about the God of Israel, he commanded that these gold and silver goblets be brought up from the treasury of Bel or Nebo so that he and his friends could use them to raise a toast to the deities of Babylon.[4]

The Apostle Paul warns us in 1 Timothy 5:24 that the Lord judges some people's sins immediately but stores up the sins of others for a sudden, unexpected judgment day. What happens to Babylon here is the latter, since these goblets were stolen from the Temple of the Lord in the opening verses of the book of Daniel.[5] The Lord was patient with Nebuchadnezzar, giving him twelve months in which to repent before judgment suddenly fell

---

[2] This isn't quite as reckless as it sounds. 6 October was a major feast day in Babylonian culture, akin to Christmas in our own. The Greek historians Herodotus and Xenophon explain that *"a certain festival had come round in Babylon, during which all Babylon was accustomed to drink and revel all night long"* (*Histories*, 1.191, and *Cyropaedia*, 7.5.15).

[3] Six times in this chapter, Nebuchadnezzar is referred to as Belshazzar's *"father"*. This is a nod to his royal propaganda, since he and his true father Nabonidus were usurpers, outsiders to Nebuchadnezzar's dynasty.

[4] When 5:4 refers to gods of gold, silver, bronze, iron, wood and stone, it is referring to idols made out of those materials, as opposed to the invisible God of Israel.

[5] It is folly to imagine that no sign of swift judgment means that God has forgotten our sin. As a clue that he hasn't, the Lord ominously describes Babylon as his beautiful golden goblet in Jeremiah 51:7.

upon him in his Hanging Gardens. In the same way, he gives the Babylonian Empire sixty-five years in which to repent before he judges it for plundering his Temple. Those sixty-five years are now up. Babylon has reached the end of the road. As soon as Belshazzar and his dinner guests use the sacred goblets of the Lord to utter blasphemies, we are told that *"suddenly the fingers of a human hand appeared and wrote on the plaster of the wall".*[6] Paul warned that this is how it often is with the Lord's judgment. Patiently waiting, but then suddenly falling.

There is nothing particularly scary about the four Aramaic words that the ghostly hand writes on the wall. The end of the chapter informs us that they are *"Mene, Mene, Tekel, Parsin"*, which on one level means simply "Mina, Mina, Shekel, Half-Shekel". It is the modern-day equivalent of "Cent, Cent, Dollar, Dime" and it sounds like something that my children might chant in one of their playground games. But Belshazzar doesn't dismiss it as child's play. His face turns pale and his knees turn to jelly.[7]

Enter the wise men of Babylon. Once again they are described using Aramaic words that can be translated as *magicians, enchanters, diviners, soothsayers, necromancers, wizards* and *conjurers.* Once again they come up short. They have no idea what those four simple words , *"Mene, Mene, Tekel, Parsin"*, can signify. Even when Belshazzar promises to make anyone who solves the riddle the third most powerful man in the empire (after Nabonidus and himself), still nobody steps forward. The wise men of Babylon have also reached the end of the road.

In Rembrandt's famous seventeenth-century painting of *Belshazzar's Feast*, the vassal king of Babylon turns around with horror to stare at the ghostly hand at work behind him.

---

[6] I love the detail in Daniel's account. He explains that the section of wall he is referring to is the bit *"near the lampstand in the royal palace."* Such eyewitness detail ought to convince us of the historicity of this chapter.

[7] The Aramaic text of 5:6 reads literally that *"the joints of his loins were loosed and his knees knocked together."*

We are told in verse 9 that, when he discovers that the prophets of Nebo and Marduk have no interpretation, he gets even more scared and his face gets even paler. There is a reason why we still refer in modern English to "the writing being on the wall" for a politician or a football manager. Belshazzar is beginning to suspect that these four words mean that Babylon has reached the end of the road.

A thousand frightened dinner guests can make an awful racket. Eventually the queen appears to ask what all the fuss is about.[8] She actually holds the key to the whole matter. She is unlikely to be the wife or mother of Belshazzar or Nabonidus, since that would make her too young to remember the heyday of Nebuchadnezzar's reign. She is much more likely to be the widow of Nebuchadnezzar or of his son Awel-Marduk or of his son-in-law Neriglissar. She remembers the events of chapter 4 well enough to inform Belshazzar that there once was a court prophet who solved Nebuchadnezzar's riddles for him. He served as *"chief of the magicians"* and *"the spirit of the holy gods"* was said to live inside him.[9] He may be out of favour with the new kings of Babylon but he is still in town.[10] If Belshazzar wants to know the answer to a riddle, then Daniel is his man.

Belshazzar's servants rush off to find Daniel, who was not invited to the feast and who as yet knows nothing of the next chapter in his life's story. As we wait, let's reflect on that as a recurring feature of the book of Daniel. God is not looking for generals who can help him find the right strategy to reach people. He knows how to capture people's attention without our advice, but he wants to deliver his Word to them in partnership with us. As the servants knock on the door of an unsuspecting Daniel, we are reminded yet again: *It is God who put you here.*

---

[8] Her traditional royal greeting – *"May the king live forever!"* – is rather ironic, given the meaning of the four words on the wall. Belshazzar is about to learn that only the Kingdom of God will truly last forever.

[9] The queen mother's words in 5:11 are meant to echo those of 4:8–11.

[10] Daniel no longer makes it into the Top 1,000 Courtiers. It is likely that he fell from favour when Awel-Marduk was murdered and the ruling dynasty of Babylon was changed.

A Long Obedience (Daniel 5:13–29)

"Then at Belshazzar's command, Daniel was clothed in purple, a gold chain was placed round his neck, and he was proclaimed the third highest ruler in the kingdom."

(Daniel 5:29)

Jesus told a lot of parables about waiting and watching. There is the parable about five bridesmaids who kept their lamps burning and five bridesmaids who didn't. There is the parable about three men who were given bags of money to invest while they waited for a day of reckoning to arrive. There is the parable about people who grew tired of waiting for their ruler to be crowned king and who incurred his displeasure when he came home. There are parables about servants keeping watch for their master and about homeowners keeping watch for burglars. All of these parables urge us to live ready for action, because it is too late to get ready when opportunity knocks on our door.[1]

Eugene Peterson describes the key to Christian fruitfulness as *"a long obedience in the same direction"*.[2] Daniel exemplifies this for us brilliantly. He was taken to Babylon as a prisoner of war in 605 BC. It is now 539 BC. That's sixty-six years of being God's man in Babylon. He must now be in his eighties and he

---

[1] Matthew 24:42–25:30 and 26:41, Mark 13:32–37 and Luke 12:35–48, 19:11–27 and 21:34–36. These parables are not just about watching for the second coming of Jesus. They are about *"the kingdom of God"* in general.

[2] This is the title of a book he published in 1980. Its subtitle is *Discipleship in an Instant Society* and it makes a similar argument to the Rule of St Benedict that the key to Christian fruitfulness is *stability*.

has probably been out of favour with the king for twenty years.[3] Nevertheless, we catch no sense in these verses that he has slipped into retirement. He is still reminding himself: *It is God who put you here.*

In verses 13–16, Belshazzar does all the talking. He does more than simply bring Daniel up to speed. His words are full of flattery, towards himself (Nebuchadnezzar is *not* his father) and especially towards Daniel. After purring about how many great things he has heard about the Jewish prophet's wisdom, he makes lofty promises about what he will do for him if he solves his riddle for him.[4] He will clothe Daniel in purple, put a golden chain around his neck, and make him the third highest ruler in the Babylonian Empire – after Nabonidus and Belshazzar, naturally.[5]

Daniel has heard it all before. He tells Belshazzar in verse 17, *"You may keep your gifts for yourself and give your rewards to someone else. Nevertheless, I will read the writing for the king and tell him what it means."* His reply is much curter than his conversations with Nebuchadnezzar, but overall we are struck by how pure Daniel has kept his heart in his obscurity. He is not resentful towards Belshazzar for having demoted and excluded him for so many years.[6] He does not begin with a monologue of resentment towards him. He recognizes Belshazzar's authority and declares that he is ready for the hour. Even in his eighties, Daniel is prepared for action. He is still God's man in Babylon.

---

[3] Daniel was closely associated with Nebuchadnezzar, so he probably fell out of favour after the violent coup of 560 BC. Not only does he not make it into the Top 1,000 Courtiers for Belshazzar's dinner party, but Belshazzar evidently has no idea who Daniel is.

[4] The Aramaic metaphor that is used for *solving difficult problems* in 5:12 and 16 means literally *to untie a knot*. It is similar to the phrase that is used in 5:6 to describe Belshazzar's *loins being loosed* out of fear!

[5] This is hardly a great incentive, given that the Babylonian Empire is going to fall before sunrise.

[6] Daniel 8:1 and 27 tell us that he was still working in Belshazzar's civil service. He was just demoted.

Daniel does not explain the meaning of the four words on the wall straightaway. He has Belshazzar's rapt attention, so first he explains to him in verses 18–21 what he told Nebuchadnezzar: *I can't, but God can.*[7] Daniel wants to know if Belshazzar truly grasps what happened to the man he calls his father. Does he know about the seven years of madness that he spent living in his Hanging Gardens? Does he know that it was triggered by his pride and that his humiliation only ended when he confessed that "the Most High God" is the sovereign ruler of every king and every kingdom?

In verses 22–24, Daniel becomes even bolder.[8] He is happy to go along with Belshazzar's propaganda that Nebuchadnezzar is his father, but does he realize how much a son of that proud tyrant he truly is? He is no stranger to what happened to Nebuchadnezzar in his rooftop garden, so why is he acting like such a stranger to the humility it taught him? By using goblets that were plundered from the Temple in Jerusalem to toast the blind, deaf and dumb deities of Babylon, he has just declared war on *"the Lord of heaven"*. The writing is on the wall for him, in every sense of the phrase. He is doomed.

In verses 25–28, Daniel therefore reveals the meaning of *"Mene, Mene, Tekel, Parsin"*. Mene does not just mean a mina of Babylonian currency. Its literal translation is numbered. Tekel does not just mean a shekel. It literally means weighed. Parsin does not just mean a half shekel. It means literally divided.[9] The four words on the wall therefore mean *"God has numbered the days of your reign and brought it to an end... You have been*

---

[7] We are not told whether Daniel has already seen the four words written on the wall when he says this. His confidence is in the Lord, and not in his own puzzle-solving skills.

[8] In his *Cyropaedia*, the Greek historian Xenophon says that Belshazzar angrily killed a courtier for shooting game on a hunting trip before he did. He also castrated a courtier because his concubine described him as handsome. Belshazzar was not a man to be trifled with, but Daniel has a bigger goal in life than survival.

[9] *Perēs* in 5:28 is the singular form of the plural noun *parsīn* in 5:25. It also looks similar to *pâras* at the end of 5:28, which is the Aramaic word for *Persia*.

weighed on the scales and found wanting . . .Your kingdom is divided and given to the Medes and Persians."

In verse 29, Daniel faces a final test. Belshazzar is so relieved to have found a prophet with a hotline to heaven that he does all he promised he would do. He clothes Daniel in purple, puts a golden chain around his neck, and declares him the chief minister of Babylon. Nabonidus is king of kings and Belshazzar is his vassal king, but every other ruler and courtier in their kingdom will answer to Daniel. It is a staggering promotion – from supreme obscurity to supreme authority in an instant.[10]

But it isn't very attractive to Daniel. He has been waiting and watching for God for so long that he has long since died to personal ambition.[11] He is happy to be God's man in Babylon and feels no need to be God's ruler in Babylon. Those who enjoy direct access to the throne of heaven feel no great pull towards any earthly throne.[12] Furthermore, Daniel just prophesied that the Babylonian Empire is on the brink of extinction. Becoming prime minister would make him a prime candidate for Persian execution! Yet even in his eighties, Daniel does not think of retiring. He still remembers: *It is God who put you here.*

For those of us who are younger than Daniel, his example is inspiring. He models for us stability – a long obedience in the same direction. For those of us who are older, Daniel's example is inspiring too. He reminds me of the words of Gordon Macdonald:

---

[10] The examples of Joseph in Genesis 41 and Haman in the book of Esther show us that the Lord can work staggering promotions and demotions in a single day.

[11] One of the great lessons of this chapter is that those who have died to the pull of fame, riches and power are the very people that the Lord knows he can trust with each of those things.

[12] Daniel is a man of prayer. He does not need to ask Belshazzar for time alone with God to interpret the writing on the wall. There is no hurried fasting and pleading here, because Daniel lived ready for action.

A long time ago I dropped the word retirement out of my vocabulary. I don't believe in it. In the ageing process, slowing up in tandem with one's diminishing strength might be a necessity. But retirement suggests, at least to me, a transition from activity to inactivity, from giving to taking. Where in the Scriptures does one find permission to do that?[13]

[13] Gordon Macdonald says this in *A Resilient Life* (2004).

Nevertheless (Daniel 5:30–31)

"That very night Belshazzar, king of the Babylonians, was slain, and Darius the Mede took over the kingdom. . ."

(Daniel 5:30–31)

Even with the Persian army camped outside its walls, it appeared exceedingly unlikely that the city of Babylon was about to fall.[1] The Persian leader was King Cyrus, and even he admitted to his officers that *"I am unable to see how any enemy can take walls of such strength and height by assault."*[2] According to the Greek historian Herodotus, its walls were twenty-five metres thick and several times higher than the Great Wall of China.[3]

Nevertheless, the city of Babylon fell to the Persians that very night. Whenever the Lord prophesies something, it surely happens. This is meant to encourage us whenever we despair of ever seeing spiritual breakthrough in modern-day Babylon.[4] If you have ever felt that a work colleague is unsavable, if you have ever imagined that a people group is unreachable or if you have ever assumed that a quagmired church or Christian

---

[1] Xenophon tells us in his *Cyropaedia* (7.5.13) that the Babylonians mocked the besieging Persian army from their city walls, *"in the belief that they had provisions enough for more than twenty years."*

[2] Xenophon records this in his *Cyropaedia* (7.5.7).

[3] Herodotus in his *Histories* (1.178). He goes on to describe the fall of Babylon in 1.191.

[4] Revelation 18–19 takes what happened to ancient Babylon in 539 BC and turns it into a picture of what will happen to any man-made stronghold which sets itself up against God's purposes and people.

ministry is irredeemable, then you need to add a new word to your vocabulary. *Nevertheless.*[5]

Nevertheless is a beautiful word. We find it in 2 Samuel 5:6–7 and 1 Chronicles 11:5, when the Jebusite inhabitants of Jerusalem boast that *"David cannot get in here"*. We are informed that *"**nevertheless,** David captured the fortress of Zion".* We come across the same word again in Isaiah 9:1, where the prophet faces up to the backslidings of Judah before declaring that *"**nevertheless**"* a Messiah will be born to David's dynasty to save them. Daniel uses the word himself in 5:17, when he tells Belshazzar that there is no earthly reason for him to help the king, but *"**nevertheless**"* he will. We can even spot the word in Luke 5:5, where an amplified translation of Peter's words is *"Master, we've worked hard all night and haven't caught anything.* ***Nevertheless,*** *because you say so, I will let down the nets."* If we want to capture spiritual strongholds and to catch souls in our Gospel fishing nets, then we need to get used to the sound of this word in our mouths: *Nevertheless.*

Daniel's prediction that the unbreachable walls of Babylon are about to be breached speaks God's great *nevertheless* over an impossible situation. This is not presumption.[6] Daniel has many specific promises from God on which to base his claim. More than a century before Cyrus was born, the prophet Isaiah had predicted that a man named Cyrus would capture Babylon.[7] Jeremiah also predicted that the city would be captured from the north by a general draining dry the mighty River Euphrates while the rulers of Babylon were drunk and drowsy.[8]

---

[5] The very name *Babylon* is Akkadian for *Gate of God*. The Lord always has a way into Babylon!

[6] There can be presumption in a man-made *nevertheless*. See Numbers 14:44.

[7] Isaiah 44:28; 45:1 and 45:13. Predicting the name of the future conqueror of Babylon was astonishing.

[8] Jeremiah 50:9, 50:24, 50:38, 51:36, 51:39 and 51:57. Just as astonishing as the fall of Babylon was Jeremiah's prediction that the city would never be rebuilt. It never was, and its Hanging Gardens are the only Wonder of the Ancient World to have disappeared without any trace.

Daniel had also prophesied personally to Nebuchadnezzar about the fall of the Babylonian Empire.

Belshazzar does not seem to take these prophecies seriously enough in verse 30. His face turned pale and his knees turned to jelly when a disembodied hand wrote on the wall of his banqueting hall, but he shows a surprising lack of repentance towards the Lord. He appoints Daniel as his chief administrator, despite the fact that the prophet has just informed him that there will be no empire left for anybody to administer. Perhaps Belshazzar is fooling himself that, with a man like Daniel by his side, he will be granted a reprieve. Nevertheless, *"that very night Belshazzar, king of the Babylonians, was slain".*

The fall of Babylon is one of the best attested battlefield moments in ancient history. The Greek historians Herodotus and Xenophon tell us how it happened. While King Cyrus of Persia was lamenting the size of the walls of Babylon, he noticed that the River Euphrates passed under them. When night fell and the sounds of Belshazzar's feast filled the night air, Cyrus instructed his soldiers to build dams upstream to divert the river's flow away from the city. While Belshazzar partied in the palace, the Persian soldiers watched in wonder as the river-bed emptied and exposed a broad and undefended passageway under the wall.[9] By the time the drunken Babylonians knew that their walls had been breached, the battle was over. Xenophon says that the Persian soldiers *"fell upon them as they were drinking by a blazing fire, and without waiting they dealt with them as with foes."*[10] The unbreachable stronghold of Babylon had fallen.

I wonder what unbreachable strongholds lie ahead of you right now. It may be a relative, a friend or a work colleague who seems hostile to the Gospel, but whom you long to lead through to salvation. It may be an ambitious church ministry or the beginnings of a church plant. It may be an attempt to reach a new

---

[9] In the same way, if we want to breach the walls of Babylon today, we need to get into the River of God.

[10] Xenophon in his *Cyropaedia* (7.5.27).

people group or nation with the Gospel. If it seems impossible to you, then add this word to your vocabulary: *Nevertheless.*

On a recent holiday in Normandy, I took a walk along the D-Day beaches with my wife and children. We came across a massive concrete gun emplacement which had a plaque on it that read, *"This was the biggest and best defended German battery on the D-Day beaches. Nevertheless, it was captured on 8:32 am on 6th June 1944."*

There it is again: *Nevertheless.* It is such a beautiful word and an essential word in the Christian vocabulary. So take a good look at the ruins of Babylon and learn to speak it out over your own new Babylons today.

Every spiritual breakthrough appears impossible until, *nevertheless,* it is done!

Déjà Vu (Daniel 6:1–9)

"It pleased Darius to appoint 120 satraps to rule throughout the kingdom, with three chief ministers over them, one of whom was Daniel."

(Daniel 6:1–2)

You can be forgiven for thinking that much of the sixth chapter of Daniel seems familiar. The Babylonian Empire has given way to the Persian Empire, but life still carries on as normal in downtown Babylon. In these verses, we catch a definite sense of déjà vu.

For a start, we still find a ruler struggling with the challenges of administering such a vast and overstretched world empire. The ruler's name is Darius the Mede, which means that he is more like Belshazzar than Nebuchadnezzar. The real "king of kings" in this new empire is Cyrus the Persian but, like Nabonidus, he has a vassal king in Babylon.[1]

We also find that Daniel remains a powerful official within the empire.[2] It is divided into 120 provinces, ruled by 120 *satraps*, which is far too many people to have a direct reporting line to the king, so Darius appoints three *sareks* to oversee forty satraps each. It's pretty much the Babylonian Empire all over

---

[1] Daniel 5:31 (which is Daniel 6:1 in the Aramaic text) is not referring to King Darius I of Persia, since that Darius did not come to the throne until 522 BC. Daniel 6:28 explains that this Darius was vassal king to Cyrus. The Babylonians and Persians had no word for *emperor*. They simply referred to a *king of kings*.

[2] Being appointed the third most powerful man in Babylon might have led to Daniel's execution. It certainly did for the first and second! Nevertheless, because he trusted in God's timing, Daniel's sudden promotion resulted in his being asked to help establish the new Persian Empire.

again. The rulers at the very top have changed but their civil servants are the same.[3]

Once again, we find that Daniel is head-and-shoulders better than his colleagues.[4] Darius even plans a cabinet reshuffle. Why have three *sareks* to oversee the *satraps* when one of them is clearly capable of doing the job of all three? Now in his eighties, Daniel's energy for serving as God's man in Babylon clearly hasn't changed. He evidently keeps on repeating to himself: *It is God who put you here.*

Another reason for our déjà vu is the fact that Daniel's favour with the king makes his pagan colleagues hate him and, with him, the God of Israel. This is interesting, because one of the biggest mistakes that we can make in trying to serve God in modern-day Babylon is to believe that "godly influence" is the same thing as "popularity". It clearly isn't, because the other two *sareks* and many of the *satraps* hatch a plan together to murder Daniel. After poring over his track record to find evidence of corruption or negligence, they conclude that the only way to topple such a faithful man of God from power is to target his commitment to obey God's Law above the law of Persia.[5]

If all of these similarities have not yet provoked in you a sense of déjà vu, then note the way that Daniel carries on his "drilling" and "blasting". When his colleagues convene to plot his death, it becomes evident that he has explained the Jewish faith to them in words that the Medes and Persians can understand. The Jewish Law is known in Hebrew as the *tōrāh*, yet this is clearly not the word that Daniel has used when sharing it with his colleagues. They refer to it as the Jewish *dāth*, which

---

[3] Five Aramaic words are used in 6:7 to describe five different posts in the Persian imperial hierarchy. They are not the same words that were used earlier to describe their Babylonian equivalents. This type of detail highlights the historicity of the book of Daniel.

[4] Daniel wasn't just a diligent worker. The Aramaic text of 6:3 can either be translated that he excelled *"because an excellent spirit was in him"* or *"because the supreme Spirit was in him"*. This echoes what we were told in 1:17–20, 4:8–9, 4:18, 5:11 and 5:14. The Lord empowered Daniel to work well by his Holy Spirit.

[5] *Corruption* refers to wrongdoing. *Negligence* refers to failure to do right. Daniel was squeaky clean in both.

is the same Aramaic word that is used in verse 8 to describe the irrepealable laws of the Medes and Persians. Daniel has evidently carried on "drilling", seeking to find the right words to proclaim the timeless Word of God in a timely manner to the new culture that now dominates his city.

Another similarity is the way in which the new Persian ruler of Babylon entertains delusions that he is godlike. Nebuchadnezzar commanded his subjects to bow down and worship a statue that represented his rule. Darius commands his subjects to desist from praying to any god for thirty days so that they can direct all their prayers to him.

As with Nebuchadnezzar, however, we discover that the king is only pretending to possess perfect power. He mimics his predecessor by devising a strange and needlessly elaborate manner of execution. It is throwing his enemies into a lions' den rather than into a blazing furnace, but it still makes him look like a James Bond baddy. For all his fury, this new Persian king is just as easily manipulated as Nebuchadnezzar. He becomes a pawn in the puppeteering power games of his courtiers.[6] He lacks even the basic power to repeal his own decrees.[7] All of this is so similar to the first five chapters of Daniel that our sense of déjà vu can feel overwhelming.

The biggest constant in these verses, however, is Daniel himself. The thing that changes least in this chapter is the prophet's godly character. Sixty-five years have passed since he became God's man in Babylon, and yet Daniel is still full of what St Benedict calls *"stability"*. Even in his eighties, he is still pursuing what, as we have seen, Eugene Peterson refers to as *"a long obedience in the same direction"*. Long past retirement age, there is still no trace in Daniel of what Eugene Peterson

---

[6] They use the same fawning greeting in 6:6 that the courtiers of Nebuchadnezzar used in 2:4 and 3:9, but they are lying to King Darius. The *sareks* do not all support this new law, since Daniel is one of the *sareks*!

[7] Supposedly godlike, the kings of Persia were considered infallible when passing certain major laws. This pretence of divinity caused them all sorts of problems. See Esther 1:19 and 8:8.

sees as the opposite of stability. *"Impatience, the refusal to endure, is to pastoral character what strip mining is to the land – a greedy rape of what can be gotten at the least cost, and then abandonment in search of another place to loot."* [8]

No, this is still the same Daniel. He may be serving a different king in a different empire in a different decade, but he is still stable, he is still enduring, he is still pursuing a long obedience in the same direction. He is still resolutely God's man in Babylon.

So if this chapter gives you déjà vu, it is intentional. Daniel is reminding us that, to serve the Lord in Babylon, means remembering the same simple thing for a very long time. Through this chapter he encourages us yet again: *It is God who put you here.*

[8] Eugene Peterson in *The Contemplative Pastor* (1989).

Secret Weapon (Daniel 6:10–11)

"Three times a day he got down on his knees and prayed, giving thanks to his God, just as he had done before."

(Daniel 6:10)

Somebody has said that *"the secret of Christianity is Christianity in secret."* What they mean by that is prayer. Regular, devoted, targeted prayer, like that of Jesus or of the Apostle Paul or of the Early Church in general. Or like that of Daniel. In these two verses, we discover that prayer was the secret weapon in the prophet's arsenal.[1]

Up until this moment, we have not been told much about Daniel's prayer life but we have seen the results of it. He is full of the Holy Spirit. He is wise. He can interpret dreams and visions better than the wise men of Babylon. He constantly seems to experience spiritual breakthrough. The closest we have come so far to observing the engine room that powered all of this fruitful ministry was in 2:17–18, where we were told that he called a prayer meeting in his home with Shadrach, Meshach and Abednego. Now, in these verses, we are finally given a backstage pass to study the secret that lay behind all of Daniel's breakthroughs. We discover that Daniel's ministry *for* God in public flowed out of his ministry *to* God in private.

Ironically, it is only when Darius makes praying to God illegal that Daniel opens up the windows on his prayer life. Quite literally. When he hears that the other two *sareks* have

[1] Ezekiel 14:14 and 20 put Daniel in the Top 3 People of Prayer in the Old Testament.

persuaded the king to make his secret strength illegal, Daniel rushes home and opens the windows of his prayer room with the result that everyone can see where his priorities lie. For Daniel, pleasing the Lord is more important than pleasing the king of Babylon.[2] The Jewish Law is much more irreversible than the laws of the Medes and Persians.

In these two verses, we can see five aspects to Daniel's secret weapon of prayer.

First, Daniel makes prayer a *lifestyle*. We are told that he responds to the king's rash decree by praying fervently *"just as he had done before."* Prayer is a habit that we acquire over time, like going to the gym or getting up when our alarm goes off in the morning. When Martin Luther was asked by his barber to share the secret of the great revival that he spearheaded in the sixteenth century, he wrote him a forty-page letter to explain.

> *A good, clever barber must have his thoughts, mind and eyes concentrated upon the razor and the beard and not forget where he is in his stroke and shave. If he keeps talking or looking around or thinking of something else, he is likely to cut a man's mouth or nose – or even his throat... How much more must prayer possess the heart exclusively and completely!... O brother, pray; in spite of Satan, pray; spend hours in prayer; rather neglect friends than not pray; rather fast and lose breakfast, dinner, tea, and supper – and sleep too – than not pray. And we must not talk about prayer, we must pray in right earnest. The Lord is near. He comes softly while the virgins slumber!*[3]

Second, Daniel gives prayer a specific time. We are told that "three times a day he got down on his knees". This appears to mean that, following the lead of King David in Psalm 55:17, the

[2] The Babylonian Empire was no more, but the Persian rulers still referred to themselves as the kings of Babylon (9:1; Ezra 5:13 and Nehemiah 13:6).

[3] Luther wrote this to Peter Beskendorf in 1535. Quoted by Walter Trobisch in *Martin Luther's Quiet Time* (1974).

prophet cleared his diary for prayer first thing in the morning, then again at lunchtime, and then finally before he went to bed in the evening. One of the reasons why we often fail to do this ourselves is that we become busy. It is therefore pretty sobering to consider that Daniel carved out three appointments each day to meet with God in prayer, despite having the needs of forty satraps constantly banging on his door.

Martin Luther continues in his letter to his barber:

> *It is a good thing to let prayer be the first business in the morning and the last in the evening. Guard yourself against such false and deceitful thoughts that keep whispering: Wait a while. In an hour or so I will pray. I must first finish this or that. Thinking such thoughts, we get away from prayer into other things that will hold us and involve us till the prayer of the day comes to naught.*

John Calvin advised something similar. To counteract our natural disposition not to pray, he advised people to schedule prayer times when they woke up, before lunch and at the end of the day.[4]

Third, Daniel gives prayer a *specific place*. We are told that *"he went home to his upstairs room"*.[5] The Aramaic word *'allīth* possibly describes a special prayer chamber on his rooftop, but nobody needs a large house to do as Daniel models for us here. I have a big log in the park behind my house where I love to go in order to pray. It doesn't matter where we choose to be our place of prayer, but simply that we choose somewhere!

Fourth, Daniel gives prayer a *specific posture*. We are told literally that *"he knelt down on his knees"*. What we do with our bodies while we pray matters far more than many of us realize. Daniel chose to kneel before the Lord, as before a king,

---

[4] He says this in a section of his *Institutes of the Christian Religion* entitled "Prayer at Regular Times" (3.20.50).

[5] Jesus echoes these verses in Matthew 6:6 – *"When you pray, go into your room, close the door and pray."* See also 2 Kings 4:8–10 and Luke 5:16.

so that his eyes would become fixed, not on himself, but on the sovereignty of God. A literal translation of the Aramaic text of verse 10 explains that he spent his time *"praying and praising before his God."* Daniel's posture helped him to spend his time worshipping, instead of worrying.[6]

Fifth, Daniel gives his prayers a *specific focus*. We are told that he prayed in a room *"where the windows opened towards Jerusalem."*[7] That's because he knew precisely what he was asking for from the Lord.[8] In chapter 9, we can read one of the prayers that Daniel prayed in his upper room. It is focused on the fact that God's Temple is a pile of rubble. It pleads with the Lord to revive the Jewish community in Babylon and to return them to the Promised Land to rebuild a dwelling place for the Lord.[9] A literal translation of the Aramaic text of verse 11 explains that this is what Daniel is doing here. His work colleagues find him on his knees, *"making requests and asking for favour"*.

So don't miss the secret of Daniel's many spiritual breakthroughs in Babylon. All of his prophecies and all of his miracles were powered by his rooftop engine room of prayer.

Even when praying to the Lord became illegal, Daniel persisted in his lifestyle of prayer. He kept the same times, the same place, the same posture and the same focus as before. He went into his prayer room three times a day, believing: *It is God who put you here.*

---

[6] Daniel's prayer in chapter 9 reveals a man who is burdened, but not depressed. His eyes are on the Lord.

[7] At the dedication of the Temple, Solomon had foreseen the Babylonian exile and had urged the exiles to pray towards the Temple site for restoration for their nation (2 Chronicles 6:36–39).

[8] Opening the windows made it likely that the other *sareks* would catch him praying, but Daniel refused to allow his personal fears to dilute his focus of his prayers.

[9] Daniel 9:1 suggests that he prayed the prayer at the same time as the events in this chapter. His prayer was answered, and King Cyrus swiftly sent the Jews back home to rebuild the Lord's fallen Temple.

Living God (Daniel 6:12–22)

"Daniel, servant of the living God, has your God, whom you serve continually, been able to rescue you from the lions?"

(Daniel 6:20)

Babylon had many gods, but they all had one thing in common. They were dead. They had no life in them and, consequently, they could impart no life to others.

The Babylonians admitted as much in 5:4, when *"they praised the gods of gold and silver, of bronze, iron, wood and stone."* The images of Bel and Nebo were constructed out of fine materials, but they were inanimate idols all the same. Daniel describes them in 5:23 as *"gods of silver and gold, of bronze, iron, wood and stone, which cannot see or hear or understand."* Every single one of the gods of Babylon was blind and deaf and dumb.

The kings of Babylon feared becoming like them.[1] That's why they forced their subjects to wish, *"May the king live forever!"*[2] There was an irony to this, since the wise men of Babylon used these words when they spoke to Nebuchadnezzar on the morning after he dreamed that his empire would fall, and the queen mother also used these words when speaking to Belshazzar on the night that he was killed. Still, it gives us a window into how much people were longing for eternal life in Babylon.

---

[1] The Bible warns us that people always become like what they worship – either negatively (2 Kings 17:15; Psalm 115:3–8; Jeremiah 2:5 and Romans 1:18–32) or positively (2 Corinthians 3:16–18).

[2] Daniel 2:4, 3:9, 5:10, 6:6 and 6:21, and Nehemiah 2:3. Note also Babylon's words in Revelation 18:7.

Darius had forgotten that the God of Israel is different. He had liked the idea when his courtiers suggested that he outlaw prayer *"to any god or human being during the next thirty days, except to you"*. He didn't expect any kickback from the mute statues of Bel and Nebo, but when his courtiers accuse Daniel, it begins to dawn on Darius that Daniel is a Jew, part of a people who are famous for having no graven images of their deity. They claim that he is the Living God, whose life-giving power would be concealed, rather than revealed, by depicting him in metal, wood or stone. Deep down, Darius knows that the God to whom Daniel prays three times a day is nothing like the gods of Babylon.[3]

The Persian king does everything within his power to save him, but it turns out that Persian kings are not as powerful as their propaganda proclaims. We are told that *"he was determined to rescue Daniel and made every effort until sunset to save him"*, but he is like one of his idols. He cannot speak against his own law because it is set in stone, like the images of Bel and Nebo. Because the Persian kings claimed to be godlike, their decrees had to be considered infallible, so Darius lacks even the basic power to undo his own law. Miserably, he is forced by his courtiers to throw Daniel into his lions' den.

Straightaway, the Lord uses this as his opportunity to demonstrate to Babylon that he is nothing like their lifeless idols. He is the Living God of Israel. Darius shouts a final blessing to Daniel as he rolls the stone lid across the hole above the lions' den.[4] *"May your God, whom you serve continually, rescue you!"*[5] The Aramaic word *tedīrā'*, which is translated *continually*, can just as easily be translated *enduringly* or *permanently* or *non-stop*

[3] Note the repetition in 6:13 that Daniel made specific times for prayer. Acts 3:1 teaches us that, because of our own weakness, Christians still need to schedule specific times for prayer.

[4] The lions' den was evidently a deep pit in the ground, accessed via its ceiling at ground level.

[5] What Darius says in Aramaic is probably a prayer, but it can also be translated as a statement of faith: *"Your God, whom you serve continually,* ***will*** *rescue you!"*

or *without end*. It isn't just a statement that Daniel has pursued a long obedience in the same direction.[6] It is a recognition that he serves a deity who is non-stop active in the world. He is not a blind, deaf and dumb idol. The God of Israel is the Living God.

After Darius and his courtiers have placed their wax seals on the stone over the lions' den, so that nobody can tamper with it during the night, Darius goes home and spends several hours in prayer and fasting. Prayer is not specifically mentioned, but it is certainly implied by the king's rejection of food and sleep and entertainment, so don't miss the deliberate irony of this scene. Darius has forbidden anyone in Babylon from praying to any god but him, yet here we find him confessing his own powerlessness in prayer, as he cries out in great distress to the Living God of Israel!

When the sun comes up in the morning, it bears testimony to the Living God. Darius hurries to the lions' den to find out if there are further testimonies to him there.[7] As the stone is rolled back from the entrance, the king calls out an anxious question which expresses the message of this chapter. Not only does Darius repeat his assertion that Daniel serves the God of Israel *continually*, but this time he states that Daniel's non-stop worship is made possible by the fact he is the *"servant of the living God"*! Clearly, Darius has not merely rushed to the lions' den to discover whether Daniel has survived. He has also come to find out if Daniel's God is everything that Darius hopes that he might be.[8]

From the bottom of the lions' den, Daniel shouts back the traditional royal greeting. Is it with deliberate irony that he prays *"May the king live forever!"*? The fact is that there is only

---

[6] In order to get close to the non-believers around us in modern-day Babylon, we often conceal our spirituality from them. It is therefore challenging that Daniel clearly wears his own faith firmly on his sleeve.

[7] The same Aramaic word *shezab* is used to describe Darius failing to *rescue* Daniel in 6:14 as is used for the Lord successfully *rescuing* Daniel in 6:16, 20 and 27.

[8] His question is *"Has your God . . . been able?"* That is, is the God of Israel unlike the mute idols of Babylon?

one eternal King, and he has spent the night with Daniel in the lions' den. The parallels between the accounts of the blazing furnace and the lions' den suggest strongly that the angel of the Lord who shut the hungry mouths of the lions was none other than Jesus.[9] He makes a second cameo appearance in the story to vindicate his man in Babylon and to prove beyond all doubt that the Lord is the Living God of Israel.[10]

So take a moment to worship the Lord for the fact that this is true. We have far more reason to believe it than the king of Babylon. The broken wax seals on the stone that kept Daniel in the lions' den have now been bettered by the broken seals on the stone that was rolled away to show that Jesus is no longer in the grave! The one who claimed to be the Living God and to bring true life to the world has now proved it beyond all doubt.[11] He cries out to us in triumph: *"I am the Living One; I was dead, and now look, I am alive for ever and ever!"*[12]

---

[9] The lions are unquestionably hungry. Just take a look at what they do in 6:24.

[10] We are given two reasons for Daniel's vindication – his innocence (6:22) and his faith in God (6:23).

[11] John 1:4, 3:16, 3:36, 4:14, 5:21, 5:26, 5:40, 6:33, 6:47–48, 6:51, 6:57, 6:63, 6:68, 7:38, 10:10, 10:28, 11:25, 14:6 and 17:2–3. Don't miss the deliberate parallel between Daniel 6:17 and Matthew 27:62–66.

[12] Revelation 1:18.

Beyond (Daniel 6:23–28)

"People must fear and reverence the God of Daniel. 'For he is the living God and he endures forever; his kingdom will not be destroyed, his dominion will never end.'"

(Daniel 6:26)

These are the final verses of the first half of the book of Daniel. The chapters of narrative are about to end and the chapters of prophecy are about to begin. Before we reach that crossover, we are meant to glean something from these final verses of what will happen next, beyond the sixty-five years that are covered by the first half of the book of Daniel.

These verses hint at Daniel's future beyond this chapter. There is no suggestion that his ministry as God's man in Babylon is about to end. In verse 23, he emerges from the lions' den every bit as healthy as he entered it.[1] We are reminded of his continued faith in God. He still has left ahead of him many years of long obedience in the same direction. Even though he is in his eighties, we are told in verse 28 that he kept on leading strongly throughout the reigns of the vassal king of Babylon and of the bigger "king of kings" beyond him. We know from Herodotus and Xenophon that King Cyrus the Great of Persia continued to reign until 530 BC.

These verses also hint at what happened to Darius beyond this chapter. The king of Babylon writes down his personal

[1] There are many deliberate contrasts in Daniel 3 and 6 between the twin deliverances from the blazing furnace and from the lions' den. The fact that Daniel hasn't a single scratch on his body is meant to echo 3:27.

testimony and sends a copy to people from every tribe and language across the Persian Empire. It closely echoes the testimony of Nebuchadnezzar, and again we are left guessing whether he was genuinely converted. We are told that *"the king was overjoyed"* to find Daniel still alive – not just because he was a gifted official, but because of what his deliverance proved about the God of Israel. The king affirms to people across the empire that the Lord is *"the living God"* – unlike the blind, deaf and dumb Babylonian deities of gold, silver, bronze, iron, wood and stone. Like Nebuchadnezzar, Darius has been yearning for an everlasting kingdom, so he rejoices that God's Kingdom will never be destroyed. He also rejoices that the Lord *"rescues and he saves"*. We couldn't hope for a clearer conversion testimony in the language of the Persian Empire.[2]

These verses hint at what happened to the wise men of Babylon beyond this chapter. They were an evil order of *occultists, enchanters, necromancers, spiritualists, conjurers* and *soothsayers*. They served as prophets to the demon gods of Babylon and they were demonized by them. They played a leading role in the destruction of Jerusalem in 586 BC.[3] They tried to murder Shadrach, Meshach and Abednego. They tried to murder Daniel too. It may be unpleasant for us to read in verse 24 that they were torn to pieces by the lions, along with their wives and children, but we must not miss that this is meant to be a picture of what will happen to the guilty on Judgment Day.[4] Tough as it may sound to our ears, Daniel says that the wise men had it coming to them.

But he also hints that this is not the end of the story. How could it be? The Gospel is not about sinful people getting what is

---

[2] The conversion of Nebuchadnezzar took over thirty years. The conversion of Darius took mere months. We need to persevere for the long haul with some people, but we should also expect a few rapid breakthroughs.

[3] The Hebrew title *rab māg*, in Jeremiah 39:3 and 13, means literally *Chief of the Magicians*, or *Chief of the Magi*.

[4] The lions' den directly parallels the blazing furnace, so Jesus confirms this by using words in Matthew 13:42 and 50 to describe hell that are taken directly from the Greek Septuagint translation of Daniel 3.

coming to them! Even while the lions are gnawing on the bones of the royal soothsayers, Daniel is granted a slate freshly wiped clean on which he can rebuild their fallen order on a better foundation. We hear no more about this order of magicians until Matthew 2:1–12, where they reappear as *"Magi from the east"*. We call them "wise men" in nativity plays because the men who saw a star in the east when Jesus was born in Bethlehem belonged to this ancient order of wise men of Persia!

Could it be that Daniel used his position to teach a fresh generation of royal soothsayers about the ancient prophecy in Numbers 24:17 that a Messiah would come to save the world, his birth heralded by a star in the sky? We don't know for sure. All that we can say for certain is that he sowed enough little seeds of faith in the hearts of the wise men of Persia for a few to come looking for Jesus as their Messiah when he finally came.

These verses therefore hint at what will happen to the Gentiles of the Persian Empire beyond this chapter. One of the most exciting verses in the final book of the Old Testament is Malachi 1:5 which promises us, *"Great is the Lord – even beyond the borders of Israel!"* It encourages us to believe that Esther 8:17 is not a one-off when it tells us that many Gentiles in the Persian Empire came to faith in the Lord. This letter from King Darius laid the groundwork for that by proclaiming to every people group in the empire that the God of Israel is greater than the lifeless deities of Babylon. His alone is an everlasting Kingdom.

We can only imagine how the Jewish exiles reacted when they received a second letter from another pagan king who had come to believe in the God of Israel. Not only must this have added fresh fuel to the revival fires that they were enjoying under Daniel and his friends, but it must have also led directly to their return to the Promised Land.[5] Only weeks or months after Daniel's deliverance from the lions' den, King Cyrus of

[5] Not just Shadrach, Meshach and Abednego, but also the prophet Ezekiel, who joined the exiles in 597 BC.

Persia would issue a decree that the Jewish exiles were to go back home to Jerusalem and begin rebuilding the fallen Temple of the Lord![6]

So let's not miss what this chapter teaches us beyond the book of Daniel. It is all about the sovereignty of the God of Israel. His greatness extends far beyond the limits of our finite minds. That's why we are forbidden from making any image of him – there is nothing we could create that would be remotely worthy of the Living God. Great is the Lord beyond the borders of Israel – and greater still is the Lord beyond the boundaries of our imagination!

That's why the first half of the book of Daniel ends with a final cry of worship to the all-powerful, all-wise, all-conquering, sovereign, eternal and Living God of Israel.

"For he is the living God and he endures forever; his kingdom will not be destroyed, his dominion will never end. He rescues and he saves; he performs signs and wonders in the heavens and on the earth. He has rescued Daniel from the power of the lions."

---

[6] Babylon fell in October 539 BC and the events of Daniel 6 took place during the political power games that followed. Out of them, Cyrus issued his decree in 538 BC. See 2 Chronicles 36:22–23 and Ezra 1:1–11.

Part Two

God's People in the World (Daniel 7–12)

Fantastic Beasts and Where to Find Them

(Daniel 7:1–28)

"Four great beasts, each different from the others, came up out of the sea."

(Daniel 7:3)

The first half of the book of Daniel presents him as a missionary. The second half presents him as a prophet and a man of prayer. The first half is narrative, written largely in the third person. The second half is more personal, as Daniel's *"he"* turns into *"I"*.

The first half of the book of Daniel is history, which is a style of writing most of us find easy to follow. The second half is prophetic and apocalyptic, two styles of writing that we find far more difficult to understand. As a result, the first half of Daniel is famous and read widely, while the second half is often overlooked and ignored.

Let's make up for that together. Let's trust that these chapters of Daniel make essential reading for today. They are encoded because, had the Babylonians and Persians understood them, they would have accused Daniel and his readers of treason, but God enables us to decode them through his Holy Spirit. He explains to us in 12:10 that his goal was that *"None of the wicked will understand, but those who are wise will understand."* In the first half of Daniel, he taught us how Daniel lived as God's man in Babylon. In the second half he teaches us how we can also live as God's people in the world.

Chapter 7 begins by informing us that Daniel received his first prophetic vision in the same year that Nabonidus appointed his son Belshazzar to rule in Babylon as his vassal king. That dates the chapter to around 553 BC. Although it echoes Nebuchadnezzar's first dream, it recounts a separate and subsequent dream of Daniel's own. Daniel sees four fantastic beasts emerge out of the ocean and crawl up onto the shore.[1] They correspond to the four sections of Nebuchadnezzar's enormous statue and they have a similar effect on Daniel as they had on the king of Babylon. He confesses in verse 15 that he is *"troubled in spirit"*. Even after an angel interprets his dream to him, he confesses again in verse 28 that he remains *"deeply troubled by my thoughts."*[2] Clearly, Daniel didn't see this vision as unimportant. It really matters to him that his readers can identify these four fantastic beasts and know their place in the pages of history.[3]

The first beast looks like a lion but has the wings of an eagle. It represents the Babylonian Empire, since Nebuchadnezzar built statues of winged lions everywhere as a graphic symbol of his fierce and fast-expanding rule.[4] Daniel watches as the Lord strips this first beast of its powers. Its wings are torn off and it is given the mind of a man, which represents the seven-year humiliation of Nebuchadnezzar, followed by the return of his sanity and his surrender to the Lord.[5]

---

[1] *"The great sea"* in 7:2 is a Babylonian and Persian way of referring to the Mediterranean Sea (Ezekiel 48:28). Here it serves as a picture of the nations of the world jostling with each other for power (Revelation 13:1–3).

[2] The angel interprets Daniel's dream for him in the same way that Daniel interpreted for Nebuchadnezzar.

[3] The angel explains to us in 7:17 that the four beasts represent four *kings* or, more accurately, four *kingdoms*.

[4] This is why the Lord depicts Babylon as a lion or eagle in Jeremiah 4:7, 25:38, 48:40 and 49:22. See also Ezekiel 17:3.

[5] Some readers are confused by the fact that 7:17 says that *"The four great beasts are four kings that **will** rise from the earth"*. Surely the Babylonian Empire had already fallen? Yes, but to the Lord that was merely the first paragraph in a long chapter of history that would culminate in the birth of his Son in Bethlehem.

The second beast looks like a ferocious bear, raised up on one side with three chunks of flesh hanging from its mouth. This represents the Medo-Persian Empire, and its imbalance reflects the fact that the Persians dominated the Medes. The three chunks of flesh represent its three great conquests – the empire of Lydia (in modern-day Turkey) in 546 BC, the empire of Babylon in 539 BC, and the empire of Egypt in 525 BC.

The third beast looks like a leopard or cheetah, and it has four wings. It represents the Macedonian Empire of Alexander the Great, which conquered Persia and then the rest of the world with astonishing speed. This beast's two pairs of wings predict its rapid rise from 336 to 323 BC but, along with its four heads, the four wings also predict its equally rapid fall. When Alexander died suddenly, his empire was split between four of his generals and the world descended into a bitter and protracted civil war.

The fourth beast is the most terrifying of them all. Verse 19 says that it was the sight of this beast's iron teeth and bronze claws that troubled Daniel the most. The fourth beast represents the Roman Empire, which crushed every nation that it trampled. Its ten horns correspond to the ten toes in Nebuchadnezzar's vision which were like iron mixed with clay. They represent the Roman emperors, who were powerful yet corrupt – mighty in battle yet mightily foolish at home. At the peak of Rome's power, its emperors begin fighting one another – when suddenly another empire appears out of nowhere. This corresponds to the rock which suddenly struck the feet of the statue in Nebuchadnezzar's dream. It is the mountain that filled the whole earth.

Daniel's dream is therefore a fresh prediction that God alone can establish a Kingdom that will last forever. *"His dominion is an everlasting dominion that will not pass away, and his kingdom is one that will never be destroyed . . . His kingdom will be an everlasting kingdom."*

There is a lot of detail in this dream, so let's take a step back and note the three main lessons that Daniel evidently wants his readers to discern from it.

First, it reassures us that *the Lord is sovereign over history.* Whenever we feel a bit frustrated in the second half of Daniel that some of the detail seems obscure, it is intentional. Daniel's visions are meant to teach us that God knows every detail of the future, so we don't have to. He tells us just enough to help us trust him, but no more. That's because faith is less about knowing what the future holds than it is about knowing who holds the future.[6] The most important thing about these four beasts is revealed in verses 6 and 12. The Lord alone grants them authority to rule.[7]

Second, this chapter reassures us that *the Lord has placed us here for a reason*. Right at the heart of this chapter, in verse 22, we find *"the holy people of the Most High, and the time came when they possessed the kingdom"*. This is the only chapter in the second half of Daniel which is written in Aramaic because it contains a message for every nation.[8] The Lord wants the whole earth to believe in his Son. We are God's people in the world!

Third, this chapter tells us that *these two truths ought to fuel our prayers*. The chapter ends with Daniel telling us that he shared nothing of his dream with Belshazzar (since it wasn't given him to play politics) or with his friends (since it wasn't given him for idle chatter). Instead, he spoke only to God about it. The Lord had granted him insight into where to find these fantastic beasts on the pages of history so that he could pray God's plans for the world into being. The Lord invites us to follow Daniel's lead on this today.

---

[6] The level of detail in this chapter is meant to build our faith that God knows what he is doing. Ironically, it makes some readers doubt that Daniel prophesied it – even though Jesus insists he did (Matthew 24:15).

[7] Human empires are not all-powerful. They are raised up to act as mere tools in the hands of Almighty God. See 4:17, 4:25, 4:32 and 5:21; Jeremiah 51:7 and 51:20; Habakkuk 1:6 and Romans 9:17.

[8] Aramaic was the global language in the days of Daniel. Daniel 2:4b – 7:28 is written in Aramaic, as a message for the world. Daniel 1:1–2:4a and 8:1 – 12:13 are written in Hebrew, as a message for God's people.

God Has a Son (Daniel 7:9–14)

"I looked, and there before me was one like a son of man, coming with the clouds of heaven. He approached the Ancient of Days and was led into his presence."

(Daniel 7:13)

It can't have been easy for first-century Jews to hear Jesus claim to be the Son of God who had come into the world. Theirs was such a strict monotheistic religion that it sounded to them like blasphemy for anybody to claim that God has a Son.[1]

In order to help them grasp ahead of time that he is God-in-three-Persons, the Lord scattered the Old Testament with clues about the Trinity. Right from the start, in Genesis 1:26, he declares, *"Let **us** make mankind in **our** image, in **our** likeness".* Later, Proverbs 30:3–4 asks, *"I have not learned wisdom, nor have I attained to the knowledge of the Holy One . . . What is his name, and what is the name of his son?"* The response to that question comes in Isaiah 9:6 – *"For to us a child is born, to us a son is given. . . And he will be called Wonderful Counsellor, Mighty God, Everlasting Father, Prince of Peace."*

Perhaps even greater than all of these is the clue that we are given in the prophecy of Daniel 7:13. That verse is referenced five times explicitly in the New Testament, and many more times implicitly, because in this rather obscure chapter lies hidden one of the clearest prophecies about the coming of God's Son.[2]

---

[1] Mark 14:61–64; and John 5:18, 10:30–39 and 19:7.

[2] Matthew 24:30; Mark 13:26; Acts 7:56; and Revelation 1:13 and 14:14.

Let's backtrack for a moment. We have already seen that the first eight verses of Daniel 7 describe four beasts that represent four great empires that will rise up over the next six centuries. The Babylonians will give way to the Persians, who will give way to the Macedonians, who will give way to the Romans, who will finally give way to God's everlasting Kingdom. Verses 9–14 therefore describe the founding of that Kingdom. They are so important that we really need to stop and read them slowly.

We have already seen that one of the big themes of the first half of Daniel is that only the Lord will reign forever. What Daniel sees here is therefore obviously a vision of God. When Daniel describes the one who sits on the throne of heaven as the *"the Ancient of Days"*, or *"the One Who Is Aged In Days"*, he is reminding us that God has existed from eternity. Much of the imagery here echoes Ezekiel.[3] Some details are open to interpretation. For example, does God's white hair represent his age or his purity or both? Other details can only be read one way. The Lord commands armies of 10,000 times 10,000 angels, which can only speak of his colossal, irresistible power. So does the fact that the books of history are laid open before him. This means that there is nothing hidden from him and nothing is forgotten by him. He doesn't merely know the future. He authors it.[4]

Suddenly a new figure appears in Daniel's vision. *"I looked, and there before me was one like a son of man, coming with the clouds of heaven. He approached the Ancient of Days and was led into his presence."* This figure is clearly distinct from the Ancient of Days, yet at the same time he is clearly God himself. *"He was given authority, glory and sovereign power; all nations and peoples of every language worshipped him. His dominion is*

---

[3] For example, Ezekiel 1:15–21, 1:26–27, 10:2–7 and 47:1–12.

[4] Daniel sees the *Book of History* again in 10:21. It also appears in Ezekiel 2:9–10; Zechariah 5:1–3 and Revelation 5:1–14. This scene in Daniel 7 is also echoed by Revelation 20:11–15.

an everlasting dominion that will not pass away, and his kingdom is one that will never be destroyed." [5] So who is he?

When Jesus began his preaching ministry, almost six centuries after Daniel dreamed this dream, people began noticing that he liked to refer to himself as the *"Son of Man"*. He does it eighty times in the four gospels. The crowds were divided. Was Jesus simply telling them that he was a human who spoke for God, like the prophet Ezekiel, who is called a *"son of man"* ninety-three times in his book of prophecies?[6] Or was he claiming to be something far greater than that? Was he claiming to be the mysterious figure in Daniel's dream? Was he telling them that he was the promised Messiah, who would establish God's everlasting Kingdom on earth, calling people from every nation and people group and language to worship him as God, alongside the Ancient of Days?

That was the beauty of Jesus choosing to use the name *"Son of Man"* as his calling card. It was at one and the same time both missable and momentous.

Little by little, Jesus began to use the detail of Daniel's dream to reveal what he truly meant by *"Son of Man"*. He linked it to the authority that he wielded to forgive sins and drive out sickness. He linked it to his prophecies about the end of history and to his claim that God had given him authority to judge the world.[7] As it began to dawn on the Jewish leaders that such claims were preposterous for anybody other than God, they arrested Jesus and put him on trial before the Sanhedrin. When they asked him to *"Tell us if you are the Christ, the Son of God,"* he finally revealed the true significance of that title. *"Yes, it is as you say, but I say to all of you: In the future you will see the Son*

---

[5] The language here deliberately echoes 3:4–5, 3:7, 3:29, 4:1, 5:19 and 6:25. Nebuchadnezzar and Darius had craved to be worshipped alongside God. The Son of Man is freely given what they craved.

[6] The angel Gabriel addresses Daniel this same way, as a *"son of man"*, in 8:17.

[7] See Matthew 9:6, 13:41, 16:27–28, 19:28, 24:30 and 25:31. These verses make no sense whatsoever except as a direct claim to be the Messiah, Daniel's great King of kings, who would receive the worship of the nations.

of Man sitting at the right hand of the Mighty One and coming on the clouds of heaven."[8]

Andrew Wilson comments on this scene that

> *It doesn't sound as if Jesus is downgrading [from Son of God to Son of Man], does it? It doesn't sound like they are asking if he is fully God, and he is saying, 'Yes, but I am also fully man.' It sounds like he is upgrading, dramatically. It sounds like a schoolboy who has just been secretly cast as the lead part in a Hollywood blockbuster – when the bullies ask him, Did you come top of the class in Drama?' he replies, 'You said it; but from now on you will see me as Harry Potter, on billboards and film screens all over the country!"*[9]

No wonder they screamed that they had all the proof they needed to convict him of blasphemy. Little by little, Jesus revealed what the "Son of Man" meant on his calling card. When he finally did so, it got him killed.

The second half of Daniel is encoded because it predicts the emergence of a new, everlasting empire right under the noses of Daniel's Babylonian and Persian masters. The coding makes these chapters harder to read, because some deciphering is needed, but it is worth it. When Daniel prophesies about the Son of Man, look beneath the code.[10] He is revealing to us the greatest secret of history: *God has a Son!*

---

[8] This is the original NIV translation of the Greek text of Matthew 26:63–64.

[9] Andrew Wilson in his book *Incomparable* (2007).

[10] The four empires may be represented by beasts because humankind lost its authority on earth to a snake in the Garden of Eden. As a result, people became beastly themselves. The *Son of Man* restores the image of God to humanity and wins back for them all of the authority that Adam and Eve forfeited to the snake.

Apocalypse Now (Daniel 7:15–28)

"But the holy people of the Most High will receive the kingdom and will possess it forever – yes, for ever and ever."

(Daniel 7:18)

There are many different genres of writing in the Bible. There are history books. There are poems and prophecies. There are letters and sayings of the wise. But by far the toughest genre in the Bible to read is what is known as "apocalyptic literature". This includes passages like Daniel 7. What it says is vital, but we need help to decipher it.

The term "apocalyptic literature" comes from the Greek word *apokalupsis*, which is the name of the final book of the Bible in the Greek New Testament. It means *revelation* or *disclosure* or *unveiling*, which ought to encourage us. The apocalyptic chapters in the second half of Daniel and in Ezekiel, Zechariah and Revelation are not obscure in order to conceal things from us. God inspired them in order to reveal his secrets to us! The authors of Scripture wrote apocalyptic literature when they were living under violent regimes that were hostile towards God's people, where it was paramount that God's secrets didn't fall into the wrong hands. Daniel 12:10 explains that the Bible uses this genre in order that *"none of the wicked will understand, but those who are wise will understand."* Rather than give up in frustration, we simply need to ask the Lord to give us wisdom to crack the code that unlocks the secrets of these chapters.

The old English name for the final book of the Bible is the *Apocalypse*, so we should think of the second half of Daniel as *Apocalypse Now*. It reveals to us the same sweep of history as Revelation does, and that book therefore holds the key to deciphering this one. While it is true that the Apostle John focuses mainly on Rome, because the empires of Babylon, Persia and Macedon had been and gone by the time he wrote Revelation, we must not miss how much he intermingles all four of Daniel's beasts into one. In Revelation 13, a leopard beast comes up out of the ocean with the feet of a bear, the mouth of a lion, and the ten horns that Daniel says symbolize Rome. In Revelation 11 and 17, John refers to Rome as "Babylon" and "Sodom" and "Jerusalem" and "Egypt".[1] John is not challenged in his geography. He simply understands the message of Daniel 7 far better than we do, and he wants to show us how to crack the code.

John's cipher is actually very simple. If Daniel 7:9–14 describes the coming of the Kingdom of God into the world, then Daniel 7:15–28 must describe the resistance of the world to God's Kingdom. If Daniel 7:9–14 describes the reign of Christ, then Daniel 7:15–28 must describe the resistance of the Antichrist. In English, the prefix *anti-* means *"opposed to"* (as in anti-ageing, anti-aircraft, anti-clockwise and anti-social), but in Greek the prefix *anti-* also means *"instead of"*.[2] The Antichrist is therefore the evil spirit at work behind any human ruler who seeks to usurp the Kingdom that rightfully belongs to Christ. The rulers of Babylon, Persia, Macedon and Rome all attempted to do this, and Daniel predicts that the same spirit will continue to inspire others to do so after them.[3]

---

[1] John's first readers would have immediately recognised *the city on seven hills* in Revelation 17:9 as Rome, yet he also gives it these other names in 11:8 and 17:5. See also 1 Peter 5:13.

[2] One good example of the Greek word *anti* being used in this way is in Matthew 20:28 – Jesus did not come to be served *but instead* to serve.

[3] Note that, although the spirit of antichrist can work through governments and societies, it is primarily active through people. Paul speaks of the Antichrist as *"the man of lawlessness... the man doomed to destruction"* (2 Thessalonians 2:1–12). He refers to him as *"he"* rather than as *"it."*

Many readers of Daniel 7 pore over the history books and conclude that the *little horn* which topples three of the *ten horns* is Julius Caesar seizing power from Crassus, Pompey and Cicero in order to lay the foundation for the Roman Empire. By their reckoning, the little horn's boasting predicts that the emperors of Rome will destroy Jerusalem and attempt to destroy the Church too. What John shows us in Revelation is that, while some of this may be true, this chapter speaks of a far bigger spiritual battle.[4] Every human government that sets itself up against God's people is merely the flesh-and-blood embodiment of a demon which opposes the Lord's rule.[5]

John explains that *"every spirit that does not acknowledge Jesus is not from God. This is the spirit of the antichrist, which . . . even now is already in the world".*[6] Such a spirit has been at work in the world since before the days of Daniel, and it still continues its old work through new individuals today. It influences some of them so much more than their contemporaries that they can be described as the Antichrist. It influences others to a lesser extent – more like an antichrist, without the capital "A". So rather than looking in these verses for Julius Caesar and his rivals in the Roman senate, or for our own pet enemies today, we ought to understand the ten horns to be a plethora of antichrists throughout history and the little horn to be the greatest among them. John explains that *"Whoever denies that Jesus is the Christ. Such a person is the antichrist." "The antichrist is coming, even now many antichrists have come."*[7]

---

[4] We mustn't become like the eighteenth-century British Christians who became convinced, on the basis of 7:25, that the *little horn* must be the Pope, since he had just switched Europe over to the Gregorian Calendar. These chapters deal with far bigger matters than tussles between Britain and Europe!

[5] In Ephesians 6:10–18, Paul uses the armour of a Roman soldier to teach first-century believers that their real battle is not with the flesh-and-blood Roman Empire that they can see, but with the spiritual forces behind it.

[6] 1 John 4:3 and 2 John 7.

[7] 1 John 2:22 and 1 John 2:18.

This is the map and compass that we need to avoid getting lost in the detail of Daniel 7. This dream was given to the prophet in order to teach us three fundamental things.

First, that *the world will not receive the Kingdom of God gladly.* We must not be surprised by this. The Roman Empire crucified Jesus and tried to stamp out Christianity. Inspired by the same spirit, our own generation will resist the coming of his everlasting Kingdom too. We surrendered our lives to Jesus because the Holy Spirit overcame an evil spirit that had blinded us.[8] When we did so, we became embroiled in a spiritual war.

Second, that the *course of the war will not always run smoothly.* There will be periods in history when the world will look as though it has defeated the Kingdom of God. For long swathes of history, it will look like game over for the Jewish nation and for the Christian Church that was birthed from it.[9] Daniel urges us not to panic about this. It is all part of God's death-and-resurrection plan to defeat and plunder the Devil.

Third, that *the world will only be able to resist God's people for as long as the Lord permits it, and not for a single day more.* Daniel reassures us in verse 25 that the spirit of antichrist has only been granted authority to defeat God's people *"for a year, two years and half a year"*.[10] Whenever you are tempted to panic, just remember: *It is God who put you here.*

So don't skim read this chapter because you find apocalyptic literature tricky to understand. View it, instead, as *Apocalypse Now.* Let the book of Revelation help you to decipher these verses, and be encouraged! All of the setbacks of Church history are merely setting up the day described in verse 18, when *"The holy people of the Most High will receive the kingdom and will possess it forever – yes, for ever and ever."*

---

8 2 Corinthians 4:4–6.

9 John also depicts the Church being seemingly defeated by the world in Revelation 11 and 13.

10 My translation. These *3½ years* are expressed elsewhere as *42 months*, as *1,150 days*, as *1,260 days*, as *1,290 days* and as *1,335 days*. See Daniel 8:14, 12:7 and 12:11–12, and Revelation 11:2–3, 12:6, 12:14 and 13:5.

Manifest (Daniel 8:1–27)

"A fierce-looking king, a master of intrigue, will arise. He will become very strong, but not by his own power."

(Daniel 8:23–24)

Daniel's Jewish readers didn't understand what he wrote in chapter 7 about the Christ. That's why they failed to recognise him when he came. Many modern readers struggle equally to understand what he writes about the Antichrist, which is why it helps that he received a second dream, two years later, that gives a real-life example of what he means.

Daniel's second dream is similar to his first dream, but don't miss the fact that two big things change. First, Daniel suddenly stops writing in Aramaic and starts writing in Hebrew. It was pretty dangerous to expose a powerful ruler as an antichrist, so Daniel switched back into the language of God's people so that his insights would be understood by the Jews alone.[1] The second big difference is that Daniel says nothing here about the empires of Babylon and Rome. Nor does he say anything spectacularly new about the empires of Persia and Macedon. The purpose of his second dream is to reveal to us what the work of the spirit of antichrist will look like throughout history.

---

[1] Daniel 2:4b – 7:28 is written in Aramaic. Daniel 1:1–2:4a and 8:1–12:13 are written in Hebrew. An angel suggests in Daniel 10:14 that this may be because these last five chapters contain secrets for God's people alone.

Daniel dreams that he is in Susa, a leading city in the Persian Empire which would go on to become its capital.[2] It forms the perfect setting for Daniel's second dream, because it starts with a vision of that empire's heyday. Few people today remember that it was technically the Medo-Persian Empire, because it was a partnership in which the Persians dominated the Medes. This was represented by an imbalanced bear in Daniel's first dream, and it is echoed here by a ram with one horn longer than the other.

Suddenly a goat appears with a single massive horn between its eyes. This represents the Macedonian Empire of Alexander the Great. It crosses the earth without its hooves touching the ground in order to predict Alexander's shock defeat of Persia and his swift conquest of almost all of the known world in the years that followed. The goat's single massive horn is snapped off and replaced by four smaller horns, because Alexander would die suddenly in 323 BC, only thirteen years into his reign, and his empire would be split between four of his generals. These are known to history as the *Diadochi*, or *Successors*, and they were named Ptolemy, Seleucus, Cassander and Antigonus. They would slug it out together for the next fifty years, in a bloodthirsty war of attrition.

We know all of this detail from our history books, but to Daniel it was something of a mystery. That's why the angel Gabriel makes his first appearance in the Bible to explain to him what the vision means.[3] Gabriel quickly explains about the Persians and the Diadochi because what he really wants to focus on is one of the successors of Seleucus.[4]

---

[2] Originally the capital of Elam, Susa was made capital of Persia by King Darius I. The events of the book of Esther take place there. The Ulai Canal connected its two great rivers – the Choaspes and the Coprates.

[3] Gabriel helps Daniel again in 9:21, then disappears until he announces the births of John the Baptist and Jesus in Luke 1:19 and 26. His name is Hebrew for *Mighty-Warrior-of-God*, and the sight of him terrifies Daniel, Zechariah and Mary.

[4] The one who issues a command to Gabriel in 8:16 is probably the *"one like a son of man"* from 7:13. It is therefore significant that Gabriel addresses Daniel as *"a son of man"* – a human messenger for Jesus – in 8:17.

Antiochus IV ruled the Seleucid Kingdom from 175 to 164 BC. He was known to his subjects as *Epiphanes*, which means *God-Made-Manifest*, which makes it pretty easy for us to spot that he was an antichrist – a human ruler who wanted people to worship him as the Son of God. While marching south from Syria to attack Egypt, he conquered Israel, which is described in verse 9 as *"the Beautiful Land"*.[5] Victory over Egypt was within his grasp when, in 168 BC, a Roman ambassador suddenly appeared and commanded him to retreat or else consider the Seleucid Kingdom to be at war with Rome. Epiphanes retreated with such fury that people began calling him *Epimanes*, which means *Madman*, instead. He directed his anger towards his new Jewish subjects in Israel, forcing them to renounce the God of Israel and to adopt his own Greek ways. He suspended sacrifices in the Temple and erected a statue of Zeus in its sacred courtyards.[6] He waged a bitter war against God's people and he might have destroyed them had not the Lord raised up the Maccabee brothers against him. Defeated and fleeing, he died a horrible death from what appears to have been an aggressive form of bowel cancer.[7]

Gabriel is less interested in the detail of the life of Antiochus IV Epiphanes than he is in what it teaches us about how the spirit of antichrist works in the world. He emphasizes three times, in verses 17, 19 and 26, that Daniel's vision of the events of 168–164 BC is really all about what will happen to God's people in *"the distant future"* and at *"the appointed time of the end"*. Yes, it describes the reign of Antiochus Epiphanes, but it

---

[5] Daniel's third vision will tell the story of Antiochus IV Epiphanes in much more detail. It will also describe Israel as *"the Beautiful Land"* (11:16 and 41).

[6] Antiochus Epiphanes would stop the evening and morning sacrifices in the Temple for a total of 1,115 days during 167–164 BC. This corresponds to the *3½ years* that are variously described in Daniel 7:25, 12:7 and 12:11–12, and in Revelation 11:2–3, 12:6, 12:14 and 13:5. They symbolize something far greater.

[7] The humiliation of Antiochus IV Epiphanes and his subsequent intrigues against the Roman Empire are recounted by Polybius in his *Histories* (29.27 and 31.5–11). His persecution of the Jews and his death are told in 2 Maccabees 5:1 – 9:28 in the Apocrypha, which comments wryly that this *"indeed made God manifest to all."*

also predicts the attacks of many other antichrists against God's people throughout history. Such a person will never prosper *"by his own power"* (verse 24). His victory over God's people will always be empowered by the demonic spirit of antichrist, as part of a much larger battle in the heavenlies.[8] The Lord will permit such attacks to refine his sinful people and because he knows how to use such persecution to revive them.[9] He will ensure that the spirit of antichrist's demon army is defeated by his own far greater angel army.[10] *"He will be destroyed, but not by human power."* The Lord gave this vision to Daniel to reassure his people that he knows what he is doing, even when everything seems to be going wrong.

The Lord still has much more to reveal to us about how to follow Christ in the face of many antichrists. He will answer more of our questions through Daniel's third vision, which is still to come. For now, let's simply note that, whenever we find ourselves persecuted for our faith in Jesus, he points us back to Daniel's visions in Matthew 24:15 and Mark 13:14. He clearly expects this description of the work of the spirit of antichrist to strengthen our resolve in the face of the world's hostility towards God's people.

Jesus reassures us through Daniel's second vision: *it is God who put you here.*

---

[8] *"The commander of the army of the Lord"* and *"the Prince of princes"*, in 8:11 and 25, refers to Christ himself. Antiochus Epiphanes would not be just a nasty human ruler. Behind him would be the spirit of antichrist.

[9] The *rebels* and *rebellion* described in 8:12 and 23 predict that the second-century Jews would sink back into idolatry in the Promised Land. The Lord would use these attacks to judge and bring them back to him.

[10] These angels are described as "holy ones" in 8:13. The reality of this invisible *"host of the heavens"* (8:10) is underlined by the appearance of the angel Gabriel (8:16) and of the archangel Michael (10:13, 10:21 and 12:1).

Weapon #1: The Main Thing (Daniel 8:26–27)

"Then I got up and went about the king's business. I was appalled by the vision; it was beyond understanding."

(Daniel 8:27)

The first half of Daniel consists of several stories that describe his ministry as God's man in Babylon. The second half of Daniel consists of three visions that describe our ministry as God's people in the world. It is significant, then, that halfway through these visions Daniel takes a break in order to teach his readers how to respond to them. He has just informed us that a fierce spiritual battle is raging in the heavenlies for the fate of God's people on earth, so he now takes a halftime break in order to model for us how we can wield the six spiritual weapons that the Lord has given us to play our part in that battle.

I don't know how you feel when you hear the words "spiritual warfare". Last night, I was chatting with one of my white friends who is married to a black African. He started complaining that his mother-in-law is constantly rebuking the Devil and "binding and loosing" demons. Then the strangest thing happened. As he carried on complaining about her, he began listing some of the spiritual breakthroughs that she had encountered. He ended our conversation by expressing his wish that he could be a bit more like her!

Many of us share my friend's ambivalence towards "spiritual warfare". We have been brought up in a culture which denies the reality of angels and demons, so we can feel a little crazy talking and praying about them. Daniel challenges this by assuring us that angels and demons are very real. This is confirmed by the rest of the Bible, which mentions angels almost 300 times and demons over a hundred times. Having made it clear that angels and demons are very real, Daniel then agrees that we are right to feel cautious about seeing them lurking behind every corner. That isn't how we are to engage in spiritual warfare. Daniel teaches us to keep the main thing the main thing.

There is a famous story about a postman who was terrified of guard dogs. If he heard the tiniest of barks, he would drop his letters and run. Then one day he discovered something very exciting. He was walking up a garden path when a guard dog came running towards him. Instinctively, he held up the long, thin parcel he was holding and began wielding it like a sword. The dog stopped abruptly, let out a whimper and ran away with its tail between its legs.

The postman could hardly believe what had happened. When he tried it again at the next house, he discovered it was true. So long as he wielded a stick in his hand, the dogs were afraid of him. As time went on, he left his mailbag behind so that he could wield his stick with both hands. That was when his manager called him aside and pointed out that he was no longer delivering any letters. Chasing off guard dogs is all well and good, but it isn't the main thing that postmen are called to do! It was time for him to pick up his mailbag again. The first weapon that Daniel models for us is therefore very simple. We win the spiritual battle by remembering to keep the main thing the main thing.

First, Daniel explains in verse 26 that the angel Gabriel told him to *"seal up the vision"*. This is significant because, at the end of his first vision, he also explained to us, in 7:28, that *"I, Daniel, was deeply troubled by my thoughts, and my face turned pale, but I kept the matter to myself."* Spiritual warfare doesn't mean constantly talking about angels and demons. Such talk can often be the opposite of "drilling" and "blasting" in Babylon. It alienates people who have grown up in a scientific culture before we can bring the explosive power of the Gospel close to them. As Christians, we are to believe everything that the Bible says to us, but we are never to blurt out its spiritual secrets unwisely.[1]

Next, Daniel reminds us in verse 27 that even the best of us understands relatively little. He is the one who received these visions, with the angel Gabriel as his interpreter, yet even he confesses that he found it *"beyond understanding"*. We therefore ought to be quite cautious about pontificating too much about hierarchies of angels and demons.[2] Yes, there is a spirit of antichrist at work in the world – but is that one demon or a multitude of demons with a similar agenda? Yes, there is an angel called Gabriel – but we know little else about him. He isn't called an archangel and he doesn't command the armies of heaven.[3] He is mentioned twice in Daniel, twice in Luke 1, and then never named again. If we are meant to learn anything from the angels in Daniel's vision, then it is what one of them explains to the Apostle John in Revelation 22:9 – *"I am a fellow servant with you and with your fellow prophets and with all who keep the words of this scroll. Worship God!"* Our focus isn't to be on angels and demons, but on the Lord himself. Daniel insists that the first big weapon of our spiritual warfare is to keep the main thing the main thing.

Consequently, Daniel is extremely practical in his own response to his first two visions. He tells us that *"I got up and went about the king's business."*[4] That's an excellent summary of how we are to go about defeating the Devil's work in the world.

---

[1] 1 Kings 22:19–24; Proverbs 9:7; Matthew 7:6; Mark 4:33; John 16:12 and 1 Corinthians 3:1–2.

[2] A good example of this is 8:13, where the Hebrew word for *another* is *palmōnī*. Some Jewish rabbis create elaborate angelic hierarchies which include one named Palmoni. See Colossians 2:18 and Jude 8–10.

[3] That role belongs to the archangel Michael. See Daniel 10:13, 10:21 and 12:1, Jude 9 and Revelation 12:7.

[4] The events of chapter 8 take place before Daniel's sudden promotion in chapter 5 (8:27). Daniel was still a lowly and sidelined civil servant, yet he worked hard for his earthly king as worship to his heavenly King.

We don't know whether Daniel had a wife, but what we do know from 1 Peter 3:7 is that, if we are inconsiderate towards our spouses, our prayers will have no effect in the heavenlies, no matter how loudly we shout them.[5] We don't know what Daniel did with the wealth that the rulers of Babylon gave him, but what we do know is that the New Testament teaches us that how we use our money is spiritual warfare too.[6] Daniel wants his readers to know about the war that is raging in the heavenlies, but he doesn't want them to become ethereal in the way they fight it. We conduct our warfare through daily acts of obedience to Jesus. We get up and we go about the King's business. We keep the main thing the main thing.

Last of all, Daniel urges us to count the cost of entering into spiritual warfare at all. The way that some Christians talk about engaging with the Devil and his demons reminds me of the warning posters of people with damaged faces that get posted before Fireworks Night. I'm not sure people are fully aware of the forces they are challenging. Daniel confesses that he was *"worn out"* and *"exhausted for several days"* by what he saw of the spiritual battle. Let's therefore not be flippant about how we join it.

Daniel is about to show us five other weapons in our God-given arsenal, including the double-edged sword of the Word of God, the fiery missile of prayer and the battering-ram of fasting. But before we learn to wield such powerful weapons, he issues a warning: Whatever else you do, never forget to keep the main thing the main thing.

[5] Nor do we know whether Daniel had any children – although parents might suggest that his being able to lie down for several days without being disturbed in 8:27 is proof that he did not have young children!

[6] Jesus warns in Matthew 6:24 and Luke 16:13 that money can easily become *Mammon* to us – a demon god that usurps our worship. Hebrews 13:5–6 suggests that financial generosity is a real act of spiritual warfare.

Weapon #2: Scripture (Daniel 9:1–3)

"I, Daniel, understood from the Scriptures. . . so I turned to the Lord God and pleaded with him in prayer and petition..."

(Daniel 9:2–3)

In the classic 1980s movie *Crocodile Dundee*, the outback Australian travels to the sophisticated streets of New York. There, amidst the cosy trimmings of downtown Manhattan, he is attacked by a mugger with a pocket-knife. His New Yorker girlfriend advises him to hand over his wallet quickly because the man has got a weapon. *That's not a knife*, he assures her as he draws the huge knife that he uses for skinning crocs back home, ***this** is a knife!*

As Daniel shows us the second weapon that we are to use in our spiritual warfare, I can't help feeling like that New York mugger, who quickly turns and runs away. When I see how Daniel wields Scripture, I feel convicted that I have treated the Bible's many promises as a little pocket knife, when Scripture tells us to, *"Take. . . the sword of the Spirit, which is the word of God"*; it also states, *"For the word of God is alive and active. Sharper than any double-edged sword, it penetrates."*[1]

One of the dangers when we receive prophecies and visions through the Holy Spirit is that it can make us chase after those things, instead of studying the Bible as God's Word. Daniel clearly sees this as a false dichotomy. His two prophetic

---

[1] Ephesians 6:17 and Hebrews 4:12. See also Psalm 149:6; Isaiah 49:2; Acts 2:37 and Revelation 1:16.

visions have made him hungrier than ever to go deep into the Scriptures. At the start of chapter 9, we find him poring over the Old Testament and wielding its promises like a double-edged sword in his hands. We can tell from verse 1 that this took place only a few weeks or months after the fall of Babylon, so Daniel is in the early days of his new job of overseeing forty *satraps* in the Persian Empire. He is clearly determined that this busy role will not distract him from his daily Bible readings. When he gets to Jeremiah 25:11–14 and 29:10, he suddenly gets very excited. The Lord has made a promise to the Jewish exiles:

"These nations will serve the king of Babylon for seventy years. But when the seventy years are fulfilled, I will punish the king of Babylon and his nation, the land of the Babylonians, for their guilt." "This is what the Lord says, 'When seventy years are completed for Babylon, I will come to you and fulfil my good promise to bring you back to this place.'"

Daniel has just witnessed the fall of Babylon, so he quickly does a sum in his head. If he went into exile in 605 BC, then there can be only three years left until this prophecy is fulfilled. He is about to see the glorious return of the Jewish exiles to the Promised Land!

That's where I might have stopped. I might have written the promise down in my notebook and then taken a few moments to worship the Lord for his promises. But Daniel doesn't see the Scriptures as a ceremonial sword, to be admired. He sees them as a double-edged sword to be wielded against the forces of darkness through our prayer. He writes that *"I, Daniel, understood from the Scriptures, according to the word of the Lord given to Jeremiah the prophet, that the desolation of Jerusalem would last seventy years.* ***So I turned to the Lord God and pleaded with him in prayer and petition****."*[2]

The Hebrew text can be translated, *"So I set my face towards the Lord God"*. There is a steely determination here in Daniel.

[2] He also turned to the Lord with *fasting*, but we will examine that as our third weapon in the next chapter.

He doesn't treat the promises of God as a done deal. Scripture doesn't make him retreat into passivity. It inspires him to go to war! He reasons that, if the Lord has revealed that the Jewish exile will only last for seventy years, then he must have done so in order to inspire the Jews to pray for their exile to end. He therefore makes those promises the subject of intense spiritual warfare.[3]

I love the way that the famous nineteenth-century preacher Charles Spurgeon highlights this as the secret of how he led tens of thousands of non-believers to salvation. Using the language of old-fashioned banking in Victorian England, he urges us to see that:

> *A promise from God may very instructively be compared to a cheque payable to order. It is given to the believer with the view of bestowing upon him some good thing. It is not meant that he should read it over comfortably, and then have done with it. No, he is to treat the promise as a reality, as a man treats a cheque. He is to take the promise, and endorse it with his own name by personally receiving it as true . . . This done, he must believingly present the promise to the Lord, as a man presents a cheque at the counter of the bank. He must plead it by prayer, expecting to have it fulfilled. If he has come to Heaven's bank at the right date, he will receive the promised amount at once. If the date should happen to be further on, he must patiently wait till its arrival; but meanwhile he may count the promise as money, for the bank is sure to pay when the due time arrives. Some fail to place the endorsement of faith upon the cheque, and so they get nothing; and others are slack in presenting it, and these also receive nothing. This is not the fault of the promise, but of those who do not act with it in a*

[3] In the same way, the promise in Daniel 7:13–14 should stir us to pray *"Your Kingdom come!"* (Matthew 6:10).

> *common-sense, business-like manner. God has given no pledge which He will not redeem, and encouraged no hope which He will not fulfil.*[4]

The most remarkable thing about Daniel's prayer in this chapter is that he has actually misunderstood the verses that he is reading in Jeremiah – but the Lord answers his prayer anyway! Daniel assumes that the passage is talking about his own experience of exile, which began in 605 BC, but the Lord is actually referring to the destruction of Jerusalem in 586 BC. He is prophesying that Babylon, which fell in 539 BC but which was largely preserved, will rebel against Persian rule and be utterly destroyed in 516 BC. That same year would also see the dedication of the Temple rebuilt by Zerubbabel and his friends. Daniel has misunderstood the promise, but God rewards his faith anyway.[5] Shortly after praying in this chapter, Daniel was thrown into the lions' den, which made the king of Babylon witness the greatness of the God of Israel and send out a letter to the empire, which helped persuade King Cyrus to send the Jewish exiles home![6]

So let's learn from Daniel to treat the promises of Scripture as a double-edged sword in our hands. Let's go to war with the forces of evil through our prayers. Let's learn from Hudson Taylor, the British missionary to China, who saw the same Gospel breakthroughs in China that his friend Charles Spurgeon saw back at home. Hudson Taylor concluded that *"There are three great truths: First, that there is a God. Second, that He has spoken to us in the Bible. Third, that He means what He says. Oh, the joy of trusting Him!"*[7]

---

[4] He writes this in the preface to his book *Chequebook of the Bank of Faith* (1893).

[5] For another example of this, see the chapter entitled "Faith" in *Straight to the Heart of Matthew*. God loves our faith so much that he will answer our misguided prayers – but not the insightful prayers we never pray!

[6] See Zechariah 1:12, spoken in 519 BC. Daniel's prayer is answered in 2 Chronicles 36:22–23 and Ezra 1:1–11.

[7] Quoted by A. J. Broomhall in *Hudson Taylor and China's Open Century – Volume 6* (1988).

Weapon #3: Fasting (Daniel 9:3)

"I turned to the Lord God and pleaded with him in prayer and petition, in fasting, and in sackcloth and ashes."

(Daniel 9:3)

When Daniel read the promises in Jeremiah, he did more than simply pray. He tells us in verse 3 that he accompanied his prayers with *fasting*. So what exactly does that mean?

Put simply, fasting means going without food as an intensification of our prayers. It is not a hunger strike, whereby we force the hand of a reluctant God. It is like kneeling to pray, only more so. It is a way that God has given us to side with him in prayer, not just with our spirits and our voices, but with our bodies too. Andrew Murray likens fasting to firing our very selves at our spiritual enemies in prayer. *"Fasting helps to express, to deepen, and to confirm the resolution that we are ready to sacrifice anything, to sacrifice ourselves to attain what we seek for the kingdom of God."*[1]

First, Daniel fasts in this chapter because he wants greater revelation from the Lord as to how he should pray for the return of the Jewish exiles from Babylon. We are told in verse 22 that, as a result of his prayer and fasting, the angel Gabriel appeared a second time and told him, *"Daniel, I have now come to give you insight and understanding."*[2]

---

[1] Andrew Murray in his book *With Christ in the School of Prayer* (1895).

[2] This is echoed by the New Testament when the Apostle Paul describes his frequent fasts before recounting his *"visions and revelations from the Lord"* (2 Corinthians 11:27 and 12:1).

Second, Daniel fasts in this chapter because fasting is a powerful way for us to humble ourselves before the Lord. Fasting is more than "prayer plus". It serves a mighty purpose of its own by fostering real humility.[3] The Bible warns us that a full physical stomach invariably leads to spiritual pride. The root of Sodom's sin was not sexual perversion, but an excess of food: *"Now this was the sin of your sister Sodom: she and her daughters were arrogant, overfed and unconcerned."* The sins of the Israelites were also rooted in their full bellies: *"He humbled you, causing you to hunger . . . to teach you that man does not live on bread alone but on every word that comes out of the mouth of the Lord . . . Be careful . . . Otherwise, when you eat and are satisfied . . . your heart will become proud and you will forget the Lord."* Those of us who live in prosperous, well-fed and spiritually lukewarm nations particularly need to take this lesson from Israel's history seriously. *"When I fed them, they were satisfied; when they were satisfied, they became proud; then they forgot me."*[4]

Daniel is God's man in Babylon. He can see the danger of living in one of the wealthiest cities in the world.[5] My question is: *Can we?* I know that talk of fasting is unfashionable these days. I know that many Western Christians tend to view it as ascetic, outdated and unnecessary. But when I read about Daniel's prayer in this chapter, it makes me wonder whether Jesus was particularly thinking about prosperous Christians when he taught his followers about *"when you fast"* (not *if* you fast).[6] Was it for our benefit that he taught them, *"Blessed are those who hunger and thirst for righteousness, for they will be filled"*?[7]

---

[3] Daniel 10:12 sees the purpose of fasting as *"to humble yourself before your God"*. See also Psalm 35:13 and Ezra 8:21.

[4] Ezekiel 16:49; Deuteronomy 8:2–3 and 8:11–14; and Hosea 13:6.

[5] Daniel fasts completely here. In 10:2–3, he fasts only from luxury food so that he can fast for longer.

[6] Matthew 6:16–17.

[7] Matthew 5:6.

When we fast, we make an active decision to empty our earthly bellies for a season to increase our hunger for the things of heaven. We choose to embrace the path of poverty and lack to feast, instead, on the promises of God. Daniel has learned this from King David, another great prayer warrior, who writes that *"I wept and humbled my soul with fasting"*.[8] Ezra would learn it in turn from Daniel, proclaiming *"a fast, so that we might humble ourselves before our God."*[9] Fasting is a God-given corrective to the pride that so easily infects the heart of any well-fed human. I wonder if the reason we neglect fasting is rather more basic than a fear of asceticism. Are we too wedded to this world to deny ourselves the things of earth as an expression of our devotion to the things of heaven?

Third, Daniel fasts in this chapter because he is genuinely grief-stricken about the fortunes of God's people. Fasting was a major element of the elaborate mourning rituals of Israel.[10] As a result, it became a way in which the Jews would express to God the profound sorrow that they felt about their nation's sin against him. Samuel had led the Israelites in one such fast of repentance. The wicked King Ahab and the pagan citizens of Nineveh had fasted in repentance when the Lord's prophets warned them that God was about to judge them.[11] On each of these occasions, the threatened crisis was averted. Daniel fasts here because he longs to see this happen for the Jewish exiles now.

I know that certain Christians in the past have treated fasting in the way that Muslims treat Ramadan – as the accrual

---

[8] This is a literal translation of Psalm 69:10. It is surprising that David doesn't make it into Ezekiel's list of the Top 3 Prayer Warriors in the Old Testament, alongside Daniel, in Ezekiel 14:14 and 20.

[9] Ezra 8:21. This suggests that fasting is more than just a powerful accompaniment to prayer. It also has a powerful effect on its own. See James 4:6–8.

[10] 1 Samuel 31:13, and 2 Samuel 1:12 and 3:35. So were wearing *sackcloth* and putting *ashes* on one's head, as Daniel also does in these verses. Jesus uses *"fasting"* and *"mourning"* as equivalent terms in Matthew 9:15.

[11] 1 Samuel 7:6; 1 Kings 21:25–29 and Jonah 3:4–10. Ezra and Nehemiah would go on to follow Daniel's lead in this matter too (Ezra 9:3–6 and 10:6; and Nehemiah 9:1–2).

of "good deeds" to tip the scales of divine judgment in their favour. I know that fasting has frequently become a source of pride to its practitioners, like the Pharisee in Luke 18:11–12. I know that medieval priests taught that fasting is a "penance" that can top up what is lacking in the work of Jesus on the cross for us. I totally reject that false teaching as much as you do, but the remedy for *abuse* is never *disuse*, but rather *proper use*.[12] As I read about how Daniel prayed for the Jewish exiles, I can't help feeling that fasting is a vital weapon for our own day too. We mustn't allow the mistakes of others to rob us of a powerful weapon that God has given us to activate deep humility in our hearts and to express sincere repentance for our sin.

Arthur Wallis encourages us to learn from the example of Daniel:

> *Mourning over personal sin and failure is an indispensable stage in the process of sanctification, and it is facilitated by fasting. However, God wants to bring us beyond the place of mourning only for our personal sins, to where we are moved by the Spirit to mourn for the sins of the Church, the nation, and even the world... In giving us the privilege of fasting as well as praying, God has added a powerful weapon to our spiritual armoury.*[13]

Daniel's fasting changed his nation's history. So can ours. Let's rediscover the powerful weapon of fasting. Let's dust it off and let's learn to wield it again in our prayers.

---

[12] The Hebrew word *tahanūn* in 9:3 means literally *a request for grace*. Daniel's fast was not a religious endeavour, but a means of expressing his passionate faith in the grace of God.

[13] Arthur Wallis in his classic book *God's Chosen Fast* (1968).

Weapon #4: Prayer (Daniel 9:4–19)

"I prayed to the Lord my God. . . 'Lord, listen! Lord, forgive! Lord, hear and act!'"

(Daniel 9:4, 19)

People are willing to pay huge sums of money to be coached by an expert in their field. An after-dinner speech from the British entrepreneur Richard Branson or the American fashion guru Anna Wintour is said to set you back $100,000. If you think that's expensive, then you haven't seen how much Barack or Michelle Obama charge for something similar. Thirty minutes of their wisdom can cost you anything up to $400,000.

On that basis, the ninth chapter of Daniel is pretty much priceless. When the Lord looks back over the Old Testament in the book of Ezekiel and names his Top 3 Prayer Warriors, Daniel is right up there on the podium, and in this chapter he pulls back the curtain to let us into the secrets of his prayer life.[1] He offers to teach us how to wield prayer as the fourth deadly weapon in the arsenal of our spiritual warfare.

First, Daniel shows us how to structure our prayers in a way that will secure an answer. This comes as quite a surprise, because many of us have been taught that the more informal our prayers are, the better. Daniel clearly disagrees. If a barrister takes the time to prepare his legal argument before he steps

---

[1] The other two are Noah and Job. What is remarkable about Ezekiel 14:14 and 14:20 is that Daniel is still alive and known by Ezekiel when the Lord says this to him. He was a prayer hero in his own lifetime.

into the courtroom, and if a business executive takes the time to prepare her presentation before she pitches to a customer, then God's people should not simply saunter into his presence with chitter-chatter. Daniel structures his prayer carefully to present his case in the most forceful way:

9:4	Confession of God's perfect love and faithfulness
9:5–6	Confession of the Jewish nation's sin and unfaithfulness
9:7–14	Glory belongs to the Lord and shame belongs to the Jewish nation
9:15–19	But unless God revives the Jewish nation, their shame will belong to him

We are to view Daniel's careful construction of his prayer as the equivalent of a mighty warrior carefully sharpening the edge of his sword. Hosea 14:2 encourages us to do the same thing with our own prayers, even writing them down beforehand if it helps us to express our hearts more forcefully: *"Take words with you and return to the Lord."*

Second, Daniel teaches us to pray with our eyes wide open. In verses 4–6, he makes no attempt to play down the sinfulness of the Jewish nation.[2] He confesses it freely, while declaring that he also sees something bigger than Israel's sin.[3] The Lord is as awesome as Israel is awful. The Lord is as attentive to the cries of his people as they are deaf to his Word. The Lord is as faithful towards Israel as Israel is unfaithful towards him. Daniel teaches us that effective prayer never denies the unpalatable truth of

[2] Some people question whether it is right for Christians to repent of the sins of their nation, rather than just their own personal sin. Daniel 9:5–6 and 9:20 clarify that God has called us to confess our national sins too.

[3] Although he is one of the godliest men in the Old Testament, Daniel confesses his own sin freely too. His refrain throughout this prayer is always *"we"*, rather than *"they"*. See also 9:20.

our earthly reality. It simply declares that such earthly truth is trumped by a far greater heavenly reality.[4]

Third, Daniel teaches us to focus our prayers on the Lord, rather than on ourselves. The most surprising thing about this prayer is that Daniel never mentions his bad experiences in Babylon or his conviction that the exile must end after seventy years. We were told that it was prompted by Daniel's reading of promises in the book of Jeremiah, but he never mentions those promises explicitly. Instead, he keeps his prayer focused on the Lord, because his hope is based entirely on God's character and on God's purposes – not on any sense that Israel is entitled to intervention from the Lord.[5] In verses 7–14, Daniel contrasts the glory that belongs to the Lord with the shame that belongs to the Jewish nation, confessing that both of these two belongings are just and fair.[6] The Lord promised in the Law of Moses that he would put Israel to shame if they disobeyed his Word, and he has done just as he promised. The destruction of Jerusalem and the exile of the Jewish nation is not a blot of God's character. It is evidence of his righteousness.[7]

Fourth, Daniel teaches us to reason with the Lord in prayer. When he finally makes his request in verses 15–19, he brings it with a very forceful logic. The Lord has a history with the Hebrew nation. Everybody knows the story of how the God of Israel rescued his people from slavery in Egypt. Everybody knows that Jerusalem is *"your city"*. Everybody knows that

---

[4] The New Testament would describe this as an appeal to *God's grace*, rather than to *human works*. Israel will not be saved by its own faithfulness to God's covenant, but only by God's faithfulness to his covenant (9:4).

[5] Daniel confesses in 9:13–14 that the Jews have not fully repented of their sin, even after seventy years. Their hope is not in rehabilitation through exile, but only in receiving undeserved mercy from the Lord.

[6] This contrast comes out even more clearly in the original text of 9:7–9. Ten times Daniel uses the Hebrew prefix *le-*, which denotes *belonging*, to state that glory *belongs to* the Lord and shame *belongs to* his people.

[7] Leviticus 26:14–45 and Deuteronomy 28:15–68. Note the difference here between Daniel's prayer and our own prayers. We tend to complain that God is unjust for judging us, whereas Daniel sees it as proof of God's righteousness. This is the frank confession of faith that moves the hand of God.

Zion is *"your holy hill"*. Everybody knows that the Hebrew nation is *"your people"* and that its ruined Temple is *"your desolate sanctuary"*. And therein lies the problem. Like it or not, Daniel informs the Lord, the reputation of God's name on earth is inextricably bound up with the fortunes of the Jewish nation. Since Jerusalem lies in ruins and its people are exiled, the nations have naturally assumed that the God of Israel is a loser. But if, against all odds, the Jews were to return home from exile to rebuild Jerusalem and its Temple, then the world would be forced to conclude that the God of Israel is stronger than any of its idols. Daniel insists that it is really very simple: *"For your sake, my God, do not delay, because your city and your people bear your Name."*[8]

Fifth, Daniel teaches us to pray with passion. If you aren't slightly surprised by the way that he talks to the Lord in verse 19, then go back and read that verse again. He cries out, *"Open your eyes and see!"* – as if the Lord could ever be blind. He cries out, *"Lord, listen!"* – as if the Lord could ever be deaf or distracted. He cries out, *"Do not delay!"* – as if the Lord could ever be lazy. Daniel is so consumed by the glorious reality of God that he burns with passion in his prayers. He refuses to take "no" for an answer and, as a result, he gets what he asks for. So will we, if we learn to imitate Daniel in his prayers.[9]

So you can keep your money, Richard Branson and Anna Wintour. We don't need your after-dinner speeches, Barack and Michelle Obama. We have found something far more valuable in the ninth chapter of Daniel. One of the greatest prayer warriors of the Bible has let us into his prayer room and has coached us in how he prayed three times a day. He has taught us how to wield prayer as a mighty weapon in our own spiritual warfare.

---

[8] This is not a one-off lesson in how to pray. Note how much it echoes Exodus 32:11–14, Numbers 14:13–16; Deuteronomy 9:26–29 and 32:26–27; Joshua 7:8–9; Psalm 79:9–10; and Ezekiel 20:9–22 and 36:19–23.

[9] This is what God does in response to the prayers of a single person – *"your servant"* in 9:17. How much more, therefore, will God surely answer the united prayers of an entire church!

Faster Than Angels Can Fly (Daniel 9:20–27)

"As soon as you began to pray, a word went out, which I have come to tell you."

(Daniel 9:23)

The English poet Tennyson believed that *"more things are wrought by prayer than this world dreams of."*[1] That's what Daniel discovers here. Although there are times when we need to persevere long and hard in prayer, our prayers are always heard in heaven instantly and the Lord answers them faster than angels can fly.[2]

Daniel explains that the prayer he prayed in verses 4–19 was interrupted by Gabriel. Maybe he was about to mention the prophecies he had found in the book of Jeremiah. We will never know, because the angel who guided him through his second vision suddenly reappears to explain what happens in the heavenlies whenever we pray on earth. The final verses of chapter 9 are not part of Daniel's three visions. They serve as a conclusion to the prophet's prayer and as a stand-alone encouragement for us to wield prayer as a powerful weapon in our hands to engage in our own spiritual warfare.

The angel Gabriel arrives to tell Daniel how much the God of heaven prizes his earthly prayer warriors. He uses the Hebrew

---

[1] Alfred, Lord Tennyson in *Morte d'Arthur* (1842).

[2] Daniel 8:27 and 10:2–3; Luke 18:1–8 and 1 Thessalonians 3:10. Even when the answer to our prayers seems delayed, Daniel explains in 10:12–13 that our prayers are overcoming deep-seated demonic strongholds. We persevere in prayer, not because God is slow to answer, but because we believe we are affecting weighty heavenly realities that can only be shifted by the cumulative effect of many answered prayers.

word *hamûdôth* to inform Daniel that he is among God's *most highly desired things* in the world. Better than any beautiful sunrise, better than any lofty mountain view, and better than any magnificent creature, the Lord prizes people who devote themselves to prayer. In 10:3, this same word will be used to describe the tastiest food in the palaces of Babylon, so take a moment to think about how amazing your favourite food tastes to you. That's how God feels about your prayers.[3]

The angel Gabriel also arrives to tell Daniel how quickly God answers our prayers. Note how keen the prophet is for us to grasp this. He tells us that the angel appeared *"while I was speaking and praying"* (verse 20). In case we miss it, he repeats a second time that Gabriel appeared *"while I was still in prayer"* (verse 21). In order to emphasize still further how quickly the Lord answers our prayers, he explains that the angel *"came to me in swift flight"* (verse 21) and explained that *"As soon as you began to pray, a word went out, which I have come to tell you"* (verse 23). Take a moment to meditate on what that means. Daniel's prayer was heard and answered instantly. The only delay was in how long it took for Gabriel to reach him and to tell him that this is true. We may not always see the immediate results of our prayers, but this does not mean that they are not answered immediately in the heavenlies. Our prayers are answered faster than angels can fly.

Daniel knows that this isn't always our experience of prayer, so he continues. He informs us that the angel interrupted his prayers at *"about the time of the evening sacrifice."* That's a very odd way of telling the time during a period of history when the Jewish Temple lay in ruins! There was no altar of the Lord and no priest to offer sacrifices on it, so we are meant to make a link back to a similar strange statement in 6:10, which told us that Daniel prayed *"towards Jerusalem"*, despite the fact that the city lay in ruins. Daniel was a prophet who glimpsed some of the

---

[3] This isn't a throwaway statement. The Lord calls Daniel one of his *hamûdôth* again in 10:11 and 19.

deeper spiritual realities which lay behind the architecture of the Temple in Jerusalem.[4] He grasped that the Temple sacrifices pointed to a greater blood sacrifice which would one day be offered by the Jewish Messiah.[5]

When the Messiah finally came, he would never teach his disciples about unanswered prayer. Jesus would warn them that they needed to persevere in prayer. He would warn them that they needed to pray with the right motives. But he would never lead them to believe that their prayers might ever merely bounce back off the ceiling. On the contrary, he assured them that *"Everyone who asks receives"* and that *"My Father will give you whatever you ask in my name"*.[6] Even when we ask for the wrong things, Jesus assures us, our heavenly Father is wise enough to know how to answer our flawed prayers in the right way, because *"Your Father knows what you need before you ask him."*[7]

The extra information that the angel gives to Daniel in verses 24–27 is a little hard to follow.[8] Gabriel is informing him that the Lord will grant the Jewish nation 564 years to repent fully between King Cyrus issuing his decree that the Jews can return to their homeland and the public appearance of their true and better King – the long-awaited Messiah.[9] The number

[4] See also 1 Kings 18:36; 2 Chronicles 6:36–39; Ezra 9:4–5; Matthew 27:46; and Acts 3:1 and 10:3.

[5] Daniel grasped that this was the only way a holy God could forgive his sinful nation. The Hebrew words that are used for his prayers in 9:20 and 23 are *tehinnāh* and *tahanūn*. Both mean literally *a request for grace*.

[6] Matthew 7:8; Luke 11:10, and John 14:13, 14:14, 15:7, 15:16, 16:23, 16:24 and 16:26.

[7] Matthew 6:8. When we ask from sinful motives, it does affect our prayers (James 4:2–3), but the main thing by a mile that hinders our prayers is a lack of faith that they will truly be answered (James 1:5–7).

[8] Nevertheless, it is important that we try. Jesus quotes from 9:27 in Matthew 24:15 and Mark 13:14, where he says that *"the abomination that causes desolation"* will be a constant sign of the spirit of antichrist throughout AD history. We will examine what this phrase means in much more detail when we encounter it again in Daniel 11:31 and 12:11.

[9] The Hebrew word that is translated *Anointed One* in 9:25 and 26 is *Messiah*. The reference to anointing the *Most Holy Place* in 9:24 is best understood as a call to recognize the Messiah as the true and better Temple.

seven is used in apocalyptic literature to convey a sense of God's perfection, so Gabriel's *"seventy 'sevens'"* are intended to communicate that the period between Cyrus issuing his decree (in 538 BC) and the Romans destroying the Temple (in 70 AD) will be the perfect quantity of time to satisfy both God's mercy and his justice.[10] It will grant the Jewish nation sufficient time to repent of their sin and to receive their Messiah as King, even though the Lord already knows that they will squander it and crucify him, fulfilling all that was prefigured by the blood sacrifices offered in their new Temple.[11] Even after the crucifixion of Jesus, the Lord would still mercifully grant them forty more years in which to repent, before he would permit the Romans to destroy their new Temple and city, just as the Babylonians had done in 586 BC.

If you find some of this historical detail a bit confusing, don't worry. We will be told much more about it in Daniel's third vision. For now, what really matters is quite clear. Daniel encourages his readers by saying that his prayers were answered the very moment he started praying. He is teaching us to believe that, the instant we start praying, our own prayers are answered too. We may not see the visible fruit of it immediately, but we can rest assured that it is true.

Our prayers travel to heaven's throne room at breakneck speed and they are dealt with just as quickly. Daniel tells us that our prayers are answered faster than angels can fly.

---

[10] 538 BC to 70 AD is technically 607 years. The "sevens" are therefore to be taken figuratively.

[11] Daniel 9:26 can be translated as a prediction that the Messiah *"will be put to death, but not for himself"*. In other words, that he will die as a substitutionary sacrifice for the sins of the world.

Weapon #5: Authority (Daniel 10:1 – 11:1)

"The prince of the Persian kingdom resisted me twenty-one days. Then Michael, one of the chief princes, came to help me, because I was detained there with the king of Persia."

(Daniel 10:13)

If we want to understand the introduction to Daniel's third and final prophetic vision, then it helps to understand what the Bible teaches us elsewhere about spiritual authority.

Although the earth belongs to the Lord, the Bible informs us that he has firmly decided to rule it in partnership with humanity. *"The earth is the Lord's, and everything in it"*, yet he created Adam and Eve in his own image and commanded them to *"Be fruitful and increase in number; fill the earth and subdue it. Rule!"* [1] If you find the idea of having been created to rule the world in partnership with God a bit mind-blowing, then you are in good company. The psalmists marvel with awestruck wonder that *"The highest heavens belong to the Lord, but the earth he has given to the human race"*, and that *"You made them rulers over the works of your hands; you put everything under their feet."* [2] Amazing though this sounds, it is totally true. When the Lord decides to heal Abraham and Job's friends, he refuses to do so unless Abraham and Job partner with him

---

[1] Psalm 24:1 and 1 Corinthians 10:26, and Genesis 1:26–28.

[2] Psalm 115:16 and Psalm 8:6.

in prayer. He still decrees that his work in the world will be contingent upon our prayers.[3]

Sadly, most people are not interested in ruling the earth in partnership with God. When Adam and Eve chose to listen to the Devil instead, they surrendered their authority on earth to him. Satan wasn't completely lying when he tempted Jesus by showing him the kingdoms of the world and promising that *"I will give you all their authority and splendour; it has been given to me, and I can give it to anyone I want to."* Jesus confirms it when he refers to the Devil as *"the prince of this world"*. The Apostle John confirms it too, when he warns that *"The whole world is under the control of the evil one."*[4]

But John also explains that the Son of God became a human being in order to undo this disaster. *"The reason the Son of God appeared was to destroy the devil's work."* Although fully God, he became fully human in order to win back the authority that God had originally given us. He announced at the house of Zacchaeus that *"The Son of Man came to seek and to save what was lost."*[5] He spoke to the crowds in such a way that *"they praised God, who had given such authority to men"* – not just to a *man*, as if Jesus were a one-off, but to *men*, because he came to restore this authority to everyone.[6] Through his life, death and resurrection, Jesus has renewed God's partnership with humanity in ruling the earth.[7] This is the Gospel, and it provides the background to the astonishing encounter with the pre-incarnate Jesus that Daniel enjoys in the introduction to his third and final vision.

It is 536 BC, three years after Daniel prayed in chapter 9, and two years after King Cyrus issued his decree that the Jewish

---

[3] Genesis 20:7 and 20:17, and Job 42:7–10. The Lord could have healed them on his own, but chose not to do so.

[4] Luke 4:5–7; John 12:31 and 1 John 5:19.

[5] 1 John 3:8 and a literal translation of Luke 19:10.

[6] The Greek *tois anthrôpois* in Matthew 9:8 means literally *"to people"*. It includes women too.

[7] Matthew 16:19 and 18:18–20; John 20:23; Colossians 2:15 and Revelation 11:15.

exiles could return home.[8] Daniel is in his mid- to late-eighties, but he we still find him faithfully wielding his weapons of spiritual warfare. He has just finished a three-week fast from meat, wine and other choice foods in order to express his deep grief to the Lord. He senses that God's people are caught up in a great spiritual war, about which he understands very little.[9] He therefore lets his hair become dishevelled, like a devastated Jewish parent praying at the graveside of their child.[10]

Suddenly, the pre-incarnate Son of God makes another cameo appearance in the book of Daniel. Don't miss the similarities between the man that Daniel sees by the banks of the River Tigris and the man that the Apostle John sees on the island of Patmos in Revelation 1:9–18.[11] Daniel sees a man dressed in a linen garment with a belt of gold around his waist. John sees Jesus dressed in a long garment with a sash of gold around his chest.[12] Daniel sees a man's face as bright as lightning. John sees Jesus' face shining as brightly as the sun. Daniel sees a man with eyes like flaming torches, and arms and legs like burnished bronze. John sees Jesus' eyes like flames of fire and his feet like burnished bronze. Daniel compares the man's voice to the sound of a massive crowd. John compares Jesus' voice like the sound of a loud trumpet and a rushing waterfall. Daniel falls facedown before the man. John does the same thing before Jesus. In verses 16 and 18, Daniel recognizes

---

[8] The is the final time that Daniel is referred to as *Belteshazzar*. He wrote in Hebrew so that only the people of God would understand his vision, but he also gave the name by which he was best known throughout the Persian Empire to enable any Gentiles who truly sought the Lord to believe the words of this vision too.

[9] Ezra 4 tells us that the kings of Persia withdrew their permission for the Jews to rebuild the Temple from 535 to 520 BC. Daniel receives revelation in 10:1 that this is due to a spiritual battle that is raging in the heavenlies. The Son of God appears to him in chapters 10–12 to explain more to him about this great battle.

[10] See 2 Samuel 14:2 and 19:24. Jesus tells us not to mimic this aspect of Jewish fasting (Matthew 6:16–18).

[11] The Hebrew name for the River Tigris is *Hiddekel*, which means *Ever-Flowing*. Daniel had to cross the river to travel from Babylon to Susa, so he may have received this vision during one of his frequent work trips.

[12] *Uphaz* was in Arabia and was famous for its fine gold. See Jeremiah 10:9.

him as the *"one like a son of man"* that he saw in 7:13. John does the same in Revelation 1:13. Make no mistake about it. This man is no mere angel.[13]

The Son of God begins by repeating to Daniel what the angel Gabriel said in chapter 9. He tells him twice, in verses 11 and 19, that Daniel is one of the Lord's *hamûdôth* – that is, one of God's *most highly desired things* in the world.[14] He assures him that his prayers were answered on the first of his twenty-one days of fasting, but that all twenty-one days were needed to shift some powerful demonic strongholds in the heavenlies.[15] The *"king of Persia"* in verse 13 is not a reference to Cyrus, but to the evil spirit that is at work behind his flesh-and-blood empire.[16] Daniel's prayers have already released into battle Michael, the archangel who protects God's people.[17] But now another powerful demon is joining the battle too – *"the prince of Greece"*.[18] The Lord can easily conquer these demons, but he is determined only to do so through the prayers of people like Daniel.[19]

---

[13] The two Hebrew phrases used 10:16 and 18 both mean *one who looked like a son of man*. Daniel never describes Gabriel in such majestic terms, nor does he tremble so much before him. See John 17:5.

[14] Daniel 9:23. This same word is used in 10:3 to describe the tastiest foods in the Persian Empire.

[15] God responds to our prayers instantly (Isaiah 65:24). We persevere, not because he is slow to answer, but because over time our answered prayers demolish deep-seated demonic strongholds (2 Corinthians 10:3–5).

[16] This is made clearer in the Hebrew text of 10:13, which tells us literally that *"the prince of the kingdom of Persia"* is commanding *"the kings of Persia"* against *"Michael, one of the chief princes"*.

[17] This is the first explicit mention of Michael in the Bible. Jude 9 clarifies that *"one of the chief princes"* means an *"archangel"*. Michael is mentioned again in Daniel 10:21 and 12:1, and in Revelation 12:7.

[18] Angels and demons attach themselves more to people than to places (Luke 22:3, John 13:27, and Matthew 12:43–45 and 18:10). In 536 BC, more Jews were scattered across the Persian Empire than were back in Judah.

[19] Daniel's prayers matter so much that we are told three times, in 10:11, 12 and 20, that they occasioned this spectacular cameo appearance from the pre-incarnate Son of God himself!

What is at issue here is not the Lord's strength. We are told that the mere sight of him was enough to bring Daniel to his knees.[20] He confesses freely that *"I feel very weak . . . My strength is gone and I can hardly breathe."* No, these verses are about the Lord's determination to rule the earth in partnership with humanity. He could destroy the Devil in a moment, but he is committed to doing so in conjunction with the authority that he has entrusted to his people. He wants to strengthen us, as he strengthened Daniel, so that we can join him in battle against demonic strongholds through our prayers.

The Apostle Paul also describes this hierarchy of angels and demons in Ephesians 6:12, but he gives us scant detail about it in order to keep us focused on what the *one like a son of man* tells Daniel in 10:21 - 11:1. He has come to earth to reveal to Daniel *"what is written in the Book of Truth"* - that is, in the true book of world history.[21] He doesn't need Daniel to understand the hierarchies of angels and demons. Daniel has already supported him, unknowingly, in his battle against those demons when he prayed two years earlier in chapter 9, during the first year of King Darius.[22] All that is required of Daniel is faith that the Lord holds world history in his hands and that he has decided to complete it, not just with the support of angels, but with the support of humans, just like him.[23]

Jesus calls us to join in this spiritual warfare too when he tells his followers that demons are overthrown *"only by prayer and fasting."*[24] So let's believe we have authority to rule the earth

---

[20] Daniel falls face down in 10:9 and, even after Jesus raises him back to his feet in 10:10–11, he falls facedown again in 10:15. For a similar effect upon demons, see Matthew 8:28–32; Luke 8:27–33 and 2 Thessalonians 2:8.

[21] The Hebrew phrase *kāthāb 'emeth* in 10:21 can also be translated as *The True Decree*, in contrast to the decree of King Cyrus in 538 BC. This *Book of History* appears again in Psalm 139:16 and Revelation 5:1.

[22] English translations can be a bit confusing here. The Son of God is speaking in 10:21 and Daniel is reflecting in 11:1.

[23] Michael leads the mighty angel army that is described in 8:10 as *"the host of the heavens"*. But 10:21 suggests God views that army as *"no one"* until it is sent into battle by a similar army of praying men and women.

[24] Matthew 17:21 and Mark 9:29. See also Matthew 16:19 and 18:18.

in partnership with God. Let's learn to wield authority as the fifth deadly weapon in our spiritual armoury. Twenty-one days of prayer and fasting were enough for Daniel to secure victory over the demon prince of Persia. We have that same authority today.[25]

---

[25] Daniel's earthly victory began when he *set his heart* to obey the Lord (1:8). His victory in the heavenlies began when he *set his heart* to play his part in the spiritual battle through prayer (10:12).

What Must Soon Take Place (Daniel 11:2–20)

"Now then, I tell you the truth. . . an end will still come at the appointed time."

(Daniel 11:2, 27)

Many modern scholars struggle to believe that Daniel truly wrote chapter 11. His third and final prophetic vision predicts the next few hundred years of history in such astonishing detail that they believe it can only have been written by a historian looking backwards, not by a prophet looking forwards. What they forget is that, for the Sovereign Lord, the future is as certain as the past. Elsewhere, Jesus describes the future as *"what must soon take place"*.[1] He wants us to sense that same level of certainty here.

A. W. Pink explains:

> *God not only knows whatsoever has happened in the past in every part of His vast domains, and He is not only thoroughly acquainted with everything that is now transpiring throughout the entire universe, but He is also perfectly cognizant with every event, from the least to the greatest, that ever will happen in the ages to come. God's knowledge of the future is as complete as is His knowledge of the past and the present, and that, because the future depends entirely upon Himself. Were it in anywise possible for something to occur apart from either the direct agency or permission of God then that*

---

[1] Revelation 1:1 and 22:6.

something would be independent of Him, and He would at once cease to be Supreme.[2]

This isn't easy to understand for timebound creatures such as us. We tend to regard the past as done-and-dusted but the future as a free-for-all. In order to reassure the Jewish nation that the future is as certain as the past to him, God gave the prophet Daniel a third vision which recounts the next few centuries of the Jewish story ahead of time. Jesus explains to Daniel in 10:14 that *"I have come to explain to you what will happen to your people in the future".*[3] He came to earth centuries before his incarnation in order to reassure his people that, no matter how dark the events of history may seem, the Lord is always in control.[4] These things must happen to hasten the coming of the Messiah.

In verses 2–4, Jesus predicts that King Cyrus will die and be succeeded by three more kings of Persia. This refers to Cambyses (530–522 BC), Smerdis (522 BC) and Darius I (522–486 BC). After them will come a fourth king of Persia who is wealthier than them all. King Xerxes I (486–465 BC) will lead a great invasion of the Greek mainland, which will fail. It will trigger the rise of Alexander the Great, who will conquer and destroy Persia. Although his Macedonian Empire will appear all-powerful, his sudden death will quickly splinter it into four separate kingdoms ruled by his four strongest generals.[5]

---

[2] A. W. Pink in *The Attributes of God* (1931).

[3] Daniel 2:4b – 7:28 was written in Aramaic in order to instruct all nations within the Babylonian and Persian Empires. The visions of 8:1–12:13 are written in Hebrew because they are primarily for the Jewish nation.

[4] Jesus says something similar in Matthew 24:6 and 24:25 – *"See to it that you are not alarmed . . . See, I have told you in advance."* God prophesies in order to encourage us: *I put you here!* See also Amos 3:7 and John 13:19.

[5] Alexander conquered the Persian Empire in 331 BC. He died in 323 BC, aged only thirty-two, in Nebuchadnezzar's former palace in Babylon, possibly by poisoning. The ancient historian Diodorus Siculus tells us that, while dying he contemptuously bequeathed his empire *"To the strongest!"* (*Historical Library*, 17.177). His four strongest generals were Ptolemy, Seleucus, Cassander and Antigonus – known as the *Diadochi*, or *Successors*.

From verse 5 onwards, the Son of God focuses on two of these four generals. *"The king of the South"* refers to Ptolemy, who made Egypt the centre of his breakaway kingdom. *"The king of the North"* refers to Seleucus, who initially supported Ptolemy but then established his own breakaway kingdom, based in Babylon and Syria.

Ptolemaic Kingdom	**Seleucid Kingdom**
Ptolemy I (305–285 BC)	Seleucus I (305–281 BC)
Ptolemy II (285–246 BC)	Antiochus I (281–261 BC)
Ptolemy III (246–221 BC)	Antiochus II (261–246 BC)
Ptolemy IV (221–203 BC)	Seleucus II (246–225 BC)
Ptolemy V (203–181 BC)	Seleucus III (225–223 BC)
Ptolemy VI (181–145 BC)	Antiochus III (223–187 BC)
	Seleucus IV (187–175 BC)
	Antiochus IV Epiphanes (175–164 BC)

Verses 5–6 predict a short-lived alliance between these two breakaway kingdoms. Ptolemy II will persuade Antiochus II to marry his daughter, Berenice.[6] In order to do so, Antiochus will agree to divorce his existing wife, Laodice, a tricky character who will take vengeance by murdering Antiochus and Berenice. She will also murder their baby to ensure that her own son is crowned as the new King Seleucus II.

Verses 7–13 predict the aftermath of this murder. Ptolemy III will march north to avenge his sister's death by killing Laodice. In doing so, he will capture his rival's capital and plunder his rival's kingdom.[7] This will lead to decades of war between the two kingdoms, with much of the back-and-forth fighting taking

---

[6] It was Ptolemy II who commissioned seventy Jewish scholars to produce the Septuagint, the first Greek translation of the Old Testament, so that it could be included in the famous Library of Alexandria.

[7] The *fortress* in 11:7 is Antioch, the capital of the Seleucid Kingdom, but Ptolemy III also entered Babylon.

place in *"the Beautiful Land"* of Israel.[8] Verses 14–20 predict that many Jews will join the army of Antiochus III in the vain hope that he will grant their nation independence. Instead, he will lay waste their nation to support his army, before betraying them by marrying his daughter to Ptolemy V in order to forge a new military alliance against Rome. It will not work. Antiochus III will be forced to fight alone against the Romans, and he will lose.[9] Seleucus IV will be forced to pay such a heavy tribute to Rome that he will send his royal tax collector, Heliodorus, to raid the Temple treasury in Jerusalem.[10] He will be punished for his act of sacrilege when Heliodorus returns, not to help him, but to assassinate him.

If you hated history lessons at school, then you might find all of this a bit bewildering. If you love history, then you might find it distracting, so don't miss the point of all this detail. The Son of God did not appear to Daniel with a third prophetic vision to deliver him a history book, but to deliver hope to the Jewish nation. When the exiles who had recently returned home to rebuild the Temple discover that the Promised Land will remain a conquered province of the Persian Empire, they must not succumb to disappointment. The Lord is in complete control of history. When their land becomes a battlefield and their people become pawns in the power games of Alexander the Great and his successors, they must not despair. The Lord is in complete control of history. These are the things that must take place in order for the Kingdom of Heaven to be established on the earth, as was predicted by the vision in Daniel 7.

---

[8] Daniel 11:11 predicts the Battle of Raphia, which took place in Gaza in 217 BC. It was one of the largest battles in ancient history and it even included elephants. It saw the defeat of Antiochus III by Ptolemy IV.

[9] Antiochus III was defeated by the Romans at the Battles of Thermopylae (191 BC) and Magnesia (190 BC). The Roman commander Scipio Asiaticus drove him back until he was killed in a minor skirmish.

[10] This took place in 178 BC and it is recounted in 2 Maccabees 3, which is part of the Apocrypha.

The Jews could rest assured that history has not gone wrong. They have it from the lips of the King of Heaven that it is going right. The troubles of the next few centuries are merely what must happen to hasten the coming of the everlasting Kingdom of God.

Twin Peaks (Daniel 11:21–45)

"Then they will set up the abomination that causes desolation."

(Daniel 11:31)

Last summer, while holidaying in the Scottish Highlands, my children and I decided on a whim to climb a mountain near our home. After huffing and puffing our way through the gorse and heather, we finally reached what we imagined was the summit – only to discover from our new vantage point that the true summit lay some way behind it. After climbing this second peak, we discovered the same thing again.

It can feel a bit like that when we read the prophecies in the Old Testament. Sometimes they appear to be talking about the events of BC history. At other times they seem to be talking about the destruction of Jerusalem in 70 AD. At other times it sounds like they are talking about the second coming of Jesus at the end of history. So which one is it?

If we want to grasp what is going on in Daniel 11, then we need to understand that the answer is: *all of the above*. Verses 21–45 predict the actions of Antiochus IV, who ruled over the Seleucid Kingdom from 175 to 164 BC. At the same time, Jesus makes it clear in Matthew 24:15 and Mark 13:14 that they also predict the actions of every other antichrist in history. Antiochus IV was known to his subjects as *Epiphanes*, which means *God-Made-Manifest*, so he was an early antichrist – a human ruler who wanted people to worship him as the Son of God. The angel Gabriel has already explained to us in chapter 8 that the events of his reign are meant to serve as a picture of the many other antichrists who will arise against God's people throughout history.[1] We need to read these verses with both of these twin peaks of prophecy in view.

Antiochus was not the rightful heir to the throne when his brother Seleucus IV was assassinated by the royal tax collector, Heliodorus, in 175 BC. He was not even living in the royal palace, but heard the news from his home in Athens. Nevertheless, verse 21 predicts that he will quickly raise an army and march to Syria to usurp the throne. The talk of *"intrigue"* here is a prediction that he will do so by offering to serve as regent for his young nephew, while making secret plans to murder him.

Verses 22–28 predict that Antiochus IV will march south against Ptolemy VI in 170 BC. As he passes by Jerusalem, he will kill the high priest Onias, who is described here as *"a prince of the covenant"*.[2] By following up battlefield victories with letters to treacherous courtiers within Ptolemy's palace, Antiochus will finally succeed where his predecessors failed. He will conquer and plunder Egypt. He will seem to have the whole world at his feet, but *"only for a time"*. His plotting will come *"to no avail, because an end will still come at the appointed time."* While Ptolemy feigns forgiveness at their dinner table, he will be sending secret messengers to plead for help from Rome. Antiochus will be forced to retreat all the way to Syria, plundering the Temple in Jerusalem on his way back home.

Verses 29–35 predict that Antiochus IV will launch a second invasion of Egypt in 168 BC. He will be furious when a Roman fleet appears and an ambassador informs him that, unless he leads his army back home, his kingdom will be at war with the Roman Empire. Epiphanes will retreat with such

---

[1] Daniel 8:17, 19 and 26 tell us to treat the actions of Antiochus IV from 167 to 164 BC as a prophetic picture of what many other antichrists will do *"in the distant future"* towards *"the time of the end"*.

[2] The word *"covenant"* appears five times in 11:22–32 because this prophetic vision is about much more than ancient power politics. It seeks to equip the Jews to fulfil their calling to live as God's people in the world.

anger that people will nickname him *Epimanes*, which means *Madman*, instead. He will vent his fury on his Jewish subjects by forcing them to renounce the God of Israel and to adopt his own Greek ways.[3] He will suspend the Temple sacrifices and erect a statue of Zeus in its sacred courtyards. Any Jew who is prepared to worship this *"abomination that causes desolation"* will be spared, but any who oppose it will be imprisoned, enslaved or killed.[4] This will be such a terrible time for the Jews that they will be tempted to imagine that God has abandoned them. That's why he predicted it ahead of time, to reassure them that *"The end... will still come at the appointed time."*[5]

Verses 36–39 encourage God's people not to lose heart in the face of such bitter persecution. Like the other individuals in history who have been empowered by the spirit of antichrist, Antiochus IV will briefly seem all-powerful. He will speak blasphemies against the God of heaven and demand to be worshipped as a god himself. The Lord will permit this in order to root out sin and compromise within his people, but his *"time of wrath"* will soon be completed and his people restored to a passionate faith in him. This is why we mustn't let our eyes glaze over as we quickly skim-read through this chapter. These verses contain a vital promise for us today, whenever antichrists arise to persecute God's people. The Lord tells us to rejoice in the midst of such hardships because we know that he uses such times to refine and revive his people. It is in times of persecution that false believers are exposed and true believers are emboldened. We are meant to grasp that persecution and revival go hand in hand.[6]

---

[3] Daniel 11:37–39 predicts that Antiochus IV will abandon the traditional gods of Syria and Babylon (such as Tammuz, *"the one desired by women"*) in order to worship the Greek god Zeus instead.

[4] 2 Maccabees 5:11–14 says that Antiochus killed 40,000 Jews and enslaved 40,000 more in three days of slaughter.

[5] See Matthew 24:6 and 24:25, and John 13:19. *"See to it that you are not alarmed... See, I have told you ahead of time... I am telling you now before it happens."*

[6] See Matthew 15:13 and 24:9–16, Mark 13:9–14 and Luke 21:12–28. See also Exodus 1:12.

Sure enough, this would indeed be what happened when Judas Maccabeus rallied the devout Jews against Antiochus IV in the Maccabean Revolt. Against all odds, the Jews succeeded in defeating the Seleucids, recapturing Jerusalem and reconsecrating the Temple to the Lord in December 164 BC. The Jewish community today still celebrates this amazing turnaround at the feast of Hanukkah. Difficult though the three years of persecution were for their nation, it was *"what... must take place"* because only through it would the Lord revive and prepare them for the coming of his everlasting Kingdom.

Verses 40–45 predict the final downfall of Antiochus IV. *"He will come to his end, and no one will help him."* Ptolemy VI will march against him from Egypt in the south, turning *"the Beautiful Land"* of Israel into a battleground once more.[7] Just when he thinks he has succeeded in warding off his enemy, Antiochus will hear that the Parthian army is marching against him from the east and that the Roman army is marching against him from the north. The one who dared to pitch his tents at *"the beautiful holy mountain"* – on the slopes of Jerusalem – will die of aggressive bowel cancer, panicked and surrounded.[8]

The returning Jewish exiles were to read these verses and see the first peak of prophecy. They were to be encouraged that the Lord knew what he was doing to their nation, even in the dark days of Antiochus IV. The New Testament encourages us to look beyond this to see a second peak of prophecy that is meant to encourage us too.[9] These verses reassure us that the Lord knows what he is doing whenever any antichrist arises and persecutes God's people. The Lord is in complete control of history and he wants to use Daniel's vision to reassure us in our own trials that *it is God who put you here.*

---

[7] Israel is called *"the Beautiful Land"* in 8:9, 11:16 and 11:41 in order to emphasize that this vision is far more than a mere history lesson. It aims to teach us how to live as God's people in the world.

[8] 2 Maccabees 9:1–28. Judea would then enjoy independence until conquered by the Romans in 63 BC.

[9] See Matthew 24:15; Mark 13:14; 2 Thessalonians 2:1–12; 1 John 2:18 and Revelation 13:11–18.

Weapon #6: Knowing God (Daniel 11:32–35)

"With flattery he will corrupt those who have violated the covenant, but the people who know their God will firmly resist him."

(Daniel 11:32)

It is far easier to talk about the fact that the Lord uses periods of persecution to refine and revive his people than it is to believe it when such times of persecution come. For Christians in the West, the reflections of persecuted Chinese pastors can appear unreal:

> *The Lord wants us to embrace suffering as a friend. We need a deep realisation that when we're persecuted for Jesus' sake it is an act of God's blessing to us... Sometimes Western visitors come to China and ask the house church leaders what seminary they attended. We reply, jokingly yet with underlying seriousness, that we have been trained in the Holy Spirit Personal Devotion Bible School (prison) for many years. Sometimes our Western friends don't understand what we mean because they then ask, "What materials do you use in this Bible school?" We reply, "Our only materials are the foot chains that bind us, and the leather whips that bruise us." In this prison seminary we have learned many valuable lessons about the Lord that we could never have learned from a book. We've come to know God in a deeper way.*[1]

---

[1] Brother Yun says this in his book *The Heavenly Man* (2002).

Strange as such reflections may sound to Western ears, the Lord tells Daniel in these verses that they are definitely true. Periods of persecution throughout history have often proved to be times of great refining and revival for God's people, which is why these verses teach us not to fear such times of testing. They inform us that the sixth and final weapon by which we win our spiritual warfare is the mighty weapon of *knowing God*.

Periods of persecution expose the reality of our relationship with the Lord. It is difficult to tell whether we are serving God for God himself, or for what we hope we can get out of God, until we discover that serving him offers us loss and hardship in return. Daniel predicts that Antiochus IV's flattery will reveal that many Jews are not devoted to the Lord at all. They are merely using him to get what they want from him. It will only take a few threats for them to abandon him and worship Zeus instead. In the same way, Jesus explains in Matthew 15:13, periods of persecution for the Church drive out false believers and destroy any ministries that were not initiated by the Lord: *"Every plant that my heavenly Father has not planted will be pulled up by the roots."*

Periods of persecution also reveal that many people are truly serving God for his own sake, and not for what they hope they can get out of him. The Hebrew text of Daniel's prophecy about Antiochus IV in verse 32 can either be translated that *"the people who know their God will firmly resist him"* or that *"the people who know their God shall be strong and perform exploits."* This is meant to encourage us and spur us on today, because the more we know God and the more we love him for his own sake, the more we find ourselves empowered to see spiritual breakthrough in the midst of savage persecution. We discover that our friendship with the Lord is like a mighty weapon in our hands.

Knowing God means *having faith in who he really is.* Daniel emphasizes in verse 33 that *"those who are wise will instruct many"* because knowing God isn't something vague or intangible. It flows out of our study of his glorious character. Knowing God is his greatest desire for us (Hosea 6:6) and his main purpose in our salvation (John 17:3 and Ephesians 1:17). It is the only true source of lasting human contentment (Jeremiah 9:23–24) and it lies at the heart of the faith by which we overcome the world (Psalm 9:10, 1 John 5:4). The study of God's character is therefore of vital importance for anyone who wants to serve him and to see spiritual breakthrough in their generation. It is the deadly weapon by which the Church keeps on advancing in the face of fierce opposition.

Jim Packer explains: *"What makes life worthwhile is having a big enough objective, something which catches our imagination and lays hold of our allegiance; and this the Christian has, in a way that no other person has. For what higher, more exalted, and more compelling goal can there be than to know God?"* Further: *"Once you become aware that the main business that you are here for is to know God, most of life's problems fall into place of their own accord."*[2]

Knowing God means *worshipping him for who he really is.* Daniel emphasizes in verse 35 that even genuine believers can stumble during periods of persecution because they have paid lip service to God's character, instead of truly grasping that having *God plus nothing* is far better than having *everything minus God.* Readers of John Bunyan's seventeenth-century story *The Pilgrim's Progress* are often struck by his deep love for the Lord without understanding how he obtained it. After three months in a Bedford jail (which was the standard sentence for anyone who resisted King Charles II's restrictions on Christian preaching), he was offered his freedom if he promised not to preach again. He responded: *"If I lie in prison until the moss grows on my eyelids, I will never make a promise to withhold from preaching. If you will let me out of prison today, I will preach again tomorrow!"*[3] It was during the twelve additional years that

---

[2] J. I. Packer in his book *Knowing God* (1973).

[3] Quoted by Charles Spurgeon in a sermon at the New Park Street Chapel, London, on 13 June 1858.

he was subsequently forced to spend in prison that he wrote *The Pilgrim's Progress.* The Lord used those years of testing to wean his heart away from the fleeting pleasures of this world and onto the lasting pleasure of deep friendship with his God. As a result, Bunyan wrote a book which has inspired millions of believers to pursue a deeper walk with God themselves.

This is why Psalm 149:6 likens our worship to *"a double-edged sword"* in our hands. Periods of persecution force us to choose between finding our pleasure in the world and finding our pleasure in the Lord himself, and the Devil has no armour that can resist the person who has firmly decided that they are now living for God and for God alone.

If the Scriptures teach us that Jesus was fruitful through deep friendship with his Father, that his disciples were fruitful through deep friendship with God too, and that we can only be fruitful if we pursue deep friendship with God ourselves, then we need to sit up and take the words of Daniel very seriously indeed.[4]

Daniel is telling us that knowing God is the Christian's secret weapon, which enables us to survive and thrive in times of persecution. He is reassuring us that what the world needs most in our own generation is men and women who know their God and who find that it empowers them to perform mighty exploits for the glory of his name.

---

[4] For example, in Mark 3:14; John 15:5 and Acts 10:38. Daniel isn't merely talking theory here. He and his friends proved how powerful this weapon is to conquer empires and cultures when they loved the Lord enough to be thrown into the blazing furnace and the lions' den.

Stars In the Night Sky (Daniel 12:1–13)

"Those who are wise will shine like the brightness of the heavens, and those who lead many to righteousness, like the stars for ever and ever."

(Daniel 12:3)

We have seen that Daniel is a book of two halves. Chapters 1–6 recount his personal exploits as God's man in Babylon. Chapters 7–12 record his prophetic visions about God's people in the world. Chapters 10 and 12 introduce and conclude his third prophetic vision, but chapter 12 also serves a larger purpose. It acts as a conclusion to the book of Daniel as a whole. It reminds us one last time that *it is God who put you here*.

The speaker in these final verses is still the pre-incarnate Son of God.[1] Daniel continues to recount words spoken by *"the man clothed in linen"* that are intended to encourage the Jews in the difficult days that lie ahead of them under Antiochus IV. As we read them, we are still expected to remember what we learned about the "twin peaks" of biblical prophecy. These final verses are intended to encourage believers under pressure in any generation of AD history too.[2]

We are encouraged to *be realistic*. There will be trouble for God's people in the world. Verse 11 warns us that Antiochus IV

---

[1] This means that when Jesus walked on Lake Galilee, it was actually the second time that he had walked on water. He had previously walked on the River Tigris in Daniel 12:6.

[2] Jesus stresses this in 12:4 and 12:9 by referring to *"the time of the end"*, a phrase that he also used in 8:17, 8:19, 11:35 and 11:40 to draw our attention to the "twin peaks" of biblical prophecy. He is not telling us in 12:4 to leave the book of Daniel unread, but to keep it away from the hostile eyes of the enemies of God's people.

will bring unprecedented distress on the Jewish nation when he sets up *"the abomination that causes desolation"* (that is, his great statue of Zeus) in the sacred courtyards of the Temple.[3] We are also meant to understand verse 11 as a warning that the suffering of 167–164 BC will be a foretaste of even greater persecution in the future for God's people.[4] Unless we take to heart the warning in verse 7 that God's people will very often appear down-and-out and defeated, we will become despondent and give up our calling to be God's people in the world.[5] Consequently, we are encouraged that, when wicked people reject the Gospel and attack us, nothing strange is happening to us.[6] Such setbacks do not mean that the Great Commission has failed. They are all part of God's perfect plan to advance the Gospel.

We are encouraged to *be cheerful*. We are protected in our troubles by the archangel Michael, who commands a vast army of warrior angels.[7] The Lord will not lose a single believer whose name he has written in his Book of Life.[8] Even those who are killed because of their faith in him will be raised to new life at the resurrection of the dead, when Jesus returns from heaven to judge the world.[9] Daniel's prophetic visions

---

[3] Daniel 12:11 echoes 8:13, 9:27 and 11:31. It is in turn echoed by Jesus in Matthew 24:15 and Mark 13:14.

[4] For example, the events of 167–164 BC seemed like nothing during the fall of Jerusalem in 70 AD, during the Jewish holocaust of 1941–45, and during some of the harshest waves of persecution against the Church.

[5] Daniel 12:7 is echoed by Revelation 11:7–11 and 13:5–7, where *3½ days* of defeat also echo *3½ years*.

[6] 1 Peter 4:12–13. See also Matthew 10:21–25; John 16:1–4; Acts 14:22; 1 Thessalonians 3:2–4 and 2 Timothy 3:12.

[7] Does 12:1 teach us that Michael protects the Jewish nation or the Christian Church? The answer is: *both*. The Church is not separate from Israel, but a continuation of the story of God's people (Romans 11:11–32).

[8] *"The book"* that is mentioned in Daniel 12:1 also appears in Exodus 32:32–33; Psalm 69:28 and 87:6; Luke 10:20 and Philippians 4:3. It is described in greater detail in Revelation 3:5, 13:8, 17:8, 20:12, 20:15 and 21:27.

[9] Daniel 12:2 is the clearest Old Testament prophecy that the wicked will be raised from the dead for judgment. This is echoed more clearly in Matthew 25:46; John 5:25–29 and Acts 24:15. The contrast between *everlasting* life and *everlasting* contempt is intended to quash any doubt that hell is both real and forever.

about the sufferings of God's people are not meant to make us anxious. They are meant to bring us happiness in the midst of troubled times. In the final verse of the book of Daniel, the aged prophet is encouraged to live out his last days in peace, confident that nothing can exclude him from the resurrection of the righteous on the Final Day.[10]

We are encouraged to *be full of faith*. When two angels ask the Man in verse 6 how long it will take for these prophetic visions to be fulfilled, he explains that it will be for *"a time, times and half a time"*.[11] This is a promise that the Lord has set a fixed limit of three-and-a-half years for Antiochus IV to defile his Temple, and it is also a promise that he has set similar limits for every other antichrist in history. The description of these three-and-a-half years as both *"1,290 days"* and *"1,335 days"* emphasizes that God alone knows the exact limits that he has set for each individual antichrist who is to come. We aren't meant to mark the days off on our calendars so much as to trust that God has a perfect calendar in heaven.[12] Troubles never befall God's people in spite of God, but only ever because of God. If we suffer, then it is always because he has determined that such trials are necessary to purify, refine and revive us to serve him as God's people in the world.[13]

---

[10] The Hebrew word for *you* in 12:13 is *you (singular)*. The Lord expresses deep care for his prophet personally, even as he prophesies a common hope for all God's people throughout BC and AD history.

[11] Deuteronomy 19:15 stipulated that a solemn oath must be made before two or three witnesses, so these two angels appear so that the Son of God can make a solemn oath to Daniel regarding God's people in 12:7.

[12] Remember, we saw the Lord holding the *Book of History* in 10:21. Although these *3½ years* are described in a variety of ways in Daniel 7:25, 8:14, 12:7 and 12:11–12, and in Revelation 11:2–3, 12:6, 12:14 and 13:5, they all use the time that God fixed for Antiochus IV to defile his Temple as a promise that he has also fixed similar limits for every other antichrist who will arise throughout AD history.

[13] The Hebrew word *tsāraph* in 12:10 means literally *to smelt* precious metal. It reminds us that God regards our faith as being of greater worth than gold and uses earthly trials to purify us for eternity. Just as a bride endures the pain of leg-waxing because her eyes are fixed on the glories of her wedding day, so too the Bride of Christ ought never to complain about the ways in which the Lord prepares her for an even greater Wedding Day (2 Corinthians 4:16–18; 1 Peter 1:6–9; and Revelation 19:7 and 21:2).

We are therefore encouraged to *be on the front foot.* The Lord has given us a Great Commission to proclaim his Gospel to the world. *"Those who are wise"* – or to translate the Hebrew text a bit more precisely – *"Those who impart wisdom to others"* will shine like the bright sky and *"those who lead many to righteousness, like the stars forever and ever."*[14] Yes, the skies of history will often grow dark above God's people. But no, this doesn't mean we are to batten down the hatches and go on the defensive, desperately hoping that Jesus will return from heaven and whisk us away to our new home. A proper view of God's sovereignty over world history always places us on the offensive with the Gospel.

Don't miss this. It's when the skies of history are darkest that God's people can shine brightest. The Apostle Paul is surely thinking about Daniel 12:3 when he encourages us in Philippians 2:15–16 that believers *"shine . . . like stars in the sky"* best as we *"hold firmly to the word of life"* in the midst of a *"warped and crooked generation"*.

So as the book of Daniel comes to an end, we are meant to do more than admire God's man in Babylon. We are meant to rise up and take our own place among God's people in the world. Even in our darkest moments, and even when we are most tempted to doubt it, the book of Daniel constantly encourages us: *It is God who put you here.*

[14] The first half of the Hebrew text of 12:3 is ambiguous. If taken to mean *"the wise"*, it is an Old Testament precursor to Matthew 13:43. But, since the second half of the verse is definitely talking about evangelism, we probably ought to read the first half to mean *"those who impart wisdom to others"*. See Proverbs 11:30.

Part Three

God's Woman in Persia (Esther 1–10)

Same Difference (Esther 1:1–8)

"At that time King Xerxes reigned from his royal throne in the citadel of Susa. . ."

(Esther 1:2)

At first glance, the book of Esther looks very different from the book of Daniel. It contains no obvious prophecies; it is narrative history all the way. It is not about a man, but a woman. It is not about a government minister, but a queen. It does not take place in Babylon, but in Susa, the new capital city of the Persian Empire.[1] It is not set in the days before King Cyrus sent the Jewish exiles back to the Promised Land to rebuild their Temple, but over fifty years later, during the reign of King Xerxes, who ruled over the Persian Empire at its peak, from 486 to 465 BC.[2]

What is more, the book of Esther makes no explicit reference to the God of Israel. The twelve chapters of Daniel refer to him as *"God"* at least fifty times and as *"the Lord"* at least twenty times. They even invent a new name for him, referring to him three times as *"the Ancient of Days"*, a name that appears nowhere else in the Bible. This amounts on average to at least six direct references to God for every chapter in the book of Daniel, whereas Esther is the only book in the Bible not to mention God

[1] *Susa* means *Lily*, and it became the Persian capital under Xerxes' father, King Darius I (522–486 BC).

[2] He is called *Ahasuerus* in the Hebrew text of the book of Esther, which the translators of the Septuagint took to mean King Artaxerxes (465–424 BC). However, modern evidence firmly points to King Xerxes.

by name at all.[3] At first glance, therefore, Esther could hardly be more different from the book of Daniel.

But that's why we need to look a bit more deeply at the book of Esther. When we examine it a little bit more carefully, we discover some remarkable similarities between these two books of the Bible. Daniel and Esther are both Jews living out their faith as exiles in an empire that is very hostile towards their belief in the Lord. Daniel serves as God's man in Babylon and Esther serves as God's woman in Persia. Susa was 350 miles away from Babylon in terms of geography, but we only have to read the first eight verses of the book of Esther to spot that they were one and the same city spiritually. The city of Babylon had fallen but the spirit of Babylon was still very much alive and well in Susa.

We are told in Daniel 6:1 that the Babylonian Empire consisted of 120 provinces, each ruled by a *satrap*. The book of Esther begins by telling us that the Persian Empire consisted of 127 provinces (everything that Nebuchadnezzar ruled, plus some more). Xerxes is as proud a ruler as Nebuchadnezzar ever was. It may only be a Hollywood movie, but we catch a little of his spirit in the film *300*, where he is seated on an enormous throne with twenty steps, all of which is made of ivory and carried onto the battlefield on the shoulders of a hundred slaves. As his herald proudly declares that Xerxes is the god of gods, the king of kings and the ruler of the world, we realize that the spirit of Babylon did not die with the destruction of its city. It merely moved home.[4]

We can spot this in the insatiable ambition of King Xerxes. Instead of being content to rule over the largest empire ever known to man, stretching from India in the east to Ethiopia in the west, the book of Esther begins with an account of the great banquet that he threw at the start of his reign to persuade his

---

[3] Song of Songs can feel equally secular, but at least the Hebrew text of Song of Songs 8:6 refers to *"the flame of the Lord"*.

[4] *300* (Warner Brothers, 2006).

noblemen and generals to help him conquer Greece.[5] For 180 days in 483 BC, he showcased the breathtaking wealth and luxury that had once marked out Babylon and that now marked out Susa as the greatest city in the world. Having secured the support of his noblemen and generals, he then threw another party for a further seven days to secure the support of the common people too.[6] As the wine flows freely in golden goblets and the guests recline on gold and silver couches in his royal gardens, we are meant to be reminded of Belshazzar's feast in Daniel 5 and of the Hanging Gardens of Babylon in Daniel 4. For all the superficial differences in the drama, the stage for the book of Esther looks the same.

Even the absence of any explicit mention of God in the book of Esther doesn't make it quite as different from the book of Daniel as we might at first suppose. The truth is that, for people living in pagan cities such as Babylon or Susa or New York or Paris or London, the Lord can feel absent a lot of the time. It is all too easy for us to mistake the invisibility of God for the non-existence of God. Before we know it, even devout believers begin to think and talk and act like non-believers. We do not know who wrote the book of Esther, but the mention of God is omitted for a reason.[7] By constantly hinting at his activity, while never naming him, the author cleverly undermines a secular view of the world. We are being taught to see the Lord's sovereign activity everywhere.

---

[5] King Darius I had been defeated in his own attempt to conquer Greece at the Battle of Marathon in 490 BC. His son Xerxes was therefore determined from the start of his reign to succeed where his father had failed. The Greek historian Herodotus recounts several days of after-discussions between King Xerxes and his noblemen and generals concerning his plans to invade Greece (*Histories*, 7.8–19).

[6] The word *partam* in 1:3 and 6:9 is a Hebrew transliteration of the Persian name for a specific type of *nobleman*. We also know that "white and bluey-purple", mentioned in 1:6 and 8:15, were the official colours of the Persian royal family. Technical details such as these testify to the historicity of the book of Esther.

[7] Although we do not know the author of the book of Esther, it appears to have been written shortly after the events it describes, since it makes no reference to Ezra and Nehemiah's great achievements after 458 BC.

A drunken married squabble creates a vacancy for a new queen of Persia. Is that a coincidence or is God at work in Susa? We are never told explicitly because that's how life often is. God is constantly at work all around us, but it takes eyes of faith to spot that *it is God who put you here.*[8] A royal beauty contest plucks a young Jewish girl from obscurity into the powerful corridors of the palace. Is that another coincidence or has heaven decreed that she must serve as God's woman in Persia? When her cousin suddenly finds himself in the right place at the right time to overhear two would-be assassins plotting to kill King Xerxes, is that a coincidence too? How about when a sleepless night reminds the king that he has not rewarded her cousin for saving his life, a matter of moments before his arch-enemy arrives at the palace to ask for permission to murder him? When that arch-enemy tries to wipe out the Jewish nation, unaware that the new queen of Persia is a Jew and is perfectly positioned to stop him, it becomes difficult to deny that the invisible God of Israel is at work behind the scenes in Susa.[9]

So as we read the book of Esther together, let's not miss how much God's sovereignty is emblazoned on its every page.[10] Let's not miss how similar its message is to that of the book of Daniel. In chapter after chapter, it reminds us that, just as Daniel was God's man in Babylon, Esther is God's woman in Persia and we are God's people where we are. Esther seeks to encourage us with the same repeated reminder: *It is God who put you here.*

---

[8] The book of Esther therefore expands on the message of Genesis 28:16; Exodus 3:1–5 and Job 33:13–14.

[9] *"The citadel of Susa"* is mentioned ten times in the book of Esther. It refers to the *royal quarter* of the Persian capital, the densely populated inner city which was somewhere between two and four football fields in size.

[10] Even these eight opening verses can be taken as a reminder that the Lord alone is seated on the true royal throne, that he alone truly rules over the nations, and that he alone possesses all true glory and majesty.

The Queen's Gambit (Esther 1:9–22)

"Queen Vashti also gave a banquet for the women in the royal palace of King Xerxes."

(Esther 1:9)

King Xerxes I of Persia was a bit of a ladies' man. It wasn't enough for him that his wife Amestris was world-famous for her beauty. He also tried to seduce his sister-in-law and had an affair with his daughter-in-law.[1] He also kept a well-stocked harem of young women so that he would never feel lonely in his royal bedroom at the palace.

One of these many women was recognised as his official queen. The book of Esther calls her *Vashti,* which appears to be a Hebrew name for Queen Amestris, just as *Ahasuerus* is the Hebrew name it uses throughout for King Xerxes.[2] While her husband was throwing a seven-day party in the palace gardens to persuade the men of Susa to join his invasion army, Vashti was charming their wives at a banquet elsewhere in the royal palace. On the final day of their twin feasts, the drunken King Xerxes ordered the eunuchs who guarded his harem to summon his wife to appear before his party guests in her best royal robes so that he could show off her beauty to them.[3] We are not told

---

[1] Herodotus tells us about Xerxes' marital infidelity in his *Histories* (9.108–109).

[2] Herodotus tells us that Amestris was Xerxes' official queen. She still appears in his *Histories* after 483 BC, but she becomes insecure, jealous and cruel, which may be explained by what happens here. As the mother of the future King Artaxerxes, she remained a powerful force in Persian politics, even after her demotion.

[3] *Eunuchs* guarded the royal harem so that the kings of Persia could be certain that any heirs conceived within the harem were definitely theirs. These castrated soldiers are mentioned nine times in the book of Esther.

what the queen hoped to achieve by refusing to pose as his trophy wife but, whatever she intended, her gambit failed. A king who was trying to convince his subjects that he was strong enough to conquer Greece could not afford to look weak in his own home.

Verses 10 and 14 name the seven eunuchs who guarded the royal harem and the seven noblemen who served as royal advisers. This confirms the historicity of the book of Esther, since the Greek historians Herodotus and Xenophon, as well as Ezra 7:14, corroborate that this was indeed the set-up in the palace of the kings of Persia. The seven royal advisers counsel Xerxes to take a tough stand against the queen.[4] Her refusal to parade her beauty before his partygoers has been witnessed by so many people that the story is bound to spread across the empire. Every man's authority to issue commands to his wife will be undermined unless the king makes an example of his queen. They therefore persuade Xerxes to issue a royal decree demoting her as queen and banishing her from the palace.[5] Since such royal decrees could not be repealed under Persian law (remember how much trouble that caused in Daniel 6?), this would send out a clear message across the Persian Empire: *"Every man should be ruler over his own household."*[6]

We are meant to sympathise with the queen in these verses. In 483 BC, she was either recovering from giving birth to the future King Artaxerxes or she was still pregnant with him. Either way, we can understand why she did not want to be paraded as a beauty queen before her husband's drunken party guests. Harriet Beecher Stowe, who wrote *Uncle Tom's Cabin* to

---

[4] The advisers are described as *"wise men who understood the times"*, which echoes 1 Chronicles 12:32.

[5] We should not take 1:19 to mean that Xerxes divorced her. A king of Persia would never let another man marry his former queen. She was demoted but remained the mother of his heir, the future King Artaxerxes.

[6] The Hebrew text of Esther 1:22 should probably be understood to mean that *"Every man should be ruler over his own household and his own language should be used in the home."* This is yet more detail that proves how well the writer understood the domestic tensions at play across the multicultural Persian Empire.

campaign against slavery, argued that her refusal was the *"first stand for women's rights"*.[7] The nineteenth-century women's rights activist Elizabeth Cady Stanton agreed: *"The disobedience of Vashti was providential." "Vashti added new glory to [her] day and generation . . . by her disobedience; for 'Resistance to tyrants is obedience to God.'"*[8]

The book of Esther doesn't state this quite so clearly. At no point in these verses does the writer mention the name of God. The Lord seems silent and disconnected from the injustice that is taking place in the palace. King Xerxes is an abusive husband, who enshrines domestic abuse in Persian law, and yet God seems to do nothing.[9] If you have ever been the victim of domestic abuse, or if you have ever supported someone who is, then you will know that one of the biggest questions that victims often ask is "Where was God while I was suffering?" That's what the book of Esther answers for us here.

The Lord is not mentioned in these verses because the writer wants us to acknowledge that this is how life often is. God can feel distant in our times of suffering. He can appear to have turned a blind eye to the injustice in the world. But if we read these verses more closely, we see signs of God's active sovereignty everywhere. Haman is not yet listed among the seven royal advisers, but he is already working his way up in the Persian civil service. It is 483 BC, so in nine years' time he will launch his attempt to eradicate the Jewish nation. We are therefore meant to see the Lord's hand at work behind the failed queen's gambit in these verses. He has just removed the queen from the great chessboard of Persia so that a Jewish pawn can be promoted to that position instead.

---

[7] She wrote this in her longer titled and lesser known book *Bible Heroines: Being Narrative Biographies of Prominent Hebrew Women . . .As Revealed in the Light of the Present Day* (1878).

[8] Elizabeth Cady Stanton in *The Woman's Bible* (1895).

[9] Some readers try to use 1:22 as a divine mandate for male domination. But these aren't the words of God. They are the words of an abusive king! Ephesians 5:22–33 teaches us that husbands should lead within their homes as servant-leaders, which is totally different from the repressive rule promoted by King Xerxes.

Furthermore, since it is 483 BC, the events of this chapter take place during a period in which the revival of the Jewish nation has sadly stalled. There is a gap of fifty-eight years between the restoration of the Temple in Jerusalem in Ezra 1–6 (in 516 BC) and the next great leap forward for the returning Jewish exiles in Ezra 7–10 (in 458 BC). The removal of the queen of Persia is therefore far more than a domestic squabble. It paves the way for a Jewish queen to shape the next chapter in the history of the Jewish nation. God may not be named in these verses but, if we look closely, we can see his fingerprints everywhere. He has just paved the way for Esther to become his woman in Persia.

God is equally active in our own world, even when we don't perceive it. He invites us to believe this and to shape world history with him through our prayers. When we think about things that way, then these verses convict us that we often play the part of Queen Vashti ourselves. We can all too often refuse the Lord's invitation to come to him and to enjoy his presence in prayer. Praise God, he never rejects us when we do. He still regards us as the Bride of Christ. He refuses to be done with us and to begin a partnership with someone else. He forgives us and continues to invite us to come into his presence to partner with him in his purposes through our prayers.

This requires us to recognise that God is with us, that God is at work all around us and that God wants us to shape world history with him through our prayers. In a world where God can often appear distant and disconnected from the events taking place around us, these verses call us to believe a simple truth: *It is God who put you here.*

Later (Esther 2:1–11)

"Later when King Xerxes' fury had subsided, he remembered. . ."

(Esther 2:1)

Later is such a little word, yet it can cover up a catalogue of failure.

Later at the start of the second chapter of Esther informs us that four years have passed since King Xerxes threw his lavish party to persuade his subjects to invade Greece with him. It is now 479 BC. Xerxes has led the Persian army into Greece and back again, and the invasion did not go as planned.[1] First, the Persian army took too long to cross the Hellespont into Greece.[2] Next, it was slowed down by King Leonidas and his 300 Spartans, who blocked its way at the Battle of Thermopylae. By the time the Persian army finally entered Athens, the Athenians had withdrawn to safety on a nearby island, forcing Xerxes to fight the naval Battle of Salamis. When the Athenian *triremes* outmanoeuvred and destroyed the Persian fleet, his invasion plans started to unravel fast. Talk of mutiny among his troops, combined with rumours of

---

[1] We are told in 2:16 that Esther met King Xerxes in either December 479 BC or January 478 BC.

[2] Herodotus tells us that its pontoon bridges were destroyed by a storm. It says a lot about King Xerxes that he responded by ordering that the waters of the Hellespont be whipped 300 times! (*Histories*, 7.33–37.)

insurrection back at home, spooked him into rushing back to his palace in Susa.[3]

Later therefore describes what King Xerxes did to salvage his hurt pride after returning home in disgrace from the battlefield. He needed to do something which would win him back the respect of his subjects. Herodotus tells us that he launched a vast construction programme, building many breathtaking palaces and civic buildings. The book of Esther adds that he also launched the first recorded beauty pageant in history. He decided to scour the 127 provinces of his empire to find a new queen who would turn people's heads even faster than Queen Vashti. The winner of this beauty pageant would become consort to the throne of the greatest empire that the world had ever seen. Even the runners-up would be rewarded with a life of luxury within the royal bedrooms.[4]

Later therefore means that the moment in the story has arrived for us to meet God's woman in Persia. Her Hebrew name *Hadassah* means *Myrtle-Tree*, which was a Jewish symbol for fertility and prosperity. It spoke about the life and fruitfulness that the Lord had promised to his people – and yet her early life was marked by death and pain. We are told that her mother and father died while she was young and that she was brought up by a cousin.[5] Mordecai means *Belonging-To-The-Babylonian-God-Marduk*, so he was probably given that name by his Persian

[3] The Battles of Thermopylae and Salamis both took place in 480 BC. Xerxes therefore found himself in the same position as his father, Darius I, who had retreated from Greece after losing the Battle of Marathon in 490 BC. This would be the last Persian attempt to invade Greece. The next great crossing of the Hellespont would be led by Alexander the Great, as the Greeks invaded the Persian Empire instead.

[4] A king of Persia would never allow one of his concubines to sleep with another man. Those who failed to win the beauty pageant would therefore never be permitted to leave the royal harem.

[5] We are told in 2:15 that Esther's father was named Abihail, which is Hebrew for *My-Father-Is-Strength*. This is meant to add to our sense of confusion. Why didn't the Lord prevent Esther's father from dying?

masters.[6] In the same way, they renamed Hadassah after the Babylonian goddess of sexual love.[7] *Ishtar* is written as Esther in English, and it literally means *Star*, but there is very little else about the life of this little Jewish orphan girl to remind us of God's promise in Daniel 12:3 that he will make his people shine like stars in the darkness of their pagan world. Esther's early life was tragic.

These verses make no comment on the rights and wrongs of this royal beauty pageant. We can read them superficially and regard it as nothing more than an ancient version of a reality TV show. After all, who wouldn't want a chance to be catapulted from obscurity into the palace of the most powerful man in the world? Alternatively, we can read a bit more slowly and recoil with horror at the casual cruelty of the Persian Empire. The beautiful virgins who are brought to the king's palace are not given any choice in the matter. This beauty pageant is rape on royal scale. King Xerxes is a serial sexual predator and there is no *#metoo* movement to advocate for Esther. As we read these verses, we ought to weep over Xerxes' sordid abuse of his royal power.

Once again, these verses make no mention of God. He appears to be horribly distant and disconnected from Esther's pain. She is forced to hide her Jewishness from everybody in the palace, because her cousin rightly warns her that there is too much anti-Semitism at the royal court for her to come clean that she is God's woman in Persia. We can only guess at how devalued and used this must have made Esther feel, but we are given a couple of insights into how much it tortured her cousin. First, the Hebrew word *'ōmēn* in verse 7 describes

---

[6] The exile of the Jews under King Jehoiachin took place in 597 BC (2 Kings 24:10–17). Since it is now 479 BC, we should understand 2:5–6 to mean that *Kish* was part of that exile, not Mordecai.

[7] *Ishtar* corresponds to Aphrodite and Venus in the Greek and Roman pantheons. God's man in Babylon and God's woman in Persia were therefore both renamed after pagan deities by their foreign masters (Daniel 1:7).

him as more than just her *foster-father*.[8] It tells us literally that he was her *pillar* or her *supporter*. Mordecai had spent much of his life raising his beautiful cousin to become the bride of a good Jewish boy, not to become a sex slave in the Persian harem. Second, we are told in verse 11 that Mordecai paced the street outside the courtyard of the harem every day. He knew it would be fatal to them both to resist King Xerxes in this matter, but he surely asked himself the same questions that we would ask: *"What do you think you're doing, God? Does this vile injustice mean nothing to you?"*

The writer's omission to mention the name of God is meant to speak into the darkest moments of our own lives as God's people in the world. The truth is that we can all feel bamboozled and abandoned by the Lord. We can all feel as though events have turned against us. We can all feel as though our plans are in tatters. That's why we need these verses to inform us that the hand of God is always busy at work in our lives, even when we don't perceive it. However dire our own circumstances may be, they are rarely worse than those of Esther when she was imprisoned in the palace of a sexual predator.

God is invisible, but these verses assure us that this does not mean he is inactive. There is no mention of the Lord by name. There is no angelic visitation. There are no bright lights in the sky. There isn't even a paltry word of encouragement from a prophet among the Jewish exiles. And yet Esther's anguished cries within the palace are definitely heard by God. Mordecai's prayers as he paces about on the street outside are definitely answered too. It may appear to them both that their lives are unravelling, but these verses assure us that the invisible God always knows precisely what he is doing.

[8] The Bible consistently takes a very positive view of fostering and adoption. It isn't second best, but a beautiful Gospel picture of how God himself adopts the lost and lonely as his children. See Ephesians 1:5.

Perhaps that's another reason why this chapter starts with the word *later*. We can rarely tell what God is doing at the time, but *later* we discover that he knows what he is doing, even in our darkest hours. As we follow Esther into the claustrophobic corridors of the Persian palace, these verses continue to encourage us: *It is God who put you here.*

Beauty Queen (Esther 2:12–18)

"The king was attracted to Esther more than to any of the other women . . . So he set a royal crown on her head and made her queen. . ."

(Esther 2:17)

The Devil has never created anything. He is a mere creature, who only possesses power to deface the beautiful creation of God. For that reason, when we read about King Xerxes, we are meant to do more than just recoil in horror at his abuses. We can also look beyond them to catch a glimpse of the defaced beauty of the true King of kings.

When we meet Xerxes sitting on his royal throne and ruling over the world, we can catch a glimpse of the Lord sitting on the throne of heaven and ruling over every tribe and nation. When Xerxes summons his wife to be with him and she refuses, we can catch a glimpse of God inviting us into his throne room to shape world history with him through our prayers. When Xerxes loses his temper, rejects his wife and begins searching for another, we are meant to praise God for his grace towards us, for he never rejects us as his Bride when we fail to obey him. Each of the successes and the shortcomings of Xerxes in the book of Esther can serve as fuel for our worship of God.

For that reason, we mustn't rush over the account of Esther's preparations for her first night with the king. There is much that is sordid here. The Devil has defaced the image of God so thoroughly in Xerxes that many readers find these verses distasteful. But if we are willing to dig a little, then we will find great treasure here. These verses can inspire us to embrace God's sanctifying work in our lives.

Justification describes God counting us righteous by *imputing* the righteousness of Jesus onto us. *Sanctification* describes God making us righteous by *imparting* the righteousness of Jesus into us. Modern Christianity majors on justification. It offers people forgiveness and encourages them to keep on coming back to God for more. Biblical Christianity majors equally on sanctification. It informs us that the purpose of forgiveness is to bring us into a relationship with the Lord which results in ever-increasing holiness.[1] In other words, justification is only half of the Christian Gospel. The other half is sanctification. Forgiveness *for* our sin is always meant to lead on to a life of freedom *from* our sin.

The second chapter of the book of Esther hints at her own need of sanctification. Verse 5 says that she belonged to the tribe of Benjamin, a tribe so wicked that the Lord almost allowed it to be wiped out altogether in Judges 19–21. It also says that two of Esther's immediate ancestors were named *Shimei* and *Kish*, which reminds us of two of the greatest rogues in the terrible history of the tribe of Benjamin.[2] We can only be justified if we confess our need of forgiveness for sin, and we can only be sanctified if we recognize our need of freedom from sin. It is helpful that the writer confesses a few of Esther's shortcomings because the preparation of the Bride of Christ always begins there.

Verse 7 informs us that Esther *"had a lovely figure and was beautiful"*. Nevertheless, verse 9 insists that she still needed to be given *"beauty treatments and special food"* to make her ready for her first night with the king. Verse 12 explains that this involved six months of having her skin anointed with oil and subjected to careful scraping. It then required six further

---

[1] 2 Corinthians 3:17–18 and 2 Peter 1:5–9.

[2] *Kish* was the father of the sinful King Saul (1 Samuel 10:21). *Shimei* was the man who cursed King David (2 Samuel 16:5–13). Two of Esther's recent ancestors in exile bore the same names.

months of having her skin anointed with perfume and scraped carefully some more.[3] If all of this sounds a bit elaborate and painful, then that's because God's sanctifying work very often is. He doesn't just *declare* us to be righteous by the blood of his Son. He also does what it takes to *make* us righteous by the exacting oil of his Spirit.

Very often that hurts. The English hymnwriter John Newton reflected on his own experience of being sanctified by God when he penned one of his most famous hymns.

I asked the Lord that I might grow in faith and love and every grace;
Might more of His salvation know and seek more earnestly His face.
I hoped that in some favoured hour at once He'd answer my request,
And by His love's constraining power subdue my sins and give me rest.
Instead of this, He made me feel the hidden evils of my heart;
And let the angry powers of Hell assault my soul in every part.
Yea more, with His own hand He seemed intent to aggravate my woe;
Crossed all the fair designs I schemed, blasted my gourds, and laid me low.
"Lord, why is this?" I trembling cried, "Wilt Thou pursue Thy worm to death?"
"'Tis in this way," the Lord replied, "I answer prayer for grace and faith.
These inward trials I employ from self and pride to set thee free;

[3] The Hebrew words *mārūq* and *tamrūq* are used four times in 2:3, 2:9 and 2:12. Both words mean *scraping* or *rubbing*, which appears to describe the ancient practice of cleansing the skin using oil and a strigil.

And break thy schemes of earthly joy, that thou may'st seek thy all in Me."[4]

Esther is assisted in this painful purifying process by a guard named Hegai, who grants her seven maidservants to help her. Can we see in this a picture of the Holy Spirit, who is described in the book of Revelation as *"the sevenfold Spirit of God"*?[5] The book of Esther leaves us guessing. It merely tells us that she trusted him implicitly to lead her. Although she was permitted to choose her own clothes for her first night with the king, she wore only what Hegai instructed her to wear. As a result, we are told that she inspired *"deep love"* and *"grace"* in all who witnessed the radiance of her pure beauty.[6]

Finally the moment arrives for Esther's first night with the king. It is such a crucial moment in the story that verse 16 dates it for us to late December 479 BC or early January 478 BC. Arduous though her preparations were, she now discovers it was worth it. King Xerxes marvels at her pure beauty and announces that he has found his new queen. He places a royal crown on her head and throws a great wedding banquet for her. He commands the world to take a holiday and to celebrate with him that a bride has finally been made ready to share the royal throne with the king.

John Newton is right. The process of sanctification (of being *made* righteous by the Holy Spirit's work within us, rather than simply *declared* righteous by Christ's blood shed for us) can be painful. But as we read these verses, we have to conclude that it is worth it.

The book of Revelation prophesies that a greater wedding feast is coming for the true King of kings. It tells us that we are

---

[4] John Newton published the hymn *I Asked the Lord That I Might Grow* in 1779.

[5] Revelation 1:4, 3:1, 4:5 and 5:6.

[6] *Hēsēd* in 2:9 and 17 is the normal Hebrew word used to describe God's *covenant love* towards his people. *Hēn* in 2:15 and 17 is the normal Hebrew word used to describe God's *grace* towards his people.

the Bride of Christ and that God's Spirit is at work within us to prepare us for the day when heaven will sing: *"Let us rejoice and be glad and give him glory! For the wedding of the Lamb has come, and his bride has made herself ready."*[7]

[7] Revelation 19:7. See also Revelation 19:8–9, 21:2, 21:9–11 and 22:17.

Providence (Esther 2:19–23)

"During the time Mordecai was sitting at the king's gate, Bigthana and Teresh, two of the king's officers who guarded the doorway, became angry and conspired to assassinate King Xerxes."

(Esther 2:21)

The book of Esther has been described as *"the romance of Providence"*. We have already witnessed together how much this is true. Although it never mentions God explicitly, every page of the book of Esther trumpets his providential intervention in the lives of men and women. It warns us never to mistake God's invisibility for his inactivity.

Mordecai is struggling to believe it. Although his cousin has become queen of the Persian Empire, his heart is clearly still troubled. He remains on the street outside the royal palace.[1] Xerxes may have proclaimed his love for Esther and he may have toasted her as his new queen, but verse 19 tells us that he still proceeded to summon the virgins a second time to swell the numbers of his harem. Verse 20 also reveals that Esther cannot truly be herself with her new husband. She dares not reveal her Jewishness to him because she suspects that his anti-Semitism will dilute his affection towards her. Esther is living in the greatest palace in the greatest city of the greatest empire that the world has ever seen, but her life is full of heartache. She is married to a husband who is so self-absorbed and sinful that

---

[1] It is possible that the reference to Mordecai *"sitting at the king's gate"* in 2:21 means that Esther secured him a position as a junior royal official. This certainly seems to have been the case four years later, in 3:2.

it probably never even crosses his mind that she might regard increasing the size of his harem as an act of unfaithfulness towards her.

In the novel *Captain Corelli's Mandolin*, the heroine's father reflects on what he perceives to be God's failure to intervene against the injustice of their lives. He prays angrily, *"Is it any wonder that I lost my faith? What are you doing up there, you idle God? Do you think I am so easily fobbed off? . . . Do you think I'm stupid? Do you think I have no eyes?"*[2] That's how Mordecai must be feeling as he looks up at the palace windows from the street below.

The writer does not confirm or deny what Mordecai is feeling. He shifts the spotlight, instead, onto God's woman in Persia. This is her equivalent of the moment when Daniel resolves in his heart not to defile himself with meat and wine that have been sacrificed to pagan idols. She finds herself at a crossroads moment that will determine what happens in the rest of the story. Will she grow bitter towards God for abandoning her into the clutches of King Xerxes? Will she grow disobedient towards Mordecai, now that she is a queen and he remains a commoner outside the palace walls? Since she can no longer live openly as a Jew, will she inwardly abandon the faith of the Jewish nation too?

Esther resolves in her heart to be God's woman in Persia. She decides to match her unrivalled physical beauty with unrivalled inner beauty too. We were told in verse 10 that she honoured the instructions of Mordecai as her adoptive father. We were told in verse 15 that she honoured the instructions of the eunuch Hegai as her new guardian in the palace too. Now we are told for a third time in verse 20 that she continued to follow Mordecai's instructions even after she became queen. In the absence of any explicit mention of God, these three verses are meant to convey to us that Esther remained submissive to the Lord. Instead of raging about her misfortunes and rebelling

---

[2] Louis de Bernières in *Captain Corelli's Mandolin* (1994).

against the God of Israel, she trusted in his Providence. The Lord must know what he is doing.[3]

No amount of human planning could have engineered what happened next. Only divine Providence could arrange events so perfectly. Mordecai's constant presence at the palace gate has turned him into part of the furniture for the eunuchs who guard the royal harem.[4] Two of them, named Bigthana and Teresh, barely notice him as they vent their anger to one another against the king. He can hardly believe his ears when he overhears them plotting to assassinate King Xerxes. He scuttles away to send a warning to Queen Esther, who in turn sends a message to her husband, naming Mordecai as the source of this life-saving information.[5] If an angry conversation between two eunuchs in the palace gateway in 478 BC feels like a bit of a storm in a teacup to you, then you may not be aware: Xerxes was murdered later by another eunuch, named Aspamitres, in 465 BC.

There is no immediate clue for either Esther or Mordecai that the hand of divine Providence has just set the scene for another great revival for the Jewish nation. A scribe records what has happened in the royal annals, but Mordecai receives no immediate reward for having been in the right place at the right time with the right attitude towards God. The two eunuchs are either *"impaled on poles"* or *"hanged on gallows"* (the Hebrew phrase in verse 23 can mean either), but there is no hint that what has just happened will deliver Mordecai from suffering a similar fate himself in chapter 6.[6]

---

[3] See Exodus 20:12. Because Esther submitted to God's instructions when they came to her through others, the Lord was able to trust her to pass on his instructions to other people later too (4:17).

[4] The Hebrew word *sārîs* means more than simply *officer*. It refers specifically to the *eunuchs* who were in charge of the royal harem (1:10).

[5] The Hebrew text of 2:22 tells us literally that Esther sent this news to the king *"in the name of Mordecai"*. Her refusal to steal any of the credit that belonged to her cousin would prove vital later on in chapter 6.

[6] The phrase simply means *to suspend from a piece of wood*. The Persians impaled corpses on poles in order to shame the dead, which is why 9:14 recounts that Xerxes did this to people who had been killed 9:7–10.

For now at least, the writer of the book of Esther says nothing, because that's how life is. We rarely grasp at the time how significant many of the details of our lives will eventually prove to be. We rarely spot the ways in which the hand of divine Providence uses what we dismiss as coincidences to work out our destiny before our very eyes.

So, with that in mind, put down this book and take a moment to tell the Lord that you trust his wisdom in every aspect of your life right now – the bits where you can see his hand at work quite easily, and the bits where he does not seem to be at work at all.

Tell him that you believe that his hand of Providence has placed you in the right place at the right time for the right reason right now.[7] Tell him that you believe the message of the book of Esther. Tell him that, in everything, you trust that *it is God who put you here.*

---

[7] Acts 17:26–27 can be translated as *"God ordained the exact times and places where each person should live. He did this so that they might look for him and perhaps feel after him and find him – though he isn't far from any one of us."*

Assassin's Creed (Esther 3:1–15)

"Haman looked for a way to destroy all Mordecai's people, the Jews, throughout the whole kingdom of Xerxes."

(Esther 3:6)

One of the greatest proofs that the Bible is true is the way that people throughout history have consistently tried to kill the Jews. Did you ever hear about a pogrom against the Belgian community in a city? Did you ever hear about a Final Solution to eliminate the Portuguese? And yet, from Pharaoh down to Antiochus IV, and from the Crusaders down to Adolf Hitler, people have consistently attempted to wipe out the Jewish nation.

One of the earliest attempts to do this takes place in the book of Esther. We should read this chapter through the lens that Daniel gave us. The same evil spirit that was at work in Babylon now seethes with hatred towards God's people in Susa. Jesus explains in John 8:44 that *"the devil . . . was a murderer from the beginning"*. Since Satan cannot touch the Lord, he seeks to slaughter anyone who worships him. During BC history, the Devil hoped that by destroying God's people he might prevent the coming of God's Messiah. During AD history, the Devil now hopes that by destroying God's people he might extend the time allotted to him before Jesus returns from heaven and he is destroyed.[1] So don't miss the spirit at work

---

[1] Matthew 8:29 and Revelation 12:12. The same evil spirit appears to have prompted Herod to kill the baby boys of Bethlehem in Matthew 2:16.

behind Haman's attempt to wipe out the Jewish nation. We are meant to grasp that he is dancing to the tune of a far greater Assassin's creed.

The words *"after these events"* at the start of chapter 3 signify that the action has fast-forwarded four years, from 478 BC to 474 BC.[2] King Xerxes has appointed a new chief minister, whose authority trumps even that of his seven royal advisers who were named in 1:13–14. Xerxes even seats Haman upon a throne and commands his other courtiers to bow down and worship him together. Haman is evidently more than just chief minister. These actions communicate that Xerxes has granted him a share in his honour as king.

Just as the Holy Spirit grants peace and contentment to everyone who partners with him, evil spirits tend to make their victims perpetually dissatisfied.[3] It didn't matter that King Xerxes ruled over 127 provinces in 1:1. He still felt that he could never be happy unless he added Greece to the pile. Nor does it matter to Haman here that he is worshipped throughout the empire. It only takes one stubborn Jew to send him off into a violent rage. Rather than simply murder Mordecai, he resolves to wreak his vengeance on the entire Jewish nation. First, he consults the gods of Persia by casting lots to determine the perfect date to commit this genocide.[4] Then, having set the date as 7 March 473 BC, he quickly hurries to the palace to enlist King Xerxes in his evil master plan.[5]

---

[2] *The first month of the twelfth year of King Xerxes* in 3:7 dates this chapter to late April or early May 474 BC.

[3] Proverbs 27:20; Habakkuk 2:5 and 3:17–18; Philippians 4:11–12; 1 Timothy 6:6–17 and James 3:14–18.

[4] The Hebrew word *pūr*, which means *lot*, in 3:7 gives us our first clue that the book of Esther will explain the origins of the Jewish festival of Purim. This festival still takes place today on either 14th or 15th Adar (that is, in late February or early March) among Jewish communities all around the world.

[5] The month and year are given in 3:7. The day is added in 3:13. Proverbs 16:33 tells us that the Lord is sovereign over every single dice roll, and we can see that very clearly here. It is only because the lot falls on a date almost a year away that Esther is given enough time to scupper Haman's plans.

The writer of the book of Esther is no more likely to name the Devil than he is God, but he gives us plenty of clues here that Haman is inspired by a demonic agenda. What else could make such madness fall upon him that he plots a global massacre in order to deal with one solitary Jew under his nose in the citadel of Susa? What else could convince him to offer the king 340 tons of silver in order to cover the costs of such a genocide? Herodotus informs us that this was equal to two thirds of the annual revenue of the entire Persian Empire – a vast fortune![6] Such madness cannot be merely human. There is a spiritual force at work here. Haman is motivated by a far greater Assassin's creed.

We are also meant to spot an evil spirit at work in the heart of King Xerxes. Why else would a ruler acquiesce so easily to the massacre of tens of thousands of his subjects? Why else would he turn down Haman's offer to pay for it and, instead, reallocate two thirds of his annual imperial budget towards a needless campaign of murder?[7] There can be no other explanation for the ease with which Xerxes slips his signet ring off his finger and grants carte blanche to his chief minister to make a bloodbath of his empire.[8] Verse 15 tells us that while Xerxes and Haman sat down to drink wine together to celebrate their plans for slaughter, the citizens of Susa were *bewildered* or *perplexed* or *confused*. They simply could not understand the madness that had gripped their rulers. It made no earthly sense to them because it was inspired by hell.

The writer gives us several further clues that Haman and Xerxes are dancing to the tune of a greater Assassin. First, the Hebrew word *tsārar* in verse 10, which describes Haman as the *enemy* of the Jews, is used elsewhere in the Old Testament

[6] *Histories* (3.95). Such a sum would bankrupt Haman, but he planned to recoup it by plundering the Jews.

[7] Xerxes says literally to Haman in 3:11, *"The money is given to you"*. This could potentially mean "It's your money so do what you want with it", but a more natural way of reading it is Xerxes offering to pay instead.

[8] The two dates given in 3:12–13 are 17 April 474 BC and 7 March 473 BC.

to describe Satan.[9] Second, the decree is sent out *"in the name of King Xerxes"* using his signet ring, which is quite clearly a demonic parody of the Lord's invitation for his people to pray big prayers and to issue bold commands in his name.[10] Third, the royal decree goes out through runners who proclaim it in every language of the empire, which appears to be a demonic parody of the Great Commission.[11] Fourth, the triple command in verse 13 that the Persians must *"destroy, kill and annihilate all the Jews"* feels like an Old Testament precursor to Jesus' triple warning in John 10:10 that the Devil *"comes only to steal and kill and destroy"*. Haman and Xerxes are merely earthly believers in a hellish Assassin's creed.

The Devil is still real. We may not think about him very often. He prefers to remain invisible, not just in the book of Esther, but in our own lives too. These verses wake us up to what is happening in the world, whenever God's people are hated and persecuted. God's Word has not altered, and nor has the Assassin's creed.

[9] For example, in Psalm 8:2. This Hebrew word is again used to describe Haman in 8:1, 9:10 and 9:24.

[10] Haggai 2:23; Mark 16:17; John 16:23–26; and Acts 3:6 and 16:18.

[11] In 3:13 and 13:15, the decree goes out via *runners* to the *satrap* who rules over each of the 127 provinces of the Persian Empire and to the team of *governors* that assist him. See 8:10 and 8:14; Psalm 68:11 and Luke 24:47.

The Answer is "No" (Esther 3:2–6)

"But Mordecai would not kneel down or pay him honour. . . Day after day they spoke to him but he refused to comply."

(Esther 3:2, 4)

When did you last say "no" to something because you love the Lord more than you love the world? I remember incurring the wrath of a Buddhist monk while sightseeing in China, for refusing to kneel before one of the idols in his temple. I remember telling my boss, while working in business, that he had better fire me if he expected me to skip church to come into the office on a Sunday. But honestly, moments like that are pretty few and far between. I don't often have to tell people that, because I am a Christian, the answer is "no".

That concerns me, because it was clearly quite different for Daniel and his friends in Babylon. They said "no" to eating meat that had been sacrificed to pagan deities. They said "no" to bowing down before a golden statue, even if it meant being thrown into a blazing furnace. When the king forbade Daniel from praying to the God of Israel for thirty days, he opened up his windows with the result that everyone could see him saying "no" to the king three times a day. Saying "no" was part and parcel of living in Babylon.

Mordecai demonstrates here that this was also the case for those who lived in Susa. We are not told why he refused to bow down before Haman, since this was a pretty standard mark of respect in the ancient world from a subject towards a ruler. Was it because Haman was descended from Agag, the defeated

Amalekite ruler whose life King Saul had spared, against the orders of the Lord, and as a result had forfeited his own crown?[1] Was it because Haman was an Amalekite, one of the last remaining survivors of a people group that had persistently attempted to annihilate the Jewish nation?[2] Did Mordecai say "no" to bowing down before Haman because he personified Israel's ancient enemies?

Perhaps Mordecai sensed that Haman wanted more than just the deference of a subject towards his ruler? The Hebrew word *shāhāh*, which is used three times in verses 2 and 5, means more than merely *paying honour*. The Lord uses it in Exodus 34:14 to forbid the Israelites from *worshipping* any god other than him. The book of Psalms uses it over a dozen times to stir the Jewish nation into *worshipping* the Lord. Since the name Haman means *Magnificent*, and he clearly didn't lack self-confidence, Mordecai may have refused to bow down before him because he suspected that the new chief minister of Persia regarded himself to be some form of incarnate deity.

Whatever his precise reasons, Mordecai resolves in his heart that the answer is "no". He refuses to obey the king's command to grovel at the feet of his new chief minister. He keeps on saying "no", even when his civil service colleagues advise him that a little compromise is needed for a man to get along in Susa.[3] That's why I feel a bit uneasy about how infrequently my Christian friends and I find ourselves needing to say "no" to people in order to serve the Lord today. If saying "no" was part and parcel of serving God in Babylon and Susa, but it isn't for us today, then have we lost sight of what it means for us to live in a manner that glorifies the God of heaven in a non-believing world?

---

[1] 1 Samuel 15:7–35. Mordecai came from the tribe of Benjamin, just like King Saul (2:5).

[2] Exodus 17:8–16; Deuteronomy 25:17–19; Judges 6:3; and 1 Samuel 14:48 and 30:1–4.

[3] It wasn't clear in 2:19–23 whether Mordecai was merely loitering by the gateway. It becomes clearer in 3:2 that, by 474 BC at least, he had secured a minor position within the Persian civil service.

Verse 8 seeks to answer that question for us by explaining why the Persians were so fiercely hostile towards the Jews.[4] It explains that the Jews were *dispersed* yet *separate*. In other words, although they were scattered throughout the 127 provinces of the Persian Empire, they still remembered that, first and foremost, they were citizens of heaven. They followed *different customs* from the people around them. They rested on the Sabbath. They circumcised their sons. They avoided pagan foods. They *refused to obey the king's laws* whenever they contradicted the Law that God had given to their nation at Mount Sinai. The Persians hated the Jews because they were evidently living for a very different Master from the people of the pagan world.[5]

Does this explain why my Christian friends and I find ourselves more easily tolerated than the Jews in the Persian Empire? We are *dispersed*, but are we *separate*? Do we truly emerge from our Bible studies firmly resolved that we will follow *different customs* to the people around us? When Scripture clashes with our culture, are we quick to play down any differences, or are we happy to *refuse to obey the king's laws*?

Our willingness to say "no" to the world really matters to God. It is only when Scripture clashes with our culture that we truly discover whether we are living for God against the world, or merely using him to help us get along in the world.[6] That's why Jesus warned his followers: *"The Son of Man must suffer many things and be rejected. . . and. . . whoever wants to be my disciple must deny themselves and take up their cross daily and*

---

[4] They were so hostile towards the Jews that Mordecai told Esther to hide her Jewishness (2:10 and 20) and that Haman found it easy to gain Xerxes' consent for their mass genocide (3:8–11).

[5] Ezra 7–10 reveals that the Jewish community had compromised its holiness by 474 BC. Even so, the Jews sound more courageously different from their neighbours in 3:8 than many Christians are today.

[6] Of course, Christians are *for* the world (John 3:16). But there also comes a time when it is right for us to say with the great Church father, *"Athanasius contra mundum"* – that is, *"Athanasius against the world!"*

follow me... Whoever is ashamed of me and my words, the Son of Man will be ashamed of them when he comes in his glory and in the glory of the Father and of the holy angels."[7]

This is one of the greatest secrets of the book of Daniel and the book of Esther. We will never see revival in the Church if we attempt to blend in with the world. If we are just the same as them, then why would they convert to Christ at all? We need to take it seriously when Martyn Lloyd-Jones observes:

> *The glory of the gospel is that when the Church is absolutely different from the world, she invariably attracts it. It is then that the world is made to listen to her message, though it may hate it at first. That is how revival comes. That must also be true of us as individuals. It should not be our ambition to be as much like everybody else as we can, though we happen to be Christian, but rather to be as different from everybody who is not a Christian as we can possibly be.*[8]

Let's accept up front, therefore, that saying "yes" to God will sometimes require us to say a firm "no" to the world. Let's recognise how strange it is that many Christians live just like their non-believing neighbours, and then wonder why those neighbours have no interest in the Christian Gospel. Let's stand shoulder to shoulder with Mordecai and with Daniel and with Shadrach, Meshach and Abednego and resolve in our hearts that we will say: I have answered "yes" to serving God in a world that rejects him. I understand that saying "yes" to God means saying "no" to whatever isn't God. I have resolved ahead of time that, no matter how much it may cost me, when the world asks me to bow down and worship, the answer is "no".

---

[7] Luke 9:22–26. Note that Jesus says *whoever*. Cross-bearing isn't radical Christianity. It is simply Christianity.

[8] Martyn Lloyd-Jones in his *Studies in the Sermon on the Mount* (1959).

Weapons of Persia (Esther 4:1–17)

"Go, gather together all the Jews who are in Susa, and fast for me. Do not eat or drink for three days, night or day. I and my attendants will fast as you do."

(Esther 4:16)

In the book of Daniel, we were taught to wield six deadly weapons in our spiritual warfare. In the fourth chapter of the book of Esther, we discover that the same six weapons that breached the walls of Babylon were equally effective in Persia too.

Daniel's first weapon was *keeping the main the main thing*. Instead of focusing our attention on the Devil, we remind ourselves that binding and loosing spiritual forces in prayer is no substitute for practical obedience on the ground. In Daniel 8:27, the prophet tells us that he got up from his prayers and went about the king's business. Similarly, we are told here in verse 17 that *"Mordecai went away and carried out all of Esther's instructions."*[1] He also sent Esther away with some practical instructions of his own.

Daniel's second weapon was *Scripture*. He believed the promises that he found in the Old Testament and he allowed them to engender a steely determination within him. Instead of treating divine prophecy as an excuse for human passivity, he resolved that he would either have what Scripture promised him or die trying. Given how determined the book of Esther is to

---

[1] The fact that Esther had learned to submit to authority in 2:10, 2:15 and 2:20 enabled the Lord to entrust her with authority in 4:17.

avoid mentioning the name of God, it shouldn't surprise us that these verses reference God's Word rather obliquely. Mordecai recounts the words of chapter 3 to Esther and then summarises the Bible's teaching about God's sovereignty: *"Who knows but that you have come to your royal position for such a time as this?"* Esther responds to this summary of the Jewish Scriptures by declaring with the same courage as Daniel: *"I will go to the king . . . and if I perish, I perish."*[2]

Daniel's third weapon was *fasting*. On this point too, God's woman in Persia imitates God's man in Babylon. She hears that Mordecai's reaction to the news that Haman and Xerxes are plotting genocide was to tear his clothes, to put on sackcloth and ashes, and to fast from food.[3] She hears that many other Jews across the empire are also joining him in *"fasting, weeping and wailing . . . in sackcloth and ashes"*. She therefore decides that she too will reject the luxuries of the palace for a season in order to express her grief to God. She sends word to Mordecai: *"Go, gather together all the Jews who are in Susa, and fast for me. Do not eat or drink for three days, night or day. I and my attendants will fast as you do."*[4]

Daniel's fourth weapon was *prayer*. We know enough by now about the book of Esther to predict that the writer will not refer to prayer by name but will reference it obliquely several times. Since prayer and fasting go together throughout the Bible, we are meant to view the bitter wailing of Mordecai and his fellow Jews as a description of their fervent prayers to God. We might even take the fact that Mordecai chooses to conduct his fasting in the streets of the city, instead of fasting privately at

---

[2] 4:14, 16.

[3] Fasting, tearing clothes, wearing sackcloth and putting ashes on one's head were all ways in which the ancient Israelites mourned for their dead. Mordecai and the other Jews were therefore expressing their intense grief to God at this news. Jesus treats *"fasting"* and *"mourning"* as equivalent terms in Matthew 9:15.

[4] Note the inference here that Esther shared something of the Gospel with her pagan servant girls.

home, as a nod to corporate prayer.[5] Certainly, Esther tells him to *"gather together all the Jews who are in Susa."* The Jews are on the brink of extinction, so Esther rallies them to fight back by wielding the weapon of prayer together as a team.

Daniel's fifth weapon was *authority*, a concept that the wife of King Xerxes would understand all too well. Esther tells Mordecai that her husband possesses all authority. Even his queen would be courting death if she dared to enter his throne room uninvited, and his harem is so large that a whole month has passed since he last invited Esther. If she decides to take matters into her own hands, then her only hope of survival will be if he extends his golden sceptre towards her, as a symbol of his royal authority.[6]

But Esther has been brought up to believe that God's heavenly authority trumps the earthly authority of any man, even that of her husband. She believes Psalm 24:1 when it tells her that *"The earth is the Lord's, and everything in it"*. She believes Proverbs 21:1 when it promises her that *"In the Lord's hand the king's heart is a stream of water that he channels towards all who please him."* She therefore resolves to assert her heavenly authority by daring to enter uninvited the throne room from which King Xerxes believes he has unlimited authority to rule over the world.

Daniel's sixth weapon was *knowing God*. Again, we know better than to expect the book of Esther to name him, but knowing God is clearly the decisive factor in this chapter. Verse 14 is probably the most famous verse in the book of Esther. It is often quoted as if it speaks primarily about our destiny, but read it carefully. Mordecai isn't saying that a go-getter like Esther can change history. He is saying that, even if Esther does nothing,

---

[5] Nobody was allowed into the presence of the kings of Persia unless they were upbeat and smiling (Nehemiah 1:4 and 2:1–2). Mordecai's fasting therefore prevents him from entering the palace in 4:2.

[6] Herodotus confirms how fiercely access was guarded to the Persian kings (*Histories*, 3.118 and 3.140). Even Haman had to wait outside until invited in (6:4–5). Esther remembered what had happened to Queen Vashti.

the future is secure because of the providential sovereignty of God. *"If you remain silent at this time,* ***relief and deliverance for the Jews will arise from another place****, but. . . who knows but that you have come to your royal position for such a time as this?"* Mordecai's certainty and Esther's courage are the double edges of a single weapon. They both know the Lord.

Wielding these six weapons delivered victory for Daniel in Babylon. It delivered victory for Esther in Susa too. It will also deliver victory for us as we lay hold of these six weapons to fight the battles of today in our own spiritual Babylon and Susa.

So let's rise up with Esther's courage. Let's dare to enter the throne room of heaven right now and to make bold requests of God that are worthy of such a mighty King. Let's trust that, through the blood of Jesus, God has permanently extended his golden sceptre towards us. If it helps, let's sing the words of the old Charles Wesley hymn as we go.

No condemnation now I dread;
Jesus, and all in Him, is mine;
Alive in Him, my living Head,
And clothed in righteousness divine,
Bold I approach the eternal throne,
And claim the crown, through Christ my own.[7]

[7] This is the final verse of Charles Wesley's famous hymn *And Can It Be?* He wrote the hymn in 1738 as a celebration of his conversion to Christ on 21 May of that year.

Destiny (Esther 4:12–16)

"If you remain silent at this time, relief and deliverance for the Jews will arise from another place, but. . . who knows but that you have come to your royal position for such a time as this?"

(Esther 4:14)

There is a lot of talk in Christian circles about *destiny*. Some of it is thoroughly biblical. A lot of it is utter bunkum. The book of Esther can help us to discern between the two.

Mordecai's words to Esther teach us that *destiny is real*. God has a perfect plan for each of our lives, and a large part of our life's purpose is to discover what that plan is. Esther's life is very lonely. She is the queen of Persia, yet she has been relegated to her own rooms in the palace. A month or more can pass between each invitation to spend time with the king. When she isn't wondering which of the women in the harem are currently keeping her husband's bed warm, she battles disappointment with where her life's path has led her. Whatever happened to the little Jewish girl who once dreamed of playing her part within the Jewish community of Susa?[1]

Mordecai reminds Esther that she is doing that very thing in the palace. *"Who knows but that you have come to your royal position for such a time as this?"* By deliberately omitting to mention God here, the writer emphasizes that, even when

---

[1] The Hebrew word *hūl* in 4:4 tells us literally that Esther *"writhed in pain"* over her husband's actions.

the Lord is invisible, he is never inactive. Even now, he is still working out his destiny for the Jewish nation.

Mordecai also teaches us that *destiny isn't something that we have to find for ourselves.* Too many Christian sermons produce in us an ungodly intensity, which looks like faith but which is actually the opposite. When a sense of destiny turns inwards to become something that we can either find or lose through our own actions, then we lose sight of our Saviour and start worshipping Destiny as a goddess instead. Mordecai points out to Esther that she never made plans to become the queen of Persia. Her path into the palace was paved with domestic abuse and divorce and rape on a royal scale. The stepping stones that have brought her to this moment were not chosen carefully by her. They may not even have been the Lord's best plan for her. But they have all been transformed by his providential hand into a mighty moment of destiny for the Jews.

Just before Derek Prince died, the great Bible teacher was interviewed about what he had learned over the years about Christian teaching on destiny.

Derek Prince: *I think that word is often used today as a substitute for kingdom building or the drive for power.*

Interviewer: *But don't you believe that men are made for a purpose?*

Derek Prince: *Yes, but that purpose is to know the Lord. The meaning of life is a relationship. The future comes from pursuing Him, not pursuing the future.*

Interviewer: *You realise, don't you, that the idea of destiny and of a promised future is very much the rage in Christian circles today?*

Derek Prince: *I do. I remember reading a major Christian magazine and seeing advertisements about dynamic men and prophetic conferences and seminars to*

	know your destiny. It felt like prostitution to me. I felt as though I needed a shower when I was finished.
Interviewer:	*So it was different in your day?*
Derek Prince:	*The hope of my heart was to know the Lord and to do His will. The future, I believed, was His to fashion through my obedience.*[2]

Mordecai teaches Esther something similar here. Instead of crushing her by treating destiny as something for her either to find or lose, he takes the pressure off her shoulders: *"If you remain silent at this time,* ***relief and deliverance for the Jews will arise from another place.****"* Mordecai's point here is that Christian destiny is corporate. The Lord has made his promises to his people, as the Bride and Body of Christ, not to a few select Christian individuals who therefore have it in their hands to advance or to squander his purposes in the world. He tells Esther plainly: If you refuse it, someone else will come!

I find the theologian Carl Trueman hugely helpful on this point:

> *The belief that we are special is, by and large, complete tosh. Most of us are mediocre, make unique contributions only in the peculiar ways we screw things up, and could easily be replaced as husband, father, or employee by somebody better suited to the task . . . yet far too many Christians have senses of destiny that verge on the messianic . . . Put bluntly, when I read the Bible it seems to me that the church is the meaning of human history; but it is the church as a corporate body, not the distinct individuals who make up her membership . . . My special destiny as a believer is to be part of the church; and it is the church that is the big player in God's wider plan, not me.*[3]

---

[2] This interview is recorded by Stephen Mansfield in *Derek Prince: A Biography* (2005).

[3] Carl Trueman in his book *Fools Rush in Where Monkeys Fear to Tread* (2011).

Ironically, it is only because Esther seems to understand this that she is able to step into the destiny that God has laid before her. If she believed that destiny were something that we have to work out for ourselves, she would be fearful here instead of faith-filled. If she believed that destiny were something largely personal, instead of corporate, then she would shrink back from the dangers of entering her husband's throne room. It is precisely because she trusts that her destiny lies *in God's hands* for the sake of *all God's people* that she is emboldened to risk throwing her own puny life away. *"I will go to the king, even though it is against the law,"* she resolves in verse 16. *"And if I perish, I perish."*

This is the courage that prompted Martin Luther to continue preaching the Gospel in sixteenth-century Europe, declaring: *"If I had a thousand heads I would rather they were all cut off than revoke."*[4] This is the courage that prompted Bishop Latimer to turn to Bishop Ridley, as they were burned at the stake in Oxford in 1555 for preaching that same Gospel, and to reassure him, *"Be of good cheer, Ridley; and play the man. We shall this day, by God's grace, light up such a candle in England as, I trust, will never be put out."*[5]

This is the courage that the Scriptures commend to us and that alone leads to spiritual breakthrough. Not a burdensome destiny that we have to arrange for ourselves. Not a sense of destiny that puffs up our pride and makes us feel we are indispensable to the purposes of God. A true sense of destiny that, together with the rest of God's people, we have been promised the salvation of the nations, and the Church cannot fail to yield a harvest of thirty, sixty or a hundred times the blood that her martyrs resolve to let flow.[6]

---

[4] Quoted by Lyndal Roper in *Martin Luther: Renegade and Prophet* (2016).

[5] Quoted by John Foxe in his *Book of Martyrs* (1563).

[6] Psalm 2:8; Mark 4:8, 20; Luke 8:8, 15 and Revelation 12:11.

More Drilling and Blasting (Esther 5:1–8)

"'What is it, Queen Esther? What is your request?'. . . 'If it pleases the king,' replied Esther, 'let the king, together with Haman, come today to a banquet I have prepared for him.'"

(Esther 5:3–4)

If you have forgotten what Daniel taught us about "drilling" and "blasting" in Babylon then you will find what Esther requests from King Xerxes a colossal disappointment.

After three days of prayer and fasting, buoyed by thousands more prayers from the Jewish community, Esther puts on her best royal robes and ventures uninvited into the great hall of the king.[1] She is risking life and limb here. She knows how quickly her husband dismissed Queen Vashti when she did something which displeased him. Given how casually he agreed to mass murder, Esther must be trembling inwardly with fear.

Amazingly, however, Xerxes takes one look at Esther's beauty and instantly remembers why he chose her to be his queen. He has been a fool to neglect her for the past month and he is delighted that she has chosen to remind him of the pleasures of her company now. Xerxes extends his royal sceptre towards her, as a sign of his authority, and she touches its tip to accept his clemency. Puzzled, he enquires what could matter so much to her that she would risk her life to see him. *"What is it,*

---

[1] Esther concluded in 4:16 that her plight was too perilous for her to act without first calling the Jewish community in Susa to unite in three days of concerted prayer and fasting to God for her.

Queen Esther? What is your request? Even up to half the kingdom, it will be given you."[2]

Esther looks up at her husband on the throne. That's quite an offer. Half of the greatest empire that the world has ever seen. So it comes as a surprise when she reveals what it was worth gambling her life to request it from him. *"If it pleases the king, let the king, together with Haman, come today to a banquet I have prepared for him."*

Excuse me? Have we missed something? Has Esther forgotten about the royal edict decreeing genocide against the Jewish nation? Doesn't she know that, at this very moment, royal runners are delivering the edict to the 127 provinces of her husband's empire? Given the urgency of her need and the unexpected kindness of her husband, this is the perfect moment for her to make a big request of the king. So why doesn't she?

It is all because of what we learned in the book of Daniel about "drilling" and "blasting". Remember, Daniel was God's man in Babylon and Esther is God's woman in Persia. Theirs are parallel lives and they demand parallel wisdom. Remember what Tim Keller taught us:

> *You are building a highway and want to remove a giant boulder. First, you drill a small shaft down into the centre of the rock. Then you put explosives down the shaft into the core of the stone and detonate them. If you drill the shaft but never ignite the blast, you obviously will never move the boulder. But the same is true if you only blast and fail to drill . . . All drilling with no blasting, or all blasting with no drilling, leads to failure.*[3]

Esther isn't being foolish here. She is being exceedingly wise. She recognises that she lacks sufficient connection with her

---

[2] Mordecai encouraged Esther in 4:8 to seek the *hēn*, or *gracious favour*, of Xerxes. Their prayers are answered, because the Hebrew text of 5:2 tells us that she immediately found *hēn* in his eyes.

[3] Timothy Keller in *Center Church* (2012).

husband for her to confront him yet over his royal edict. He has so many women in his harem that he barely gave his queen a second thought until she walked into his throne room a moment ago. Sure, he has now been reminded of her beauty, but he is still much more committed to his friendship with Haman and to the fact that Persian royal decrees cannot be rescinded than he is to his friendship with her. Esther therefore finds a way to deepen the connection. She invites Xerxes and Haman to a dinner party in her quarters of the palace.

We are not told much about their dinner party, but it clearly goes well. King Xerxes begins to warm to his wife's company, and not just to her beauty. As he lies back on his couch to digest his sumptuous food and to enjoy some after-dinner wine with her, he asks her yet again: *"Now what is your petition? It will be given you. And what is your request? Even up to half the kingdom, it will be granted."*

King Xerxes is evidently intrigued by Esther. He knows she cannot have risked her life for something quite so trivial as a dinner party. For the past month, he has shown no interest in what his wife is thinking, but now he is transfixed. He has many women in his palace but his eyes and his ears are all for her. Finally, Esther dares to reveal her second big request. *"My petition and my request is this: If the king regards me with favour and if it pleases the king to grant my petition and fulfil my request, let the king and Haman come tomorrow to the banquet I will prepare for them. Then I will answer the king's question."*

We are slightly more prepared for this than last time, but it still feels like a bit of an anti-climax. Doesn't Esther realize that, right now, royal runners are enlisting the *satrap* of every province in the Persian Empire to commit genocide against her people? Does she have no sense of urgency? Was she not listening when Mordecai told her that the Lord has brought her to her royal position for such a time as this?

Of course she was listening. When the time is ripe and ready for her to begin "blasting", Esther will not disappoint us. But she is wise enough to recognise she is still firmly in the "drilling" zone.[4] Haman still hardly knows her, but he is gradually letting his guard down to her. As for Xerxes, he has never been more interested in what she has to say. Esther has a lot to teach us here about how we are to share the Gospel effectively. She encourages us to drill, drill, drill. Build bridges, build bridges, build bridges. Don't come on too strong, too fast with God's Word. If it's true that the Gospel spreads from person to person, then take the time to be personable with people.

Esther also teaches us something else in these verses. She also shows us how to pray. The prayers of Jesus were answered because he gave time to his friendship with God as his Father. The prayers of his disciples were answered because they took time to build a deep friendship with God too.[5] Might this be the reason why so many of our own prayers go unanswered? Do we rush into God's throne room and blurt out our requests to him, losing the gift because we care too little about knowing the great Giver?

If so, then don't be too surprised by the smallness of Esther's requests in these verses. Instead, let's note her reasons and let's imitate the wisdom of God's woman in Persia.

---

[4] We were told in 5:2 that Esther found *hên*, or *gracious favour*, in the eyes of Xerxes, yet she questions him further in 5:8 over whether she has truly found *hên* in his eyes. For a request this big, she needs to be sure.

[5] Mark 3:14–15 and 9:29 explain that only when his disciples learned to *"be with him"* – either in person or in prayer – could they truly begin partnering with him. Those who try to shortcut this process discover it the hard way (Acts 19:13–17).

Lasting Happiness (Esther 5:9–14)

"Haman went out that day happy and in high spirits. But when he saw Mordecai . . . he was filled with rage. . ."

(Esther 5:9)

There is an idea that many people have that the Lord wants to restrict our fun. It's the idea that his commands are burdensome and boring, and that we would be happier without them. It's the idea that prompts the rulers of the earth to rebel against the Lord and his Messiah in Psalm 2:3, saying, *"Let us break their chains and throw off their shackles!"*

It is also an idea that is entirely untrue. We can see this from the way that the writer of the book of Esther uses Haman as a walking, talking example of what happens whenever people decide to give themselves over to sin. He demonstrates that any initial freedom and happiness that people feel when they throw off the Lord's commands evaporates fast. We will only ever find true freedom and lasting happiness by persisting in unquestioning obedience to the Lord.[1]

Proverbs 27:20 gives us some important background to what the writer is teaching us through Haman in these verses. It tells us that *"Hell and Destruction are never satisfied, and neither are human eyes."* The Hebrew word for *hell* in that verse is *she'ōl*, which means literally *demanding*. The Hebrew word for *destruction* is *abaddōn*, which means literally *consuming*.

[1] We can tell from Ezra 7–10 that disobedience was a big issue for the Jewish nation at the time the book of Esther was written. That's why the writer commends unquestioning obedience in 2:10, 2:15, 2:20 and 4:17.

The proverb therefore teaches us that, just as hell is insatiable for souls, the eyes of the greedy are impossible to satisfy. When we live for the things of this world, we find that the world is never enough for us. People led by the Holy Spirit become holy, and people who are led by hellish spirits become as dissatisfied as hell.[2]

King Xerxes demonstrates this for us in the first chapter of Esther. Despite being the ruler of 127 provinces – the largest empire that the world has ever seen – he refuses to be satisfied until he has invaded Greece and added just one more province to the pile. He reminds us of the oil billionaire J. D. Rockefeller who, when asked how much money was enough to make a man happy, shot back quickly, *"Just a little bit more!"*

Haman demonstrates this principle for us even more clearly than Xerxes. He is the second most powerful man in the world. The king has given him a throne and has commanded all of his other courtiers to bow down and worship him. What is more, he alone has been selected by Queen Esther to attend her two banquets for the king. Life is as good as it gets for Haman, so it is little wonder that we are told in verse 9 that *"Haman went out that day happy and in high spirits."*

But here's the writer's point: the happiness of sin evaporates in a moment. On his way home from Esther's dinner party, Haman spots Mordecai at the entrance to the palace. Immediately we are told that *"he was filled with rage against Mordecai."* He remains respectable on the outside. We are told that *"Haman restrained himself"*. But his peace and happiness are shattered on the inside. It makes no sense that it should matter to a man who has everything that one solitary Jew refuses to bow down before him, but it clearly does. The writer uses this to highlight the astonishing fragility of the joy that the world peddles to people. Haman can boast that he has vast wealth, many sons, a brilliant government career and unprecedented

---

[2] James 3:14–15 states even more explicitly that all human covetousness and greed is inspired by hell. See also Proverbs 11:6, 14:30 and 15:27; Ecclesiastes 5:10 and Habakkuk 2:5.

access to the Persian royal family – yet he is forced to confess that *"All this gives me no satisfaction as long as I see that Jew Mordecai"*.

Proverbs 16:18 gives us some more important background to what the writer is teaching us through the life of Haman. It warns that *"Pride goes before destruction, a haughty spirit before a fall."* Everything that Haman brags about in these verses is about to rebound on his own head.[3] His wife is named Zeresh, which means *Gold*, and in less than twenty-four hours she will turn against him and predict his sudden downfall. His government position and his privileged access to the royal family will become the very means by which her prediction is fulfilled. As for the massive pole that his friends suggest he sets up outside his house to impale Mordecai, the only people who will ever be impaled on it are Haman and his ten sons.[4] The writer of Esther could hardly be clearer here. Rebellion against the Lord can never lead to lasting happiness and freedom. Haman may boast like a little god, but within a day he will be dragged down to hell.

A life surrendered to the Lord, on the other hand, leads to lasting happiness and freedom. The writer of the book of Esther emphasizes this by mentioning ten parties in ten chapters, at all of which the wine flows very freely. The Persian parties in the first few chapters are marked by discontent and discord, while the Jewish feasts in the later chapters are marked by happiness and laughter. They are full of *"feasting and joy"*. *"For the Jews it was a time of happiness and joy, gladness and honour"*.[5]

[3] Esther 6:13, 7:8–10 and 9:6–14. The Lord warns that he will always do this to the proud in Proverbs 3:34 and 16:5; James 4:6 and 1 Peter 5:5–6.

[4] We saw in 2:23 that the Persians shamed their enemies by impaling their corpses on poles, so this is a *pole* rather than *gallows*. Given its height, it was probably fixed to the top of Haman's home (1 Samuel 31:10).

[5] Esther 1:3–4, 1:5–8, 1:9, 2:18, 3:15, 5:1–8, 7:1–10, 8:15–17, 9:17 and 9:18–32. The Hebrew word that is used to describe these ten feasts is *mishteh*, which means literally a *drinking-feast*.

Mordecai is about to be promoted as quickly as Haman is toppled. The two biggest differences between the two men are that Mordecai is full of *humility* and *contentment*. Through the things that he has suffered and through the discipline of fasting, he has gained a proper perspective on his own smallness and on the Lord's greatness.[6] He has spotted the dangers of what Jesus describes in Matthew 13:22 as *"the deceitfulness of wealth"*. His eyes are no longer covetous, but contented, so the Lord is able to entrust him with the power and luxury of the Persian palace. That's the fruit of our obedience to the Lord's commands. As soon as he sees that we have truly grasped that everything is ours in Christ, and that this world holds nothing for us, then the sky is the limit for us.[7]

The Apostle Paul learned this lesson personally and he commends it to us too. Writing as a poor, single, childless prisoner, he declares in Philippians 4:11–12 that he has found true freedom and lasting happiness. The Holy Spirit who lives inside him has taught him to reject the greed that comes from hell and to embrace the contentment that can only come from heaven. *"I have learned to be content whatever the circumstances. I know what it is to be in need, and I know what it is to have plenty. I have learned the secret of being content in any and every situation, whether well fed or hungry, whether living in plenty or in want."*

So don't fall for the idea that the Lord wants to restrict your fun. Don't imagine that sin can ever bring you lasting happiness. Take a good look at Haman and recognise how fragile sin's pleasures can be. They evaporate faster than water on a sunny day.

---

[6] King David teaches us in Psalm 35:13 that this is one of the great purposes of fasting. It is one of our greatest aids towards humility. *"I put on sackcloth and humbled myself with fasting."*

[7] See 1 Corinthians 3:18–23. Recognizing what is ours in Christ lies right at the heart of Christian contentment.

Mordecai's Helper (Esther 6:1–14)

"He robed Mordecai, and led him on horseback through the city streets, proclaiming before him, 'This is what is done for the man the king delights to honour!'"

(Esther 6:11)

The date set by Haman for the slaughter of the Jews is still many months away.[1] The date set for the murder of Mordecai, however, is today. Haman has wasted no time in doing what his wife and friends suggested to him last night. He has erected a giant pole outside his house on which to impale his Jewish enemy. All that remains for him to do is to make a quick visit to the palace to obtain the king's permission for the execution.

But Haman doesn't know about Mordecai's helper. The Lord may never be mentioned by name in the book of Esther, but his fingerprints are all over this chapter. Even as Haman erects his pole and plots murder, Mordecai's helper is busy at work to save him.

First, he gives Xerxes a sleepless night after Esther's dinner party. After being wined and dined so exquisitely by his queen, there is no earthly reason why the king should suffer from sudden insomnia. It is clearly the work of heaven, because it prompts him to ask a scribe to read to him from the annals of his reign. I have read enough Persian artefacts to know that they make pretty soporific reading, but the king seems to be after

---

[1] Haman's decree went out on 17 April 474 BC (3:12) scheduling genocide for 7 March 473 BC (3:13). Since 8:9 tells us that the events of chapter 8 took place on 25 June 474 BC, the events of chapter 6 must have occurred a few days before.

more than just a good bedtime story. It is as if he suspects that one of the gods is plaguing his sleep because he has neglected some royal duty that heaven is reminding him to fulfil.

Sure enough, the scribe reads to the king about how Mordecai saved his life four years earlier. When two of the court eunuchs, named Bigthana and Teresh, plotted to assassinate him, Mordecai exposed their plot to the king. Xerxes can remember executing the two eunuchs and impaling their corpses on poles, but he cannot remember how Mordecai was rewarded. When he discovers to his horror that the man received no royal reward at all, he concludes that this must be why his sleep is being disturbed. He must waste no time in rectifying his omission. Xerxes arrives at this conclusion just as Haman arrives at the outer courtyard of the palace to seek the king's permission to murder Mordecai.[2] Nobody could ever have concocted a coincidence as large as this. It is such perfect timing that we can only conclude that the Lord is Mordecai's helper.[3]

When Haman comes in to see the king, he has no time to request permission for the murder of Mordecai. Xerxes immediately solicits his advice on how best to honour somebody who has greatly pleased the king. You can almost hear the angels laughing as the boastful Haman mistakenly assumes that the king must be talking about him.[4] Haman proposes that such a man should be dressed in the king's own clothes and placed on one of the king's own horses. He should be led through the streets of Susa by one of the most important princes of Persia, who should proclaim to the whole city: *"This is what is done for the man the king delights to honour!"* We

---

[2] The fact that even Haman needs to wait in the outer courtyard to be admitted to see the king serves to emphasize how dangerous it was for Esther to enter the king's presence uninvited in 5:1–8.

[3] For another similar example of God's perfect timing, see 2 Kings 8:5.

[4] It was not unreasonable for Haman to assume that Xerxes was referring to him. See Genesis 41:33 and 41:41. But one of the reasons why pride leads to a fall is that it warps the way in which we view the world, placing ourselves far too much at the centre of it. Haman's error is the bitter fruit of his own boasting in 5:10–12.

can imagine Haman's eyes glazing over as he begins to picture himself on horseback – when suddenly the king declares that Haman will be the Persian prince he has just mentioned. Oh, and by the way, the man that the king delights to honour is none other than Mordecai the Jew!

I hope that you have never received such tragic news that it made your head start spinning, but if you have then you know something of how Haman feels in these verses. To have come to the palace as Mordecai's executioner and to leave it as Mordecai's cheerleader is all too much for him. He has no choice but to obey the king and to act as Mordecai's little helper, but by the time he has finished parading his enemy around the city, he feels utterly humiliated. He covers his head with grief and hurries home to where the crowds can no longer see him.[5]

Haman's wife Zeresh and his friends are waiting for him. Perhaps they have gathered in anticipation of an execution. When Haman recounts to them all that happened at the palace, they are horrified. Can't he see that being forced to spend a day as Mordecai's little helper is the least of his problems? Such a reversal in fortunes, and with such comic timing, can only mean that Mordecai has another, far greater helper in heaven.

The writer of the book of Esther isn't going to name Mordecai's helper for us, but he makes it pretty clear to us through the words of Haman's wife and friends in verse 13. They effectively say: *You didn't tell us that Mordecai was a Jew! Don't you know that the Jews are the people of God? If you had told us that Mordecai had the God of Israel as his helper, we would never have advised you to impale him on a pole. This changes everything! If you think that today was tough, then watch out for what's still coming!*

[5] Esther 6:6–12 is a picture of where history is headed. When Jesus returns from heaven, many who are hated in this world will be honoured and many who are feted in this world will be put to shame.

"Since Mordecai, before whom your downfall has started, is of Jewish origin, you cannot stand against him – you will surely come to ruin!"[6]

Sure enough, while Haman is still reeling from his bad day, some royal servants arrive from the palace to escort him to Esther's second dinner party. He barely has enough time to compose himself before he is led back outside and his rapid downfall continues.[7] Haman's second visit to the palace today is going to end with his own execution. He made a fatal mistake when he failed to see that Mordecai's helper is the Lord.

[6] Zeresh and Haman's friends may sound cruel here, but they are actually being loving. What they say to Haman is true. His downfall has indeed started and he has only hours left on earth to repent of his sin.

[7] The Hebrew verb that is used in 6:14 means that they *"were anxious"* or *"in haste"* to bring him to Esther's banquet. This is meant to emphasize the speed at which his whole life is unravelling.

What Do You Want? (Esther 7:1–4)

"Queen Esther, what is your petition? It will be given you. What is your request? Even up to half the kingdom, it will be granted."

(Esther 7:2)

You probably know the joke about the man who finds a golden lamp and, rubbing it, releases a genie. The grateful genie invites him to make a wish for anything he desires.

"My wife loves horses," the man explains to the genie, "so I wish I had a unicorn so that I could give it to her as the present of a lifetime." The genie looks at him impatiently and explains to him that a unicorn is a mythical creature. It's a ridiculous wish. He needs to wish again, only this time for something easier. "Well, I don't really know what else to give. I've never really understood her. Hey, I know, I wish that I could understand what my wife wants." The genie looks at him even more impatiently than before. He scratches his head before replying: "OK, what colour did you want that unicorn to be?"

It's a stupid joke, of course. The wife of King Xerxes knows exactly what she wants. God's woman in Persia knows precisely what she intends to obtain from the king. As they sip their after-dinner wine together, he asks her, *"Queen Esther, what is your petition? It will be given you. What is your request? Even up to half the kingdom, it will be granted."* Esther spots that "drilling" time is over. She now shows us how to do some "blasting".

Esther recognises that the effectiveness of our "blasting" depends on the quality of our "drilling". The Hebrew text makes this a little bit more obvious than our English translations, so it helps here if we understand the Hebrew word *hēn*. It is the word used throughout the Old Testament to describe God's *gracious favour* towards his people. In 4:8, Mordecai encouraged Esther to go into her husband's throne room in order to seek his *gracious favour*. In 5:2, we are told that she succeeded in obtaining his *gracious favour* but, for a request this big, she needed a deeper rapport with her husband. In 5:8, she asked him for yet more *gracious favour*. Here in 7:3, she seeks to verify once more that she truly has his *gracious favour* before she makes her request of him. The little word *hēn* in these verses reminds us that real rapport is needed for a fruitful Gospel conversation.[1]

Esther recognises that the effectiveness of our "blasting" also depends on the way in which we present our message. She does not simply blurt out her request to the king. She presents it in the most reasonable of manners. Her initial request is *"Grant me my life"*. Who could possibly refuse her? Her second request is *"And spare my people"*. Note that she does not yet reveal to Xerxes that she is a Jew. She reveals the truth to him in a measured manner. She doesn't use the sovereignty of God as an excuse for lazy communication. She knows what she wants, and she knows how best to ask for it.

When my children were young, my wife and I spent many hours preparing their food for them. When they were babies, we would liquidise everything and feed it to them with a tiny spoon. When they grew into toddlers, we cut their food into small chunks and encouraged them to feed themselves. As a result, they are now old enough to cook the dinner for us, and we can see from Esther's example in these verses that this is a helpful picture when it comes to communicating God's Word to people. If we say too much to people too soon, bombarding them with Bible verses, it is a bit like giving a lamb chop to a baby. They won't know how to digest it. People need to hear the Gospel in bite-sized chunks, over a patient period of time.

---

[1] The writer emphasizes that relationships matter to requests by repeatedly referring to her as *"Queen Esther"*.

King Xerxes is intrigued by his wife's two requests. Who would dare to threaten the life of the queen of Persia? Who are her people, and how have they come to the brink of being destroyed, killed and annihilated?[2] Only now does Queen Esther reveal her full hand to her husband. She confesses that she is a Jew, a worshipper of the God of Israel, a member of the nation that Haman is plotting to destroy.

As a lesson in "drilling" and "blasting", this is perfect. Xerxes is immediately convicted of his foolishness and he is eager to make it up to her.[3] Note, therefore, how easy Esther makes it for her husband to say "yes" to what she says. She places the entire blame for the royal decree on Haman's shoulders, despite the fact that Xerxes played along with it. She even apologises to her husband for the effort it will take him to reverse it! She predicts his every objection and she deals up front with them all.[4]

The Apostle Paul does something similar when he shares the Gospel with Greeks in the book of Acts. He is aware that one of their biggest objections to faith in Jesus will be the thought that the great Greek heroes, such as Pericles and Socrates, might be in hell. He therefore assures them twice, in Acts 14:16 and 17:30, that *"In the past God overlooked such ignorance, but now he commands all people everywhere to repent."*[5] If we want to be successful in our "blasting" then we need to learn to do this too. We need to anticipate people's objections to the Gospel and defuse them, even as we share the Gospel with them.

---

[2] This triple description of the killing of the Jews echoes 3:13 and serves as an Old Testament precursor to the triple warning of Jesus in John 10:10 that the Devil *"comes only to steal and kill and destroy"*.

[3] The writer does not mention it, but Xerxes, as we discussed earlier, may well have believed that one of the gods had kept him awake the previous night in order to remind him to honour a Jew. He is now firmly on Esther's side.

[4] The Hebrew text of 7:4 can either be translated as *"no such distress would justify disturbing the king"* or as *"though no amount of compensation could offset the loss to the king"*. The first option makes more sense.

[5] Paul is not saying the Greek heroes were saved. He is simply doing what Jesus does in John 21:20–22.

There is one final lesson for us here at Esther's second dinner party. We have seen already that her interactions with King Xerxes can be taken as a picture of our own interactions with the true King of kings. We are the Bride of Christ. The Lord has extended his golden sceptre of grace towards us and has invited us to bring petitions and requests to him in prayer. In that sense, when Xerxes invites Esther to ask him for anything, even up to half of his kingdom, it isn't an exaggeration. The Lord really means it when he invites us to ask him to give us the Kingdom of Heaven.

We can therefore learn from Esther how to respond to such an offer. Although the Lord is far more gracious towards us than a Persian king, we shouldn't simply blurt out our prayers. Hosea 14:2 exhorts us to *"Take words with you and return to the Lord"* – in other words to plan our prayers beforehand, even writing them down. If we would never dream of going into an important work meeting without planning what to say, then why are we often so careless about bringing requests to the Ruler of the Universe? Esther shows us that we need to be specific, compelling and prepared. Give the Lord good reasons to say "yes" to your requests of him. If it helps you, even write those reasons down.

Six times in the Gospels, Jesus echoes the words of King Xerxes to Esther. He asks people, *"What do you want me to do for you?"*[6] He is asking that same question of you right now.

[6] Matthew 20:21, 32; Mark 10:36, 51; Luke 18:41 and John 1:38.

The Greasy Pole (Esther 7:5–8:2)

"'A pole reaching to a height of fifty cubits stands by Haman's house.'. . . The king said, 'Impale him on it!'"
(Esther 7:9)

When Benjamin Disraeli became the British prime minister in 1868, he exulted that *"I have climbed to the top of the greasy pole!"* He was likening the process of political advancement to a game played at Victorian funfairs. It was slow work climbing upwards and incredibly easy to find yourself slipping downwards fast.

Few people in history have ever slid down the greasy pole of politics with such rapidity as Haman. In chapter 5, he boasted about his vast wealth, his many sons, his political position and his unprecedented access to the private quarters of the Persian royal family. When Mordecai refused to recognize his greatness, Haman had the power to erect a pole outside his house and to impale the irksome Jew upon it. Haman saw his life as an inspiring Persian success story. He was at the top of the greasy pole.

In chapter 6, Haman's hands and feet begin slipping due to the invisible helper of the Jewish nation. Before he can ask the king's permission to murder Mordecai, the king forces him to act as Mordecai's cheerleader. When Haman's wife Zeresh hears what happened, she instantly concludes that her husband is about to continue sliding back down the greasy pole all the way. *"Your downfall has started,"* she warns him. *"You will surely come to ruin!"* [1]

---

[1] If you find the Lord unmerciful towards Haman in these verses, then consider this: the Lord inspired Haman's wife and friends to issue him this warning as a final call for him to repent of his sin.

Things get worse for Haman at Esther's second dinner party. He manages to pull himself together after the humiliation of his day with Mordecai. As he reclines with the king and queen, he may even have begun to dream that he can haul his way back up the greasy pole. All such hope ends when Queen Esther reveals her Jewishness to the king. In 2:10 and 2:20, the writer informed us twice that she kept her ethnicity a secret from everybody in the palace. There was far too much anti-Semitism in the Persian Empire for her to confess that she was part of the people of God. Haman is aghast to discover that news now.[2] His genocidal decree has made an enemy of one of the most powerful women in the world.[3] His hands and feet keep slipping quickly down the greasy pole.

The king is so furious with his chief minister that he steps outside into the garden to get a little fresh air to calm his anger and consider what to do. Haman seizes this as his final opportunity to prevent his hands and feet from slipping further. He stays behind with Esther to beg for his life. His world is spinning so fast around him that, as he leans over the queen's couch, he leans too far forward and tumbles right on top of her at the very moment when the king comes back inside! The comic timing here is as perfect as it was earlier, when the king's insomnia reminded him to honour Mordecai at the very moment Haman arrived to request permission to murder him. It is clearly the work of the Lord. The king bellows, *"Will he even molest the queen while she is with me in the house?"* The hapless chief minister can feel his hands and feet slipping even further.

Even now, the Lord hasn't finished. Haman covered his face in shame in 6:12 after being humiliated with Mordecai. Now the king's eunuchs rush forward to cover his face again, for it is obvious to everyone that Haman has become a dead man walking. The Lord ensures that Harbona is among them,

---

[2] The Hebrew word *bā'ath* in 7:6 means that Haman *was overtaken by sudden terror.*

[3] Not necessarily *the* most powerful woman. Herodotus reveals that Xerxes was manipulated by several other women. Not least was Vashti, or Amestris, who remained mother to the future King Artaxerxes.

since the eunuch heard chatter this morning about the giant pole that Haman set up outside his home yesterday evening.[4] Harbona informs the king that Haman is planning to impale Mordecai on it, adding pointedly that Mordecai is the man *"who spoke up to help the king."* Haman's pole is 23 metres tall, but it feels short compared to the greasy pole down which he keeps on slipping.

One of the scariest verses in the New Testament is 1 Peter 5:5 – *"God opposes the proud but shows favour to the humble."* Most people imagine that the Lord will either support them or act indifferently towards them. It is quite shocking to discover that pride actually turns our greatest Friend into our mortal Enemy. If you struggle to believe that, then just look at what happens here to Haman. He woke up in bed this morning as the second most powerful man in the world, but he will never see his bed again. He spent yesterday evening setting up a giant pole outside his house, and this evening his corpse will be impaled upon it.[5] Because Haman remained proud and unrepentant, even when he felt himself slipping down the greasy pole, he kept on slipping all the way down to hell.[6]

Praise God, however, that 1 Peter 5:5 contains a promise as well as a threat. Pride turns the Lord into our worst enemy, but humility lays hold of the Lord as our greatest friend. This mention of Mordecai puts an idea into the king's head about how he can fill the freshly vacant post of chief minister. When Queen Esther confesses all, revealing that Mordecai is in fact her cousin and adoptive father, King Xerxes follows through on the idea. He reclaims his royal signet ring from Haman's finger and

---

[4] Harbona was evidently one of the most senior royal eunuchs, since he is listed among "the seven" in 1:10.

[5] We can deduce from 1 Samuel 31:10 that one of the reasons why Haman's pole was so tall was that it was attached to the top of his house. He wanted to shame his enemy by impaling him where everyone could see.

[6] Not only does this warn us not to mess with Lord, but it also teaches us not to mess with his people.

he hands it to Mordecai.[7] He gives all of Haman's possessions to Queen Esther, who completes her cousin's meteoric rise to power by appointing him to act as steward over everything that once belonged to his arch-enemy. It's alright for us to stop and take a gasp here. *Wow!*

Mordecai has climbed up the greasy pole as quickly as Haman just slid down it. Like Joseph and Daniel before him, the Lord has taken him from zero to hero in a single day.

What a great advert for humility. What a great advert for obedience to the Lord. And what a great advert for the providential sovereignty of God. Without ever mentioning the Lord by name, the writer of the book of Esther has shown the truth of Psalm 75:6–7: *"No one from the east or the west or from the desert can exalt themselves. It is God who judges: He brings one down, he exalts another."*

---

[7] Archaeologists have discovered a cuneiform tablet in the ruins of Borsippa, dating to the reign of Xerxes, which refers to a senior official named *Marduka* – that is, Mordecai. Even the rocks corroborate the historicity of Esther.

Good News (Esther 8:1–17)

"That same day King Xerxes gave Queen Esther the estate of Haman, the enemy of the Jews."

(Esther 8:1)

When we read the book of Esther carefully, it is hard not to conclude that our understanding of the Gospel is far too small. We major on forgiveness for our sins, and rightly so, for that is what we need initially from God. But we mustn't let our experience of the Gospel stop there. These verses remind us why it is known as the Good News.

The eighth chapter of Esther begins with Haman's corpse impaled upon a pole. The original Jewish readers of this chapter would instantly spot this as a reference back to Deuteronomy 21:23 – *"Anyone who is hung on a pole is under God's curse."* We have further commentary on that verse from the Apostle Paul in Galatians 3:10–14. He explains that we should see Haman in these verses as a picture of ourselves: *"Cursed is everyone who does not continue to do everything written in the Book of the Law."* We should also see Haman as a picture of Jesus becoming sin for us when he was nailed to a wooden cross at Calvary: *"Christ redeemed us from the curse of the law by becoming a curse for us, for it is written: 'Cursed is everyone who is hung on a pole.'"*[1]

Paul's insight helps us to see that it is Good News when Xerxes gifts Haman's estate to Esther in verse 1. Haman is described here as *"the enemy of the Jews"* because he is merely

---

[1] Don't be surprised that Haman can be a prophetic picture of Jesus in these verses. We are told in 2 Corinthians 5:21 that *"God made him who had no sin to be sin for us"*. He is even pictured as a *snake* in John 3:14.

the human face of the Devil and his demons at work in the world. Satan loves it when believers in Jesus accept forgiveness from him, and then expect nothing more. But verse 1 reminds us that, if Jesus has saved us, we are now far more than just forgiven sinners. We have become saints of God.[2] We are no longer under the curse of sin, which means that the Devil has no further hold over us. Jesus wasn't exaggerating when he declared literally in Luke 19:10 that *"The Son of Man came to seek and to save **what was lost.**"*

The Apostle Paul isn't exaggerating either when he declares in Colossians 2:14–15 that, when Jesus died on the cross, he *"cancelled the charge . . . which stood against us and condemned us; he has taken it away, nailing it to the cross. And having disarmed the powers and authorities, he made a public spectacle of them, triumphing over them by the cross."* The Gospel is Good News because it declares our total victory over our great enemy, Satan. Everything that he possessed before Christ came has now been wrested away from him. It is all ours for the taking, through the blood of the one who became a curse for us.

In Galatians 3:10–14, the Apostle Paul adds something else important after telling us that Jesus became a curse for us when he was hung, like Haman, on a pole. Paul says that Jesus took our place *"so that by faith we might receive the promise of the Spirit."* We should therefore be reminded of this when King Xerxes offers his royal signet ring to Mordecai. In the ancient world, a signet ring signified a king's authority.[3] Anyone he gave it to could press it into sealing wax or clay and use it to issue royal edicts in his name. In 3:10, Haman used Xerxes' signet ring to send out messages commanding genocide against the Jews, which can be taken as a picture of how Adam and Eve abdicated their God-given authority to the Devil in the Garden of Eden.

---

[2] In Romans 5:8 Paul says we *were* sinners. We are sinners no longer! We have become *"the saints of Christ Jesus"* (Romans 1:7 and Philippians 1:1).

[3] Genesis 41:42; Daniel 6:17; Haggai 2:23 and Luke 15:22.

Now, as Xerxes wrestles his royal signet ring back from Haman's finger and hands it to Mordecai, it serves as a picture of the fresh authority that the Lord now gives to his Son's followers so that they can partner with him in ruling the world.

Paul explains that we are empowered to do this by receiving the promise of the Holy Spirit through faith in the Gospel. Paul likens receiving the Holy Spirit to receiving the imprint of God's signet ring upon us.[4] It marks us out as his royal agents in the world. We do not need to *beg* for God to fill us with the Holy Spirit, any more than Mordecai has to beg for any of the honours that he receives from Xerxes here. We simply need to *believe* that this is part and parcel of the Good News. Paul explains in Ephesians 3:17 that we receive this indwelling of the Holy Spirit *"through faith"*. From start to finish, our experience of the Christian Gospel is never about *begging*, but always about *believing*.

In these verses, Esther models for us how to partner with the Holy Spirit to rule on earth with God through our prayers. Most Christians know about the first time that Esther entered the throne room of King Xerxes uninvited in chapter 5. But what many Christians do not realize is that she courageously entered his throne room for a second time in chapter 8. Once again, we are told that the king greets her with *hēn*, or *gracious favour*, by extending his golden sceptre towards her. Once again, he is intrigued by her willingness to flout the conventions of the Persian royal palace in order to lay a great request before him. Esther has escaped destruction personally, but now she comes into the king's presence to intercede for the salvation of others. In the same way, we are to come into the Lord's presence repeatedly in prayer to request salvation for our friends, for our neighbours, for our work colleagues and for the unreached nations of the world.

Because of Esther's second act of courage, salvation spreads from her own family to all of God's chosen people, right

[4] He says this in 2 Corinthians 1:21–22, and in Ephesians 1:13–14 and 4:30.

across the Persian Empire. Since King Xerxes cannot repeal his first edict under Persian law, he responds to Esther's pleas by sending out another. This second edict permits the Jews across the empire to assemble together and to arm themselves on the day that Haman scheduled for their slaughter.[5] If anyone is foolish enough to attack them under the first edict, then the second edict grants them authority from the king to fight back. It will be a day for the Jews to kill and plunder their foes.[6]

The Good News of the Gospel is far bigger than many of us imagine. It isn't merely God's proclamation that we have been forgiven, but also his proclamation that the Devil has been utterly defeated, that we have been given authority to crush him beneath our feet and that we can now plunder his defeated realm.[7] As Mordecai leaves the presence of the king, dressed in royal robes and wearing a golden crown upon his head, it should inspire us to rise up with faith to start asserting the new authority God has given us.[8]

It's time for us to get a bigger view of the Good News. It's time for us to start believing what the Bible tells us: *"The highest heavens belong to the Lord, but the earth he has given to the human race." "Be fruitful and increase in number; fill the earth and subdue it. Rule!"*[9]

---

[5] The kings of Persia were regarded as messengers from the gods, so their royal edicts were viewed as infallible. This was a major headache for them in Daniel 6 and throughout the book of Esther.

[6] The triple reference in 8:11 to the Jews *destroying*, *killing* and *annihilating* their enemies echoes 3:13 and 7:4. It is echoed in turn by Jesus when he teaches about the Devil in John 10:10. The shoe is on the other foot now!

[7] Matthew 12:28–30; Luke 11:20–23; Romans 16:20 and 1 John 3:8.

[8] The reference to *"white and bluey-purple"* robes in 8:15 echoes 1:6, because these were the official colours of the Persian royal family. This type of attention to detail corroborates the historicity of the book of Esther.

[9] Psalm 115:16 and Genesis 1:26–28.

Good News Shoes (Esther 8:1–17)

"The couriers, riding the royal horses, went out, spurred on by the king's command."

(Esther 8:14)

When the prodigal son receives forgiveness from his father in the famous parable, the father doesn't merely offer him his signet ring. He also offers him a pair of sandals so that he can run the farm with him. In the same way, when the Apostle Paul describes the spiritual weapons that the Lord has given us, he doesn't merely list items of armour. He also tells us that the Lord has given us Good News shoes and has commissioned us to become runners for the Gospel throughout the world.[1]

It should not therefore surprise us that the picture of the Gospel in the eighth chapter of Esther goes beyond describing the redemption, the plunder, the anointing and the authority which now belong to us through Jesus Christ. It also encourages us that God called us to be his Gospel messengers to the nations. It tells us that, as a result of our belief in Jesus, we have each been given a pair of Good News shoes to wear.

Mordecai prepares the Gospel message in this chapter. He writes to the Jews that their great enemy has been defeated. They may not fully experience that victory immediately. People are still plotting to destroy them on 7 March 473 BC, but Mordecai insists that their enemy's power has been broken once and for all. If anybody does attack them, then they should view it as the desperate last-ditch attack of a defeated foe, because the

---

[1] Luke 15:22 and Ephesians 6:15.

Jews are now the ones who have been granted royal authority to assemble together with dangerous weapons in their hands. The Jews are the ones the king calls to go out and plunder their enemies. They need to fear the foe no longer. They are on the winning side!

Mordecai writes this Gospel message *"in the king's name"*. He seals it *"with the king's signet ring"*. But the message will not succeed in saving anyone unless a team of willing messengers take it to every corner of the world. When we think about it this way, it sheds new light on what it means for God to have entrusted his Church with the task of world evangelization. It is a privilege, and not a burden.

In verses 3–6, we are shown where we need to start if we want to succeed in our great mission. The first place to which our Good News shoes ought to take us is the throne room of the King. Before we speak to people for God, we need to speak to God for people. We are told that Esther *"pleaded with the king, falling at his feet and weeping."* We are told that she begged for *hēn*, or *gracious favour*, for the Jews. Don't miss the way she takes real ownership for the salvation of the world before the king. She has never met most of the Jews in the Persian Empire and she never will, yet she pleads for them as her beloved brothers and sisters. She sees them as *"my people"* and *"my family"*.

Esther's bold intercession for the Jewish nation in these verses ought to stir us to plead with the Lord to save the nations of the world. He still encourages us in Psalm 2:8 to *"Ask me, and I will make the nations your inheritance, the ends of the earth your possession."*

In verse 9, we are shown what to do next if we are to succeed in our great mission. Mordecai calls the royal secretaries together because this message needs to go to every people group and language of the Persian Empire. India is mentioned in the east. Ethiopia is mentioned in the west. The 127 provinces between them encompass parts of Asia, Africa and Europe, together symbolizing every nation of the world. Mordecai commands the royal secretaries to translate the edict into every person's mother tongue. Even if most people in the empire can understand Persian, this message is of such importance that it needs to come to everybody in the language of their heart.[2]

In verse 9, we are reminded that the Gospel is Good News for the Jews. There is a danger that we might miss this, amidst the talk of translating Mordecai's message into every pagan language, so note something pretty striking here. The writer uses the word *Jew* fifteen times in this chapter, which is more times than he used it in the first seven chapters of Esther put together! The Lord has commissioned us to take the Good News to the nations, but as we go to the Gentiles, we must not neglect the fact that it is Good News for the Jews. The Apostle Paul reminds us that it is *"the power of God that brings salvation to everyone who believes: first to the Jew, then to the Gentile."*[3]

In verses 10 and 14, we are reminded that praying and translating and contextualizing are no substitute for actually *going*. Mordecai sends his message out *"by mounted couriers, who rode fast horses especially bred for the king"*. We are told that *"The couriers, riding the royal horses, went out, spurred on by the king's command."*[4] The picture here is active, like an army, not lethargic, like many of our churches.[5] Clearly, there is no time to lose.

After Jesus ascended back to heaven, the apostles put on their Good News shoes and began fulfilling this picture of the Gospel going into all the world. Soon, even the Roman emperor claimed to be a Christian. Fresh generations of believers put

---

[2] This can be applied not only to Bible translation, but also to contextualisation. We need to "drill" into the heart of every community, regardless of its official language, to "blast" in a way that truly touches people.

[3] Romans 1:16. See also Romans 2:9–11 and 9:30–11:32.

[4] Proclaiming Mordecai's edict in time to people in every corner of the vast empire would be challenging. Some readers link these *horses* to the promise that God's Spirit will empower us to reach the world (Acts 1:8).

[5] The Hebrew word that is used for these riders in 8:10 and 14 means literally *runners*. This was also the case in 3:13 and 15. The writer wants to convey to us here a sense of great speed and urgency. See Psalm 68:11.

on their own Good News shoes and took the message to the lands of the barbarians. People like Ulfilas amongst the Gothic tribesmen, or like Patrick in Ireland, or like Cyril and Methodius among the Slavs. With the coming of the Reformation and the Counter-Reformation, new groups of believers put on their Good News shoes and went from Christian Europe to the world. Francis Xavier went to India, Indonesia and Japan. Matteo Ricci went to China. The Moravians went to the Inuits and Native Americans. As the world opened up further, thousands of believers put on their Good News shoes and took the message right across Africa and South America and Asia and the Pacific islands.

Most of them suffered great hardship and persecution. Many of them lost their lives. But the picture that we see here in the book of Esther reminds us why it was worth their pain. We are told that *"there was joy and gladness"* when people heard the Good News. Astonishingly, we are told that *"many people of other nationalities became Jews"*. The Gospel truly does carry heaven's power to save people. But only if we go and share it.

So whether it is over the globe or over your garden fence, whether it means crossing the oceans or merely crossing the road, put on your own Good News shoes. The Lord has placed his mighty message in our hands, but it will only save the nations if we *go*.

Case Study (Esther 8:16–9:19)

"Many people of other nationalities became Jews because fear of the Jews had seized them."

(Esther 8:17)

Mahatma Gandhi, who led India to independence from British rule, was no stranger to hatred and persecution. He was not overly concerned about either of them. He is quoted as saying, *"First they ignore you, then they laugh at you, then they fight you, then you win."*[1]

But is that actually true? I know that lots of Christian preachers will tell you that the people of God have nothing to fear from hatred and persecution, but have you noticed that they tend to say it from their comfortable offices or from the safety of their pulpits? I have argued it myself in this book from the pages of Daniel, but I am writing this book in London, which feels a million miles away from what it must have been like for the Jewish community in Babylon and Persia. That's why I am so grateful that the writer of the book of Esther uses the events of 7 March 473 BC as a case study on the effects of persecution on the people of God.

First, the writer examines what the persecution of 473 BC did *to the Jews*. Haman had hoped to exterminate the people of God, and he might have succeeded. Despite the king's second edict, large lynch mobs still gathered across the empire to fulfil the dead chief minister's plan for Jewish genocide. We

---

[1] If Gandhi said this, then he was actually quoting Nicholas Klein, the US labour lawyer, who said it in 1918.

must never be gung-ho about times of persecution. They are always horrible. We catch a glimpse of just how hard the Jews were forced to fight for survival from the fact that they kill 800 would-be murderers in Susa and 75,000 would-be murderers across the rest of the Persian Empire.

But the writer tells us that the persecution of the Jews strengthened their faith in God. In 9:2, the Jews gather together and take up deadly weapons in their hands. In our own context, we must not take this as an encouragement to return violence towards our persecutors. Jesus explicitly forbids this.[2] The most effective leaders of the Church in times of persecution have always warned against it too. During the French Wars of Religion, Theodore Beza protested that *"It belongs to the Church of God to suffer blows, not to strike them. But the Church is an anvil which has worn out many hammers."*[3] This is simply meant to be a picture of how persecution reminds the people of God that they are called to spiritual warfare, wielding the deadly weapons of God in their hands. The persecution of 473 BC made the Jews more determined than ever to keep on gathering together as the people of God in order to push back the forces of darkness in the world.

This is what has happened in recent decades in China. Instead of wiping out Christianity, persecution has intensified the faith of Chinese believers. One observer notes that

> *Mao smashed the institution of Christianity in China, but the Christians went into the homes, and there it became rubbed into Chinese culture, embedding itself in families, sitting rooms, and apartment blocs in a way missionaries only dreamt of for centuries. Said one Shanghai pastor, "Before the early 1960s, we practised Christianity in churches, and hardly anywhere else.*

---

[2] Matthew 5:39, 5:44, 10:23 and 26:51–54. This may be why the Jews are so restrained in plundering their human enemies in 9:10, 15 and 16. Our battle is not with flesh and blood, but with the Devil.

[3] Quoted by Jacques Auguste de Thou in his *Historia Sui Temporis* (1605).

After the persecutions, we practised it in our homes, and ***therefore*** *everywhere else!"*[4]

Next, the writer examines what the persecution of 473 BC did *to non-believers*. Anti-Semitism was a potent force within the Persian Empire, but when news started spreading about Haman's sudden downfall and Mordecai's meteoric rise to power, people began to take the God of Israel seriously. When the ten sons of Haman were killed in the fighting and their corpses impaled on poles, the piqued curiosity of the pagans turned into outright fear of the Lord. As a result, the writer tells us in 8:17 that *"Many people of other nationalities became Jews because fear of the Jews had seized them."* Yes, that's really what it says! Rather than destroying the people of God, persecution made them grow in number.[5] When the pagans of the Persian Empire saw how well the God of Israel protected his followers, many of them threw away the traditional idols of Persia.

The writer also examines what the persecution of 473 BC did *to government*. King Xerxes isn't the only one who changed tack to become a fervent champion of the Jewish nation. We are told in 9:3 that many noblemen and governors across the Persian Empire changed their views about the God of Israel and began to promote the interests of the Jews. Here the consequences spill out beyond the book of Esther. Ezra 1–6 tells us that the Persian government forbade the Jews from rebuilding the walls of Jerusalem because they felt suspicious towards them. The future King Artaxerxes was aged around ten in 473 BC, so we should trace the sudden change of heart during his reign back to the year in which he witnessed this miraculous deliverance for the Jews. King Artaxerxes became one of the greatest champions of the rebuilding of Jerusalem, sending Ezra and Nehemiah back to the city in 458 BC and 445 BC. He even financed the building

---

[4] Ron Boyd-Macmillan reports this in his book *Explosive Preaching* (2006).

[5] This was the case 3,500 years ago in Exodus 1:12, and it has generally been the case ever since then too.

work from his imperial treasury. That's hard to explain except as a product of persecution.

As a result, the writer ends by examining what the persecution of 473 BC did *to the Jewish vision for the world*. One of the great tragedies of Old Testament history is that the Lord called Israel to be a missionary nation, preaching his glories to their pagan neighbours, but the Jews became inward-looking and self-righteous in their pursuit of God. After the great deliverance of 473 BC, the Jewish vision for the world began to change. The writer tells us in 8:16 that they began to find true freedom and lasting happiness in the Lord. *"For the Jews it was a time of happiness and joy, gladness and honour."* As they rejoiced in the Lord, they began to catch his missionary heart towards the world. The writer tells us in 9:27 that they stopped planning purely in terms of their tight-knit Jewish community. They began planning how to receive the many Gentiles who would convert to Judaism.[6]

None of these positive products of persecution should surprise us, because they are what the prophet Daniel prophesied would happen to God's people in troubled times. If it is impossible to engender faith by force, then it is equally impossible to hinder faith by force. The more God's people are persecuted, the more they multiply. The book of Daniel tells us that this is true, but the book of Esther demonstrates it through the events of 473 BC.

"First they ignore you, then they laugh at you, then they fight you, then you win."

---

[6] The New Testament has much to say against the Pharisees, but at least they had a missionary vision (Matthew 23:15). Early Christianity came out of the synagogues they had planted across the Roman Empire.

Invisible God (Esther 8:17 – 9:3)

"Fear of the Jews had seized them. . . fear of Mordecai had seized them."

(Esther 8:17 – 9:3)

One of the games that I love to play with my children is *Taboo*. If you've never played it, then it's very simple. You are given a card with a word on it that your teammates have to guess, along with several other words that you are not allowed to say. For example, if the word on my card were *Esther*, I would have to explain it to you without saying words such as *queen* or *Bible* or *Persia* or *Mordecai*. It's a very simple game to play.

Reading the book of Esther can feel a little bit like playing the game *Taboo*. The writer has clearly decided not to mention the name of God at all in the story. It's his way of showing us that, even when the Lord appears invisible in our lives, he is never inactive. In the early chapters of Esther, this isn't too much of a problem. In chapter 4, when people start fasting and praying and talking about destiny, it gets harder. In chapters 6 and 7, when the perfect timing of Providence is unmistakable, avoiding any mention of God by name gets really tricky. Here in chapters 8 and 9, it borders on the ridiculous.

In 8:17, the writer tells us that *"many people of other nationalities became Jews because* ***fear of the Jews*** *had seized them."* To which our answer has to be: Really? Do you expect us to believe that the Persians were afraid of a group of exiles who had hidden their faith behind closed doors for years and who now huddled together with swords in their hands for fear of the lynch mobs gathered at their door? It's pretty obvious that what the writer really means is that *fear of the God of the Jews* had gripped them. I feel like I'm playing *Taboo* here with my children. We can all tell what the writer truly wishes to say.

In 9:2, the writer tells us that *"No one could stand against them, because the people of all the other nationalities were **afraid of them**."* To which our answer once again has to be: Really? Are we genuinely to believe that the proudest nation in the world, which only ten years earlier dared to cross the Hellespont and to invade Greece, is now quaking in its boots over a minor ethnic group within its own borders? Any discerning reader can tell that what the writer really wishes to say here is that they were *afraid of the God of Israel*.

In 9:3, the writer tells us that *"All the nobles of the provinces, the satraps, the governors and the king's administrators helped the Jews, because **fear of Mordecai** had seized them."* To which we have to answer yet again: Really? Are we really to believe that the Persian grandees are petrified of a man who escaped by a whisker from being impaled on a Persian pole? Are we genuinely to accept that they are afraid of a man so inconsequential that two courtiers failed even to notice him listening on the sidelines while they plotted to assassinate King Xerxes? It's obvious that what the writer truly wishes to say here is that fear of Mordecai's God spread like wildfire across the empire.

With oblique and convoluted verses such as these, we can only reasonably conclude that the writer wants to revolutionize the way in which his readers view the world. He is not playing a game of *Taboo* with us, but is challenging us that we can spend too much of our lives thinking and speaking and living like non-believers. Because we can't see God at work around us, we can easily assume that he isn't at work around us, and we could not be more wrong. The book of Esther omits any direct reference to God, whilst revealing his fingerprints everywhere, so that readers will stop using the word *coincidence* and begin to think and talk and act in terms of *Providence*.

Not every reader of the book of Esther can accept this. You may be familiar with the *Apocrypha*, which is the name given to the fifteen extra books that the translators of the Septuagint added to the Old Testament when they translated it into Greek in the third century BC.[1] Did you know that one of those fifteen books is entitled *Deutero-Esther*, which means *Second Esther* or *The Extra Bits of Esther*, and that it seeks to remedy the writer's omission of any mention of God by name? Its six extra chapters are structured:

Esther 10:4–13	Mordecai clarifies that all that happens in the book of Esther was done by the hand of the Lord and revealed to him beforehand in a dream.
Esther 11	An account of Mordecai's dream, repeating that it was definitely God who did it all. (PS Did you get that? It was God!)
Esther 12	Mordecai thwarts another plot to assassinate King Xerxes.
Esther 13	The text of the first decree of Xerxes and Haman to annihilate the Jews, plus a prayer from Mordecai which clarifies that the reason he refused to bow down to Haman was his devotion towards the God of Israel.
Esther 14	Esther's prayer in the palace at the end of chapter 4, making it clear that she put her trust in God. (PS Did you get that? I said God!)
Esther 15	Esther comes into the throne room, praying to God all the way, plus a clear statement that it was God who made the king have mercy on her.

---

[1] Two of the books are 1 and 2 Maccabees, which tell the story of King Antiochus IV. Three more books claim to record additional events from the life of Daniel.

Esther 16	The text of the second decree of Xerxes, telling everybody in his empire to worship God of Israel. (PS Did you get that this book is all about God?)

The apocryphal book of *Deutero-Esther* really is as crass as it sounds in this quick summary. At times it can feel like watching a stand-up comedian who feels the need to painfully explain every punchline. It was evidently written by somebody who could not bear the fact that the book of Esther fails to mention God by name, but that's precisely the point of the book of Esther![2] It keeps the Lord invisible because he often is to our eyes and because living as God's people in the world means learning to see the invisible. Where other people say *coincidence*, we say *Providence*.

The writer of Hebrews in the New Testament is making the same point as the book of Esther when he tells us that faith means recognizing that God's invisibility is not the same thing as God's inactivity. He teaches us in Hebrews 11 that:

> *Faith is confidence in what we hope for and assurance about what we do not see. This is what the ancients were commended for. By faith we understand that the universe was formed at God's command, so that what is seen was not made out of what was visible...*
>
> *Without faith it is impossible to please God, because anyone who comes to him must believe that he exists and that he rewards those who earnestly seek him. By faith Noah, when warned about things not yet seen, in holy fear built an ark to save his family . . . By faith Moses . . . persevered because he saw him who is invisible.*

[2] It incorrectly describes Haman as a *Macedonian* (16:10), so it was also written by somebody who wanted to discredit Alexander the Great and his successors, over 150 years after the book of Esther was written.

Purim (Esther 9:17–32)

"Therefore these days were called Purim, from the word 'pur'."

(Esther 9:26)

It is often said that the book of Esther was written to explain the Jewish feast of Purim. But that's to get things the wrong way around. It's like assuming that Jane Austen wrote her novel after watching the spoof horror movie *Pride and Prejudice and Zombies.*

The Jews had many festivals in their calendar. Virtually all of them were decreed by the Law of Moses. There was the *Passover,* which celebrated their redemption from slavery and their forgiveness from sin, and which acted as a prophetic picture of the future death of Jesus on the cross to save God's people.[1] There was the *Festival of Unleavened Bread,* which reminded them that forgiveness for sin should always lead to freedom from sin.[2] There was the *Festival of Tabernacles,* which looked back to the days when the Israelites were led through the desert by a pillar of cloud and fire and which promised that one day that same Holy Spirit would come and dwell within each of God's people.[3] There was the *Feast of Weeks* (also known as *Pentecost*) which celebrated the Lord's gift of physical harvest and looked ahead to a spiritual harvest that was yet to come.[4]

---

[1] Leviticus 23:5 and 1 Corinthians 5:7.

[2] Leviticus 23:6–8; Mark 8:15 and 1 Corinthians 5:6–8.

[3] Leviticus 23:33–43; and John 1:14 and 7:37–39.

[4] Leviticus 23:15–21; Acts 2:1–47 and 1 Corinthians 16:8–9.

The Jews also had the *Festival of Firstfruits* to remind them that the Lord brings life to any seed that we let die and be buried in the ground.[5] They had the *Festival of Trumpets*[6] at the start of each new year. They had *Yom Kippur*, the *Day of Atonement*, which reminded them that the Lord never gives up on sinful people. He allows them to begin over again.[7]

All in all, the Jews had a plethora of festivals to remind them of the different facets of the Gospel, and these are just the ones that are listed in the Law of Moses. There was also the *Festival of Hanukkah*, which celebrated the defeat of King Antiochus IV and the reconsecration of the Temple by Judas Maccabeus in December 164 BC, and which is explained to us in 1 and 2 Maccabees in the Apocrypha. Finally, last but not least, there was the *Festival of Purim*, which is explained to us here in the book of Esther.

In verses 17–19, the writer explains why the Festival of Purim is celebrated by most Jewish communities on the *fourteenth* day of the month of Adar, but by Jews in certain urban settings on the *fifteenth* day of Adar.[8] It is because the Jews in Susa had to fight off their enemies on both 7 and 8 March 473 BC, whereas Jews elsewhere in the Persian Empire only had to fight them off on the first of those two days before they partied.

In verses 20–22, the writer explains that the Festival of Purim is a reminder of the message of the book of Esther, rather than the other way around. Mordecai writes to the Jews in every province of King Xerxes to instruct them that Purim is to be an annual reminder that the invisible God of Israel is never inactive. Of course, the writer avoids mentioning him by name in these verses, but any Jew who knew their Scriptures would easily spot that verse 22 is a deliberate echo of Psalm 30:11. *"Their*

---

[5] Leviticus 23:9–14, Mark 8:35, John 12:24 and 1 Corinthians 15:20–23.

[6] Leviticus 23:23-25

[7] Leviticus 23:23–32, Romans 3:23–26 and 1 John 1:8–9.

[8] Nowadays, it is only the Jews in Jerusalem who celebrate Purim on 15th Adar. Jews around the world celebrate it on 14th Adar.

sorrow was turned into joy and their mourning into a day of celebration" is a glorious fulfilment of the promise: *"You turned my wailing into dancing; you removed my sackcloth and clothed me with joy."*

Mordecai therefore commands the Jews to mark the Festival of Purim with *feasting*, with sending *gifts of food* to one another and with giving further *gifts to the poor*. Twenty-five centuries later, Jewish communities all around the world still do those three things as three of their four main ways of celebrating the Festival of Purim. The fourth is that they also read the book of Esther to one another, in order to marvel afresh at its message.

In verses 23–26, the writer explains that the message of the Festival of Purim is to be seen as the same as that of the book of Esther. It is a celebration of the providential sovereignty of God. The word *Purim* describes the casting of *lots* by Haman. The festival is therefore a great celebration of the truth of Proverbs 16:33 – *"The lot is cast into the lap, but its every decision is from the Lord."* Had Haman cast lots and chosen a date earlier than 7 March for his massacre, Esther and Mordecai might not have had enough time to thwart him. But his lot fell on the twelfth month (the very latest month he could have chosen!) because the Lord is sovereign over every lot cast and every dice roll. If the Jews needed yet another festival on their calendar to remember this, then so be it.

In verses 27–28, the writer explains that this message of the book of Esther lies at the heart of our Gospel proclamation to the world. The Festival of Purim was to be an opportunity for Jewish parents and grandparents to teach the next generation that the invisible God is never inactive. It was also to be an opportunity for them to proclaim this truth to the Gentiles around them. It wasn't just for the Jewish community. It was also for *"all who join them . . . in every province and in every city."* The Gospel is far bigger than a promise that the Lord will forgive us for our sins. It isn't primarily a message about us, but about *him* – summarized in Isaiah 52:7 as *"Your God reigns!"*

The Gospel tells us not to worry. The Lord is entirely sovereign over world affairs. *It is God who put you here.*[9]

In verses 29–32, the writer therefore reminds us that the message of the book of Esther is for everyone in every generation. Whether or not we celebrate the Festival of Purim with the Jewish community, we must all live in the good of its message.[10] Even when it doesn't look like it, the Lord knows what he is doing. He has decreed his salvation plan for the world, and that plan will succeed. It may be opposed by many Hamans, little antichrists who are inspired by Satan to resist God's purposes, but they will always fail.[11]

The Festival of Purim proclaims that the Lord is the true King of kings, ruling over all nations, and decreeing joy and laughter for his people all over the world.

---

[9] This is one of the reasons why 9:30 summarizes the Gospel for us as *shālōm* and *'emeth* – that is, as *peace* and *truth*, or as *goodwill* and *assurance*. The Gospel is the Good News of the faithfulness of God.

[10] Many modern Jews take 9:31 to mean that they should fast on 13th Adar in preparation for the festival, imitating Mordecai and Esther's fast in chapter 4.

[11] During Nazi Germany, there were several examples of Jews being rounded up butchered, ten at a time, at the Festival of Purim, as an act of "vengeance for the death of Haman's sons". The spirit of antichrist lives on.

Final Word (Esther 10:1–3)

"Mordecai the Jew . . . worked for the good of his people and spoke up for the welfare of all the Jews."
(Esther 10:3)

The tenth chapter of Esther is one of the shortest in the Bible. Four of the psalms are shorter. One chapter of Job contains more verses but fewer words.[1] Other than those, however, the last chapter of Esther is the shortest in the Bible, but that doesn't mean it is short on meaning. The writer conveys to us a wealth of insight through its final word.

Most English translations of the last verse of Esther tell us that *"Mordecai the Jew . . . worked for the good of his people and spoke up for the welfare of all the Jews."* There is nothing wrong with that, but it fails to convey the depth of what the Hebrew text actually says. The final word of the book of Esther is *zera'*, which means seed. It explains that Mordecai and Esther did something even greater than prevent genocide and preserve their nation.

Flicking back to the beginning of the Bible, we discover how important this word *zera'* is. When the Devil succeeds in tempting Adam and Eve to sin in the Garden of Eden, the Lord proclaims the Gospel for the first time, in Genesis 3:15, as a war between the seed of the serpent and the seed of Eve. Adam picks up on this, because when the Devil entices Cain to murder Abel, Adam rejoices in Genesis 4:25 that the Gospel is not thwarted, because the Lord has granted him a new seed in his son Seth.

---

[1] Psalms 117, 131, 133 and 134; and Job 25.

Sure enough, the Lord promises one of Seth's descendants in Genesis 9:9 that the covenant belongs to his seed.

When the Lord calls Abraham to become the founder of the Jewish nation, the word *zera'* begins to feature even more prominently in the story. When he makes his covenant with the patriarchs, the Lord repeatedly tells them that the covenant belongs to their seed and that it will only reach its fullness when their seed finally comes.[2] We are helped in our reading of those verses by the fact that the Apostle Paul explains them for us in Galatians 3:16–29. "*The promises were spoken to Abraham and to his seed. Scripture does not say 'and to seeds', meaning many people, but 'and to your seed', meaning one person, who is Christ. What I mean is this: the law . . . was added because of transgressions until the Seed to whom the promise referred had come . . . If you belong to Christ, then you are Abraham's seed, and heirs according to the promise.*"

Suddenly, we begin to see that this very brief final chapter of Esther is crammed full of meaning. It highlights the fact that Haman's crime was even more vile than genocide. The Devil inspired this attempt to wipe out the Jews because he hoped to prevent the Jewish Messiah from ever coming and defeating him by being hung on a wooden cross.[3] When we start to view what happens in the book of Esther in this way, it transforms our view of history as a whole. King Antiochus IV was not merely a ruler who hated the Jewish nation. He was inspired by the spirit of antichrist to destroy the Jewish seed before the Jewish Messiah could be born to save the world. Herod was not merely a paranoid ruler who slaughtered the babies of Bethlehem to bolster his reign. He was inspired by the spirit of antichrist to launch another attempt to wipe out the seed of Abraham. Praise God, like Haman and Antiochus and Herod, such antichrists will always fail.

---

[2] For example, in Genesis 12:7, 13:15, 15:5, 17:19, 24:7, 26:3 and 28:13–14. See also 1 Peter 1:23 and 1 John 3:9.

[3] The Jews are also referred to literally as *the seed* in Esther 6:13, 9:27, 9:28 and 9:31.

The seed has now been born into the world. Due to the courage of Mordecai and Esther, the Jewish seed survived for Jesus to be born as the Son of God in a stable in Bethlehem. Just as the Lord predicted in Genesis 3:15, the serpent struck his heel when he died on the cross, but he crushed the serpent's head when he rose to life again on the third day.

Jesus is the true and better Xerxes in verse 1. He does not merely have a temporal empire which extends to distant shores. He has established the Kingdom of Heaven on the earth and it is reaching into every nation, tribe and people group around the world.[4] He is the *"one like a son of man"*, in Daniel 7:13–14, who establishes God's everlasting Kingdom.

Jesus is also the true and better King of History in verse 2. This mention of the book of the annals of the kings of Media and of Persia reminds us of what Daniel saw – that Jesus holds the true Book of World History firmly in his hands.[5] The mention of the greatness of Mordecai reminds us that Jesus is still recruiting soldiers in his missionary army to the world. His everlasting Kingdom is still ever-increasing.

Jesus is also the true and better Saviour in verse 3. We are told that Mordecai worked hard for the good of God's people and that he spoke up for the welfare of all the Jews. But Jesus laid down his life on the cross to save God's people, and right now he speaks up for them before his Father in the throne room of heaven. Mordecai and Esther made intercession with the king of Persia, but Jesus is our far greater Intercessor in heaven.[6]

The book of Esther is one of only two books in the Bible to be named after a woman. The other one is Ruth. The two books have much in common. Not only are they both love stories, in

---

[4] The Hebrew word that is used to describe Xerxes' *tribute* in 10:1 is usually used to refer to *people*, rather than *money*. People from every nation will volunteer to become part of Christ's great Gospel army.

[5] Daniel 7:10 and 10:21. See also Ezekiel 2:9–10, Zechariah 5:1–3 and Revelation 5:1–14.

[6] Mordecai was only metaphorically "brought back from the dead" in Esther 6. Jesus was truly brought back from the dead and now he intercedes for us in heaven. See Romans 8:34 and Hebrews 7:24–25.

which a woman is willing to throw away everything in order to serve the invisible God of Israel, but they both end with verses that shift the spotlight of the story onto Jesus. The book of Ruth ends by telling us that her actions led to the promised seed of Abraham being born into David's royal dynasty.[7] The book of Esther ends by telling us that her actions led to that promised seed being preserved. The Devil and his antichrists will always fail in their plans. The Lord and his Messiah will always triumph.

We have now reached the end of the book of Esther together. It has taught us much about God's sovereignty and about how to be God's people in the world. Now, as we end the book, let's take a moment to praise God that it isn't primarily about us at all. It is primarily about him. The book of Esther is the story of God's unstoppable plan to save people from every nation through the seed of Abraham.

What a book. What an ending. What a Saviour.

[7] Ruth 4:12 links God's blessing specifically to the *zera'*, or *seed*, of the Lord.

Conclusion: It Is God Who Put You Here

"Who knows but that you have come to your royal position for such a time as this?"

(Esther 4:14)

The American novelist Mark Twain tells the story of a man who died and found himself standing at the Pearly Gates. While he waits in line, he asks, "Saint Peter, I have been interested in military history for many years. Who was the greatest general of all time?" Peter points to a pretty unimpressive-looking man. He responds, "You must be mistaken. I knew that man on earth, and he was just a common labourer." "That's right, my friend," Peter smiles back. "He would have been the greatest general of all time, **if he had been a general**."[1]

I hope that our journey through the books of Daniel and Esther has taught you the same principle as Mark Twain's story. Through God's man in Babylon and God's woman in Persia, the Lord has repeatedly shown us that we, too, are his people in the world. We don't have to scrabble around to find our destiny. *It is God who put you here.*

The Devil wants to keep us focused on where God hasn't placed us. He isn't scared of what we plan to do for God in the future. That's called dreaming. He isn't scared of what we plan to do for God elsewhere. That's dreaming too. But partnering with God in the place where he has put us? That's called faith, and it makes the Devil tremble.

---

[1] John Maxwell retells Mark Twain's story in his book *Talent Is Never Enough* (2007).

Daniel was faced with a choice. He could lament the fact that he had been torn away from his beloved Jerusalem and taken into exile, or he could knuckle down in faith to serve as God's man in Babylon. He could complain about how hostile the culture around him was to the faith of his fathers, or he could remind himself: *It is God who put you here.*

Esther was faced with that same choice. Nobody would have blamed her had she doubted God's goodness when her hopes of marrying a good Jewish boy were dashed and she found herself a prisoner in the harem of a pagan king. But instead, she made the same choice as Daniel. She decided by faith to serve as God's woman in Persia.

So how about you? Do you believe the words of Acts 17:26–27, which can be translated, *"God ordained the exact times and places where each person should live; he did this so that they might look for him and perhaps feel after him and find him – though he isn't far from anyone of us"?* In a world where everyone, quite rightly, wants to make the most of their life, do you believe the message of the books of Daniel and Esther? *It is God who put you here.*

One of the people that I find the most intriguing in the Gospels is the man Jesus delivers from a legion of demons. After the demons enter a herd of pigs and are drowned in the waters of Lake Galilee, the man attempts to get into the boat with Jesus as he leaves. We can imagine the great plans that he might be making for himself with Jesus on the other side of the lake. Maybe he can help him with his ministry. Maybe he can be there for him when his disciples run away. Maybe he can even become a famous Gospel writer.

Those sound like great plans, but they are evidently not the plans that Jesus has for him. We are told in Mark 5:18–20 that

> *As Jesus was getting into the boat, the man who had been demon-possessed begged to go with him. Jesus did not let him, but said, 'Go home to your own people and tell them how much the Lord has done for you, and how he has had mercy on you.' So the man went away and began to tell in*

the Decapolis how much Jesus had done for him. And all the people were amazed.

Jesus effectively tells the man to stop fantasising about all the places where he might serve God, and to embrace the Lord's sovereignty over where he finds himself.

As we finish the books of Daniel and Esther, I believe that the Lord wants to say the same thing to us about our family and friends. I can imagine the man's heart sinking when Jesus sends him back home, because sometimes living out God's love towards our nearest and dearest is the toughest task of all. But at home was where Esther found her destiny in God. Even when her parents died and she found herself trapped in an abusive marriage, she discovered to her surprise by faith: It is God who put you here.

I also believe that the Lord wants to increase our faith that we can partner with him in our workplaces. Most of us find it easy to adopt the attitude of Ray Kroc, the founder of the McDonald's chain of fast-food restaurants, who quipped: *"I believe in God, family, and McDonald's – and in the office, that order is reversed."*[2] Before we know it, we find that we have allowed our Christian faith to become something just for evenings and weekends. But if we have learned anything from the books of Daniel and Esther, then it's how much it matters to God that we serve him in our workplaces, not just in our leisure time. He wants to help us view our whole lives with eyes of faith. It is God who put you here.

Daniel's workplace was worse than any of our workplaces. His boss really did think he was God's gift to the world. The only mission statement on the wall was one of theft and rape and slaughter. Even the food in the company canteen was displeasing to God. Daniel could very easily have compartmentalised his life, like most of the other Jews in Babylon, who didn't grasp that tiny compromise in chapter 1 will quickly lead to outright

[2] Ray Kroc in his book *Grinding It Out: The Making of McDonald's* (1977).

idolatry and betrayal of the Lord's name in chapter 3. Because he refused to leave his faith at the office door, it became where Daniel discovered his destiny in God. He found that the Lord had plans for him, even at the very heart of Babylon. He discovered: It is God who put you here.

So don't miss your calling, like the general in Mark Twain's story. Don't be so busy fantasising about what you might do for God over there and in the future that you miss out on his daily presence and his purpose for you in the here-and-now. God is invisible but he is never inactive. He is right there with you, even though you may not see any angelic choirs trumpeting in the sky.

John Lennon claimed that life is what happens to you while you're busy making other plans. That's a fitting theme tune for us as the credits begin to roll at the end of the books of Daniel and Esther. God's man in Babylon and God's woman in Persia join hands together and they cheer you on to live as God's person where he has put you.

Their final words of encouragement to you are very simple: It is God who put you here.

Other titles in the

Straight to the Heart Series